MY IMPRISONMENT, GOD'S EMPOWERMENT

A TRUE STORY

BOB GORIS

ISBN: 9781500558031

Contact the author's wife Jan at jbgoris@gmail.com

Scripture is taken from The ESV® Bible (The Holy Bible, English Standard Version®) copyright © 2001 by Crossway, a publishing ministry of Good News Publishers. ESV® Text Edition: 2011. Scripture marked NIV is taken from THE HOLY BIBLE, NEW INTERNATIONAL VERSION®, NIV® Copyright © 1973, 1978, 1984, 2011 by Biblica, Inc.® Used by permission. All rights reserved worldwide.

Cover design by Yvonne Parks at www.pearcreative.ca
Interior design and typesetting by Katherine Lloyd at www.theDESKonline.com
Publishing assistance by David Sluka at www.hitthemarkpublishing.com

DEDICATION

I want to dedicate this book to my wife, Jan, to whom I have been married fifty-two years last August. As a twenty-three-year-old man I thought I fully understood the value and the beauty I was getting in winning the heart of my wife. Fifty-two years later, I realize that I didn't have a clue as to whom I was getting when Jan said, "I do." My heart did not have the capacity to appreciate the wisdom of the "excellent wife" described in Proverbs 31.

Jan has partnered with me through all these past years, beginning with having and raising our children. Our children are such a blessing to us, and I give Jan the credit for that: "Your wife will be like a fruitful vine within your house; Your children will be like olive shoots around your table" (Psalm 128:3).

While Jan was maintaining our household and was the center of our home life, at the same time, she partnered with me in business by continually showing hospitality to clients and business associates. She made our home a wonderful place to be.

When the IRS came in and took me away, she was left alone to sift through the accumulation that comes with living in a large home for forty-eight years and moving to an apartment, which was so graciously provided for us by Lisa and Craig.

As Jan adjusted to a new life in a new community, she would anxiously wait for the questions: "Do you have a husband?" or "Are you a widow?" I left her in a hard place in a hard time having to face the shame of my imprisonment by herself.

It is true that 95 percent of wives of men with a sentence of five years or more leave their husband when they go to prison. They just can't face the situation. It seems to be easier to say, "I'm divorced" rather than "My husband is in prison." But Jan did adjust to saying it. I encouraged her to be as open as she could, and we would pray that the Lord would use her openness, and our story.

During Jan's visits to see me, we saw couples who were very angry, usually the wife angry with her inmate husband. When Jan came she was like a beam of light shinning in the Visitor Center. One older lady who came with her daughter-in-law to visit her son told us later that the first time she saw Jan she said, "I want what she has. I'd like some of whatever she is on." Jan was always showing joy and always happy to see me. She encouraged a lot of the other women who were visiting. They often stayed in the same motel at night and got to know each other quite well. That is the way Jan lives her life.

Now, she lives that way with me. I couldn't have finished my book had it not been for Jan's encouragement. In this phase of my life, dealing with cancer, Jan's workload has multiplied. I can't drive now because of the pain medications so she must also drive me everywhere I go. Sometimes as she is about to run off and get me something, I say, "Really, I can get it myself." But she just looks at me with tears and says, "I just want to do it for you."

I find Proverbs 19:14 so true: "A prudent wife is a gift. House and wealth are inherited from fathers, but a prudent wife is from the Lord." Many days I sit in my chair and watch Jan lovingly work in her garden and do the things around the house to make a nice home. I watch with tears in my eyes, and I think to myself, "this kind of wife can only be made in heaven."

I am so glad I can dedicate this book to her, and I pray God's blessing on her life through this book. I love you, Honey.

ACKNOWLEDGEMENTS

I want to acknowledge all those who have helped me with this book in such a great way. Without them it would not have been written.

The first is my wife Jan. Without Jan's support, not only would this book not have been written, but I seriously do not believe I would be alive today.

Tom has come to encourage me more in the last five years than ever before in our lives. Without me even knowing it, Tom forwarded my e-mails to our mutual friends and associates as well as additional people who I never met. Tom expanded my borders through his loving work even before I knew he was doing anything at all, and he gave me my prayer partners days before I knew he was doing anything at all.

Jill Goris has been a valuable asset to me. She is always encouraging, especially as I worked to finish this book. Her ideas about the title, the cover, and other things that have made this book stand out have been priceless. She is very talented.

I want to thank Kathy Keller. I felt as if she was sitting right beside me as I served my time. More than half of my e-mails brought a response from Kathy. Her interest concerning the theological issues that I would bring up from my discussions and teaching of inmates has been invaluable. She also transcribed many of my letters, bringing up numerous letters that I had forgotten about.

My sisters have been such a great support, especially Marcy who not only encouraged but also insisted that I write this book, even when I had given up on the idea. Marcy has always been a great encouragement since I was a baby.

My daughters are unbelievable encouragers to me. And not only did they themselves stay encouraged, but they also kept their children, my grandchildren, very encouraged and excited for the trips to come and see me. They were faithful in driving thousands of miles to see me on many, many weekends and often drove through challenging weather.

I want to acknowledge my prayer partners for their prayers and also their responses to my e-mails. It was their responses that gave me the necessary encouragement to keep writing. I really needed the assurance that someone was actually reading what I wrote, and they were so generous with their own acknowledgements.

The obvious and most important contributors is to this book were my fellow inmates. For most, I used fictitious names, but I know they will know who they are if they ever get an opportunity to read this book. In particular, I want to mention Matt Tucker. He studied with me and took several advanced courses with me. Matt is still in Duluth and spends much time training leaders so that what we started is still continuing. As well, Jeff Graham was a tremendous help in getting our classes started. He found places to meet and then recruited people to the classes. He also dealt with the administration and the chaplain, all while keeping the records that we needed to present to the Bureau of Prisons.

Thanks to David Sluka and Andy Kauth for their help in editing and publishing this book.

The memories of Amos Goris continues to live on in my mind, and I often think of him as I learn and love the theology of God. He loved it and is probably the biggest influence in my life, as he caused me to look forward to that stage in life when I would love the Bible and spend much time in it.

Finally, I want to thank Jesus, my Savior and Lord, for leading, empowering, teaching, and inspiring me. He has constantly showed me more of himself. And this has been my big gain.

PREFACE

I have always been interested in people's stories, and I have paid close attention to my story. As I grew in my faith and understanding, I began to learn how my story becomes much more important and useful as I use it as a way to see and tell God's story in my life. The first sixty years of my story are a rather nice story, and I have told parts of it many times. While it starts out a little bumpy with a boy who had a big vision and desire for God to work in his life, the man's story is more a story of unseen construction in God's story.

While God's story comes out to a degree in the first sixty-two years of the story, it is more of an acknowledgement from the man that God is good, and the man is trying to relate to God the best he can amongst a lot of apparent human success. This pattern continues through the first sixty-two years. Oh, there were bumps, disappointments, failures, and broken dreams, but they were rather short lived and the turnaround was usually close in sight.

From the age of sixty-one, there was a time of what seemed like life fulfillment in ministry, but at the same time, there were some storm clouds brewing that were to bring unknown trauma to this life. There were some hints of change at the age of sixty-five. From sixty-six to seventy, the hints really were only hints, but those hints became reality at age seventy. What seemed like only a possibility of devastation was to become a reality. It seemed that a life built on pretty good foundations was to become burned to the ground with only ashes left. It involved the IRS, a long investigation, a trial, and a fifty-four month prison sentence.

God was in the story all the time, but like most stories, it took a lot of interpretation and patience to see how God would use this story (or even know for sure that he was truly in the story). Like the first sixty-two years, I expected God's salvation to be right around the next corner, and while he was with us in many ways, he did not answer the big, ultimate prayer the way we had hoped.

I was encouraged by friends to read Job, and I did many times. I struggled with the perfection of Job and his seemingly sinless life. At first, I had a hard time being sure wither his story truly applied to me. I was not sinless, as I first

7

thought of Job. Then I discovered the content of his prayers. I was not righteous in my own eyes until I realized that Job's righteousness was imputed or declared by God, the same as mine.

I also realized that Job's trials were not just a huge challenge for him; his wife was right in it with him just as my wife was. The pain for me in my situation was to watch Jan go through this with me. Just recently I focused on Job's wife's life as he went through this, and at one point she finally said, "Curse God and die" (Job 2:9). Her advice was for him to get it over with because death could not be worse than what they were going through.

We never did think of cursing or blaming God, but at times I must admit that facing death would have been much better than what I faced. The story shows the miracle of God's grace through the trial because of friends, family, and the out pouring of God's grace. The pain of the trial and pre-trial was so great, but as you will see, God was so strongly with us. He used the night prior to the sentencing in conjunction with our family to bear us up on angels' wings to carry us through the sentencing, the incarceration, life as a convicted felon and ward of the U.S. Government, and living with and being one of the outcasts of American society.

During the early years of this experience, we had thought that facing death would be much easier, and now the Lord is allowing us to experience that as well. As I write this, I am home on compassionate release. I was diagnosed with stage four pancreatic cancer in February 2013. I was seventy-four years old and was scheduled to be released from prison in October 2013.

When the doctor in Duluth Prison told me I had cancer, he asked me if I had any questions. I said, "Yes, can I get a compassionate release?" His immediate response was that I could but that it wouldn't do me any good because it takes four months to get a compassionate release and I wouldn't live that long. Apparently, the last four men who had pancreatic cancer all died before the release came through. So God is giving us the opportunity to compare which is worse: being found guilty of two counts of tax evasion and being incarcerated or facing death.

Now, this story is not a morbid one. It is a positive one and one that I hope will encourage you who face challenges at any level of life. Everyone goes through pain, and pain and situations in life shouldn't be compared. We must be careful not to compare pain. A broken marriage or a stress in marriage may be your prison. Rheumatoid arthritis or a business or financial setback may be your prison or cancer. Nothing is small.

My hope and purpose for this book is that you may read this story and know that within your story is God's story, and he is good. He is in control of everything, and his desire is to use you and me for his kingdom purpose. The big question for us to pray about is *how can he do that? How will he do that? I am so plain. I am not interesting. My problem is so private. I can't even talk about it.* I hope you are encouraged to see your questions answered about our life. You may discover God like you never have before. You maybe didn't know him before; you maybe only knew about him. There is a big difference. Maybe you did know him and walked with him for many years as I did. Still, I have learned so much about him that I don't know if I could have learned any other way.

I wish no ill will on anyone. I don't think it's God's plan that we all go to prison or get cancer, but I hope that after you read this book you won't waste your life, regardless your prison or cancer. My prayer is that you will see that God has a purpose and a calling for you and that you can do this for the glory of God. No matter how good or bad your life has been before, God has an exciting plan for you and me. Sometimes, he just needs to put us in a place where we can take our eyes off all the cheap things around us that we value so much in order to get our eyes on his true value.

Profit is what the life of a businessman is all about; it's about profiting from each experience. Would you read this book for profit? Any value or social system that is not built on that desire, placed in the heart by God himself, will fail.

The Bible is mainly an answer to the question, "What profit is it that we have kept his ordinance?" (Malachi 3:14). Jesus himself asks, "For what profit is it to a man if he gains the whole world and loses his own soul?" (Matthew 16:26). Paul writes, "Godliness is profitable for all things having promise of the life that now is and of that which is to come" (1 Timothy 4:8).

And now, what will you profit by reading this book? I hope it will expand your vision. Life is too short to be narrow. We need to expand our horizons, sharing the joys and sorrows of our brothers and sisters in Christ.

We have entered into a new season. The Hebrew word for seasons also means festivals. The profit of godliness is that it changes all seasons into festivals. We rejoice over all the joys of all who rejoice. We have a second source of joy that unbelievers don't have, because we even rejoice in tribulations.

Disorder in the family? Losses in business? Ill health? Death of a loved one? Fill your house with the incense of prayer and the vision of heavenly

Jerusalem; God's sovereign plan will become more and more clear. Suffering born with godliness is more valuable than all the treasures of the world, if we have our eyes riveted toward the eternal profit of bearing the cross of Christ.

It is my prayer that this book will help many find relief and encouragement in the fact that God is sovereign, in control, and knows our pain: those who are in wheelchairs with no foreseeable possibility of ever getting out or becoming independent; those who face prison or getting out of prison with a felony and a mark in society that will change their future drastically; those who are alone and feel so lonely and left out of society; and those who live with pain or bear pain daily and can't remember ever being without it.

Not only does God know our pain, but he has a plan and a purpose for it and will use it to glorify himself. We must get our own understanding and familiarity with God to a point that this will make sense to us. I pray that as you read this book, it will make sense to you.

God is not just a force. He is a person, and he made us in his image so that we can relate with him, knowing his kind of happiness, joy, peace, and understanding. The best that God has for us is not controlled, restricted, or limited by our circumstances. God is greater than our circumstances, and his purposes are much greater than ours. He is going to allow us to come in and join him in fulfilling his plan for this world. When we truly understand this, we can pray with all faith and confidence, "Lord, let your kingdom come and let your will be done."

1

The sentencing is finished. The judge sentenced me to fifty-four months with thirty-six months supervised release after that. In the federal system, the sentence will be reduced 15 percent with good behavior so that will make it forty-six months, just a little short of four years. We had asked for a voluntary surrender, which would have had me turn myself in at an assigned facility in four to six weeks. The judge denied me, and they took me into custody immediately.

From Jan, My Wife

I stood in the back of the courtroom. I had Bob's Bible with me knowing he would want it with him. When I tried to hand it to him, they said, "No, he cannot take that with him; they have lots of Bibles in prison." (Bob found out later that a Bible is the single personal possession a person is allowed to take into prison with him). I thought, "How can he get along without his Bible?"

He had just been sentenced to fifty-four months in prison. My mind could hardly tally the years that would be. Our last words to him as the federal marshal escorted him from the court room were, "We love you, Dad; we love you, Grandpa; we love you . . ."—each "love you" getting louder as more voices joined in and he got farther away. He turned, smiled briefly, and was ushered out.

There were so many emotions in the past few weeks. We had endured a two-week trial, perhaps the most difficult two weeks of our lives. During the trial, I thumbed through Scripture verses I had written in a small two ring binder. Much of the trial was very technical, and I didn't understand what was being said. I was thankful to have these verses with me to keep my mind from being anxious. I was sustained. God was faithful to the promises I was reading.

Once the guilty verdict was read, it was evident we could not stay in our home. Bob would likely be going to prison.

We left the courtroom and headed home to pack, knowing we had just five weeks before the sentence would be given.

Friends and family came to help pack, throw, sort, or bring to Goodwill all we had accumulated in our nearly forty-nine years of marriage. The five weeks flew by. It was very little time to think about what lay ahead or what was in the past.

During the five weeks we were packing, our daughter and son-in-law, with the help of many friends, were finishing off the lower level of their home as an apartment for us. Bob and I were there together just three days before the sentencing. The kids and grandkids came, and we had one more night of singing, praying, and reflecting. The next morning, April 28, 2010, we once again drove to the courtroom and heard the sentence.

2

I t all started in 2003. I got a call from the IRS about a trust I had purchased in Arizona in 2000. They said they wanted to see the trust documents. I answered, as I was instructed, that they should talk to the trustee. I was neither the trustee nor the beneficiary. I purchased the trust because it was explained to me that income from the trust would not be taxed until it was drawn from the trust. The trust, however, could make charitable contributions, and that was what I was interested in. They accepted that answer, so it seemed. A month later they called again, and I gave them the same answer. I received a third call from them, this time saying they were withdrawing their request to see the documents.

I heard nothing more from them for three years. That was when they made a surprise visit at our house with a SWAT team and took all my files, computers, and other personal items, which made no sense.

At that time, I was asked a lot of questions about a large donation I had made to a ministry. I had supported this ministry for more than fifteen years, but when I sold my business, I made a large donation to the ministry. Later, I worked for them for three years, during which time they paid me a consulting fee.

I heard nothing more from the IRS for three years. During that time, I made forty-two attempts to communicate with them. They did not answer my letters, e-mails, or phone calls. They were going to people and businesses telling them what a bad guy I was—that they might be either part of the problem or part of the solution. It was very intimidating for them. My CPA dropped me because he said they do not work with people who are "under criminal investigation." This was the first time I heard these words. It shocked me to know that I was under criminal investigation.

They went to the ministry to which I made the donation several times unannounced, and they demanded copies of all correspondence they had with me in the last eight years. Later, I was to find out I was being charged with having an illegal trust as well as a second charge of money laundering because of the gift. I felt very sure of winning my case because when I found out the trust was illegal I stopped using it. The money laundering charge because of the gift seemed so far-fetched I just didn't think there was any way a jury would ever believe that was money laundering. It was very definitely a gift. I drew compensation for the three years I worked for them but not a penny since.

During the three years of not hearing from the IRS and wanting to find a way to solve this, I went to some guys who had worked for the group that set up the trust. They told me they knew how to get me out of this. I hired them. They did a lot of paper work that I signed, but I found out their work only made matters worse. I found out in court that all my e-mails and letters were just accumulating in a file in Salt Lake City to be used as evidence against me.

I felt very sure I would win my case in court. My attorney told me I just had to tell my story and to be as honest as I could be. I felt I could do that well. I've done a lot of speaking during my business years, and I felt sure about myself in this case.

What surprised me was that the court was not at all what I expected. I was on the witness stand for two days. I could tell about my life, but when it came to telling how hard I tried to communicate with the IRS (forty-two times), the prosecutor would object saying it was irrelevant. Their accusations carried up through the years I was sending in documents. I wasn't allowed to answer them, because they were after the year of the event (2001 and 2002). So, they could bring in material up to 2009, but I couldn't rebut them because it was after 2002. That was only one of the many things that surprised me. I never knew that courts worked this way. I was expecting a not guilty verdict right up to the time they said, "Guilty on two counts of tax evasion."

3

*The following is an account of my time in jail,
as told through e-mails and letters to family and friends.*

I am in Sherburne County Jail now, which is in Elk River, Minnesota. I am just a few minutes from Jan and my family. While I am close to them, it is strange when they visit. The security level is so high here that visitation is only by video screen. It is still nice to see Jan and the family though. I have had lots of visits.

I will be at Sherburne County only temporarily—possibly two to seven weeks until the B.O.P. (Board of Prisons) decides where I will go. I am hoping for Duluth, which is a minimum security camp. I have been told that the first forty-eight hours is the worst. I just finished my first forty-eight hours, and this is what I want you to know. In observing others and paying attention to my own case, these things never go the way we think they should go. I have decided that the following would be my thinking and philosophy, even my theology. I can say things about attorneys, the trial, and the judge, and I have; I will not anymore. God is in charge of all of them. He can move their hearts and minds. The verdict and sentencing passed through the hands of our gracious, loving heavenly Father. He has heard and answered many prayers the way we asked. This verdict and sentencing he did not. Therefore, I see that this is his will for me and even my family. I still feel responsible, but he has approved and even designed it for reasons either for my benefit or for others. I pray that he will help me do it well in a way that I can please and serve him. This is the backdrop of my first forty-eight hours.

The jail is not a bad place. The corrections people are nice, for the most part. The rules are tight for everyone's protection. It is kept very clean, and I am not afraid. The first night was hard. I struggled with meaning, purpose, and God's presence. I had determined I would see God early here. I didn't feel that. Our unit was in lockdown when I arrived. It was 9:00 PM. I lay down on my concrete bunk, and the pad felt thin. I prayed, but it was difficult finding reality in it. I am not allowed a clock. They took my watch away. Lights stay on all night. I fell asleep. I woke up hearing toilets flushing and thought it must be morning. I wait for an eternity. It must still be night. I tried to pray some more. I recited some psalms. God is not here. It was the longest night of my life.

Morning finally came. We are allowed into the day room for one-and-a-half hours. I make some contacts. The next night I asked God to show me who he would have me connect with. I tell God that I don't deserve any miracles for my sake, but I ask him to please not let me be here aimlessly: please God, show me your work. I fell asleep and slept the night through, concrete bunk and all.

5/12/10

Tonight is the end of the eighth day. I will be here for another two to six weeks.

My son, Tom, tells me of the concern he hears. I feel it has been a time of loss upon loss, death upon death. All of it was surreal; it was difficult for me to believe it was going to happen.

The first level of loss was dealing with the government over a four-year period and becoming aware I was losing. It was a very difficult time. The second level of loss was the publicity and the shame and loss of reputation that goes with it. The third level of loss was realizing that I would be losing everything I had worked for my whole life. The fourth level was losing my freedom and leaving my family without a husband, dad, grandpa, uncle, and friend who could function as they were all accustomed to seeing me function.

After I had finished my first night in jail, I was disappointed with myself. I had difficulty in my praying. I didn't feel as close to God as I thought I would. I couldn't remember the psalms that Jan and I had learned. It was a long lost night with no sleep, no clock, and no reality. I felt caught in a vacuum. Thursday was a little better. I looked over the 100 prisoners (fifty of whom I had access to). I sat with them, ate with them, and listened to a lot of foolish, hateful, and dirty talk. I heard a lot about drugs, crime, law, and prostitution. Here and there some would say, "But now I want to be a family man." I made a mental note of who was saying that, feeling this might be a door into their lives. One guy said, "When I get out, I want to get me one of them square jobs and barbecue in the backyard at night." One group, at dinner, was talking about their cases, their attorneys, prosecutors, and judges. They got around to me and asked me how I felt about being there. At the table was RJ, a pimp; Monty, a con man specializing in women; Irvine, addicted to marijuana and a drug dealer; and Doug, a drug dealer. When they asked me how I felt, what came out of my mouth was what I have found will be my story because it caught their attention. This is what I said.

"I'm a Christian. As my problems increased, my wife and I prayed. God heard and answered many prayers. We have had loss of jobs in our family, need for homes, and broken relationships; God heard and answered many prayers for us. When it came to my trial, we had hundreds of people praying for the trial—people from all over the world. God didn't answer this prayer the way we asked him to. We asked for a "not guilty" verdict; therefore, I believe God has a purpose for me to be here. It may be for me; it may be for others. I am hoping that I can be a help to some others."

Their response surprised and amazed me. The first guy said, "I respect that." The second guy said, "That's a good attitude." They started calling me "Pops." That name stuck. Thursday night I asked God to please work in their hearts and make me to know what he is doing. The table that took me in was a group of leaders in the unit, and I could tell they had the interest of many of the others. I noticed that Irvine was not at our table. I decided I wanted to talk further with Irvine, but I needed him alone. I asked God for that.

There is a catwalk above the day room where we can walk for exercise. I was up there walking when Irvine came along side. I noticed earlier he was always sweating. I asked him about it, and he said he was really suffering from addiction to marijuana. I said I've always heard it's not addictive. He said he was very addicted. He told me how much control it had over him. I told him he needed Jesus in his life. He said he believed in Jesus and God, but he prayed and claimed to change so many times. He had hurt his wife so much and was afraid to do it again. He told a friend that he flushed the marijuana down the toilet. (He had it in his cell.)

5/15/10

I just finished my second week. I have been moved to a different unit. It's the most desired unit because all the cells are individual. The lock down time is less, with more time in the day room.

Visitation is still by video only. I'm limited to having ten visitors on my list so in my case that is only family. The video shuts off in twenty minutes. I have lots of visitors. The guards know my family. The inmates are curious about my many visits. They like to sneak behind me and see what they look like. They always remark how nice they look. I finally have a phone card and have talked to distant family. It is so good, but the good-byes are hard. The phone shuts off in fifteen minutes. The hardest part of this life is the good-byes.

There were eleven at our Bible study. After the study I sat with a man, "Raven," who I sensed was interested. He seemed to have no resistance as I have been warming him up. Tonight he said he would like to be a Christian but had so much confessing to do. We were in the big room with a lot of his friends watching from a distance and laughing. So I told him we would pray with our eyes open. He said he had so many sins. He said, "I stole $2,000 from my parents, and I killed a man." He said he would like to go to his cell and confess. I said he could but that first I would help him to pray his prayer to accept Christ and then he could confess his sins. He truly was like a little child. He was smiling, no resistance, and very happy for the good news. Later, his friends who were laughing called me over and asked me some questions. They began to get serious. I know I will have more conversation tomorrow.

The guy who I think is their leader called me over and told me part of his story. I had him pegged as hard-boiled. He has a very sad story.

From Jan

My mind was flooded with question. Where were they taking Bob? How would he be treated? When would I visit?

By late evening I had a call from a friend. A young man Bob had mentored who had served time in prison. He was able to get tracking information on prisoners. He called to tell me that Bob was in a temporary holding place in a jail in Sherburne County, Elk River. That was just where we had moved. It was a relief to know he was only ten minutes from me. One of many blessings we saw from God.

The next morning our daughter Amy drove with me to the jail. After filling out paper work, our names were called. We walked to the little two seat booth, picked up a phone, and saw Bob on a type screen with a phone in his hand.

Bob looked better than I expected. He seemed to be calm and at peace with the accusations he had been dealing with. The phone was shut off after fifteen minutes. This was to be what our next seven weeks of visiting would be like. We talked fast. Each day I had a list of questions and things I wanted to cover. We couldn't waste precious time. This became our routine. Bob informed me that if I came to visit on a Wednesday and he was not there, they would have sent him to Oklahoma City. If it happened on a Tuesday, he was likely headed for Duluth Federal Prison Camp.

Seven weeks later, I was relieved to hear, "Robert Goris is not here." It was Tuesday morning, and I was sure Bob was on his way to Duluth and not going south.

Duluth Federal Prison Camp would be our connection point for the next four-and-a-half years.

5/19/10

We just finished Bible study. We have a steady thirteen now and are getting more organized. We agreed that the discussion after the message should stay on the topic of the message. (Big improvement!) It has been like herding cats and playing Bible Trivia. While I was in the study, they put on a movie. Movies pull everyone in. Off to the side was a new guy, really old with white stubble hair and worn down teeth.

His name is Joseph. Joseph is from Scotland and has been in the US for thirty-four years. While I thought I had found someone older than me, he is only fifty-four. I asked if he had a family. He said, "No, just an ex-wife and two kids that don't want anything to do with me." I asked him if he wanted to walk and talk. He said he would. He had never been in jail before and said he had not committed a crime. He said, "I am very nervous about this place." I assured him he is safe. He is just such a little old man and has a heavy accent. He said he hopes he gets deported because he wants to go and see his mother who is ill. I turned the conversation to God. He said he believed. I asked him his church. He said Methodist but that he had not been there for three years.

I left for a meeting, but when I came back for our prayer time, Joseph was there. The guys had already recruited him. Jail does amazing things to people. Another new guy even showed up, Miguel, a twenty-one year old who had accepted Christ two months ago in this jail. He seems well grounded for two months.

5/21/10

Saturday night Joseph was called out to the outer office. He missed our fellowship time. When he came back, I could see he was troubled. I asked him if he was okay. He said, "No." They called him up front to tell him his youngest daughter was killed in a car accident. We talked a little, and a nurse came in and gave him some medication. She told me she was sure he would want to be left alone and that they would check on him later. I said we have a support group for him, and I knew he would want to see us. He did, and we all gathered around him, laid hands on him, and prayed for him. Sunday morning I helped him fill out a request for a two-day furlough to attend the funeral. They turned down the request.

Miguel and Gomez just came over to talk. This morning Gomez told me that he was married for three months to a nice girl. Three years ago she left him because of his drinking. I told him how, now that he is a Christian, God will want him to marry only a woman who loves God and that God has someone already chosen for him and that she is living someplace right now. He should be praying for her well being and spiritual development. He was fascinated with the idea. I had the privilege of taking him through Ephesians 5, which shows what a marriage should look like. He went and got Miguel and asked me to go through it again; so we did a second time.

Gomez has been sentenced to four years. It is his first offense so he is eligible for Duluth Camp. I told him I think I am going there. He said he is going to pray that he can go there too so we can be together. I would love that. I would love to have him be an assistant for me in teaching some classes in Duluth based upon the *First Principles* Bible study book.

When I walk to booking I'm greeted along the way as "Pops" or "Mr. Goris." The young guys almost always come and take my tray away after meals. When they walk by my door, they give it a hit to say, "Hi Pops." It's kind of nice. Last night they showed the "JESUS" film. Sixteen guys watched and were really glued to it. This is a good place for ministry; there is a lot of fertile ground.

4

6/5/10

I think this might be my last week with these guys. I want to leave them with something important. In the Bible, Joshua is one of my favorite leaders. I especially like his talk that he left his people with when he knew that his time was up because he was about to die. I decided earlier in this week to use Joshua 23 and 24. The story is about how Joshua calls the people to remember and decide and about how his house will serve the Lord."

I used "Little Joseph" as a first testimonial. Joseph had never given a testimony and had never prayed aloud. The guys had been after Joseph to talk in a meeting. He was always too shy, too scared. I had helped him through this experience last week. This is his story.

Joseph, an immigrant from Scotland, lived in the US for thirty-four years. He was married for seventeen years, divorced, and had two adult daughters. He had neglected to fill out the paperwork to become a citizen. Joseph worked in a dry cleaning store. He got a call that Immigration (ICE) was coming to get him to question him. They came with two guys in a van, handcuffed Joseph and took him to jail. ICE was not going to allow him to go to his daughter's funeral. We all prayed for Joseph, and this is what happened. Someone heard about it and called a senator in Washington, and ICE changed their mind. ICE took him to the funeral. Someone at the funeral heard what was happening to Joseph and put one hundred and fifty dollars in his account in jail.

The day after the funeral, Joseph was so happy. I never saw anyone smile so much and be so happy. The next day, Joseph was really sad again. I asked him what was wrong, but he wouldn't talk. That night, just before lock down Joseph asked me if we could talk. We went off in a private place, and Joseph said he thought God was judging him for the way he was acting. I asked him what he meant; he said he shouldn't have been so happy because his daughter had just died. I asked if his daughter was a believer. He said she was, and I said it was okay to be happy about that. I told him that what he was feeling was either coming from God or from Satan. I told him if it's from God he could confess it and even unknown sins. And I told him if it's from Satan that we could command Satan to leave in the name of Jesus.

He liked that. I said, "Let's pray that right now; can you just say that right now to God?" He said he would so we prayed. Joseph got rid of his guilt and thanked God for his joy.

That was Joseph's first testimony, told as an example of what Joshua would have Joseph remember as God's goodness. We then went through the list of Joshua's "remembrances." Then I asked the guys to share the things in their own lives that they think God wants them to remember. The sharing was tremendous. Of course Gomez and Miguel headed it off. It was great.

Martin, who had never shared, wasn't going to this morning, either. I asked him to. He said he is so thankful to be in this jail. He said, "I feel so safe and respected here. I am an alcoholic. Every night after work I pick up a twelve-pack of the big cans. By the time I got home, I would be drunk, eat supper, and fall asleep. I have a seventeen-year-old son and a fifteen-year-old son. They have never seen me sober. I am so embarrassed. I wanted them to see me sober, but I just couldn't help myself. I would just like to stay here. I'm so happy here. Afterwards, we prayed individually in a circle. With joined hands, everyone prayed. This was a first.

Today is Gomez's twenty-second birthday. We arranged a birthday party for him. Everyone contributed something—a package of noodles, a sausage, a pickle, a package of tortillas, a tuna package, etc. We sang "Happy Birthday" and celebrated with burritos.

6/11/10

The life stories of these guys are incredible. Alee is forty-four years old. At age nine he found his way north from El Salvador to California by himself. He started using drugs and sold drugs since the age of seven. His father gave him bus money to Mexico City and airplane money to Tijuana. He lived on the streets. As a boy, he saw men and women shoot heroine in body parts you can't imagine just so there would be no needle marks when police caught them. Three months ago he was in a federal prison in Grand Forks and went crazy. He was getting in fights because he thought everyone wanted to attack him. He requested the hole and spent a month there. He came to a meeting here and showed interest but always very defensive. Over a two-week period he started to open up. He is now saved but still needs a lot of development. He left for El Salvador this morning on a federal prison plane.

Gomez and Miguel are both new Christians, only about two-months old and growing so amazingly. Miguel had Joe as a cellmate. Joe is from Peru and came from Peru by himself at age eight. He is now forty-three and had been working in a quarry. He beat up his girlfriend's mom (he told me this himself), thought she was dead, rolled her up in a blanket, duct taped the blanket, and left her in the trunk of his car. Miguel was his cellmate. Joe gets crazy and likes to be the center of attention. When people laugh, he gets real vulgar and nasty. Miguel is just a small guy, but he said to Joe, "You aren't funny and you're acting like a fool. You should be ashamed of yourself." Joe calmed down a lot. Joe had a custody battle over his children and wanted Miguel to pray for him. Miguel told Joe he could pray himself so Joe knelt by his bunker and prayed. He won't pray for salvation, but he is friendly now toward me. He is a wild man. I don't know if I have enough faith to see him through. He has a lot of pride and wants to be seen as wild. He would have to really change.

George is fifty-four years old and quite distinguished and well-educated. He came to the US at age nineteen and has a degree in physics and a master's degree in education administration. He owned a good-sized auto repair business. He's been here thirty-four years but is not a citizen. Due to a business problem, ICE put him here a month ago, and they didn't tell him anything. He is in here with no money. He had some but spent it all on phone calls to lawyers and immigration people who put him on hold. He came to my table and was calling me "father." I asked him why he called me father. He said, "Aren't you a priest?" I said, "No." He said someone told him I was a holy man. I asked him if he knew Jesus. He is coming to fellowship tonight. The justice system isn't working very well for many of these guys. It's quite an eye opener.

David, a believer, is beginning his third "ninety day wait." He has been in the US twenty years and has a wife and three children who are all legal. He is being deported to Sudan, Africa, and is afraid of getting killed when he gets there.

My new cell is in a perfect location. I have a table right outside my door. I get my mail and start reading. The guys just come to me now to talk. I can do so much encouraging and strengthening all morning without moving.

Yesterday morning I woke up at 3:30 a.m. as usual. I found myself thinking, "I hope this day goes fast," almost like I was willing to waste it just to get through it in a hurry. The Lord checked me in that thought. In my spirit, I was convicted of not treasuring and using each day as a gift of God. At the same time, I confessed to the Lord that while I'm okay for today I was concerned for tomorrow. Can I maintain my interest? Will life stay meaningful? Will I get tired of people? Will my prayer partners get tired of my e-mails? As time goes on, will I run out of things to write about?

I was walking the catwalk and Miguel came to walk with me. He said, "Pops, I want to know what's on your mind today." His question brought me into a confrontation with myself. How could I answer him? When I was weak, there was a form that kept me from going my own way, from wasting the day. Miguel was part of that form. My speaking at our fellowship is part of that form. I can't just waste a day, because I want to. God has placed people, activities, and expectations around me that help me sanctify my life. Miguel's question was part of what got me back on track; it was a realization "that I am not my own, that I've been bought with a price."

A few guys from the fellowship stopped by to ask questions. We are starting to talk about baptism. We decided I need to teach on that. They want to know about the amount of water. I tell them that we will need to talk about the "forms" and the "functions" in the Christian faith. These men are going to prison for several years. We need to talk about whether the "forms" (the amount of water) should rule over the "function" (the heart of baptism). They want to be baptized. After my teaching they will need to decide whether we can do a biblical baptism right here in the jail.

As we were talking a man by the name of Montose sat down. Montose showed up three days ago. He looks about seventy but is only fifty-two. He looks like he was fashioned to be a little wind-up toy and should be standing on someone's bookshelf. Montose was picked up by ICE in North Dakota. They were planting onions for a farmer. ICE came with a big helicopter that hovered over the fields to make sure that no one would escape. Men with guns came from all sides and corners of the field, rounded them up, handcuffed them, locked them in a bus, and brought them here.

Montose looks very weathered; he is sweet but doesn't smile. He has no expression and is very quiet; he just looks bewildered. I tried to talk to him but had no response, no English, and no expression. The next night he walked into our fellowship meeting when it was half over. He came again last night and was very shy.

By questioning him, I learned he is from Mexico; he has a wife and eleven children. He hasn't seen them for four years. When I asked how long he has been a Christian, he said he went to a church in Washington but not since he was in North Dakota. I asked him if his wife and family are Christians; he said they were not. I asked him if he was scared when he got arrested. He said no because now he will be going home to Mexico. I asked him if he would like to learn the gospel message so he could teach his family. He said yes and smiled for the first time.

I got to my room totally amazed at what God is doing. I don't want to read and don't want to write. I just sing on my bunk with tears in my eyes that God is letting me take this all in and that I am close to the hand of God. I love these guys. I told Miguel that I feel like Abraham and that God is giving me many sons. I have not initiated any of this. God has done it all.

We had a great time in fellowship. I talked about baptism. Most of the guys had never heard teaching on it. Miguel and Gomez were both baptized. Tomorrow I'm teaching about how the gospel moved forward through the planting and establishing of churches and how Paul worked to establish leaders and churches, moved on, checked back, and wrote letters. I think these guys see themselves doing that. We agreed to stay connected. Tomorrow night I will also introduce communion, and we will have communion. We expect that several of us will be leaving Tuesday morning so communion will be very meaningful.

6/12/10

I observed that as the guys took turns with the messages and prayers they were all so similar. They are always about temptation, not sinning, and not falling away when they get out of prison and just staying strong while they are in prison. It was coming to me that their picture was so focused on themselves and so short term that we needed to begin talking about the bigger picture of becoming a disciple: what disciples do, the Great Commission, and what Jesus taught the disciples to do. In becoming a disciple, we needed to talk about baptism.

I asked Miguel how he felt. He said he felt good. He was really glad he was baptized, but he said a lot of people were talking. He couldn't answer all their questions. We moved over to a corner to talk. Joe, who is mad at God for all the things that are happening to him, came with a chair and sat down right in front of us and said he didn't think it was right to do what we were doing. That baptizing should only be done in a church. We had a very good discussion, and he left saying he really appreciated what we were doing.

Later, Raven came to me and said, "People are talking, Pops. You shouldn't have done that. People are talking about you." I said, "That's good, Raven. Tell them to talk to me." He said, "No, they don't like what you did." Just then they called "lockdown" and our conversation ended.

I was sitting by my table. Suddenly seven tough guys with Raven came with chairs and sat around the table. Raven said, "They want to talk to you." I said, "Good." It was a little like a mob. They had a spokesman, and it wasn't Raven. One of the hardcore guys who I detected was the leader of this little uprising said, "You had no business doing that without holy water." I responded that what we did is what Jesus told us to do in the Bible. He said, "It says in the Bible that you are supposed to do that in a church." I said, "Let's see what Jesus did." I turned to Matthew and read where Jesus was baptized in the Jordan River. I asked, "Was that holy water?" The next guy said, "Well, I'm a Christian, and only John the Baptist could baptize." I said, "Well, many baptized after John the Baptist." He said, "You have to go to school a long time and be a priest. Are you a priest or a minister?" I said, "No, I'm a disciple. Jesus taught the disciples what he wanted them to do. Then the last thing Jesus told them before he left was the Great Commission." We read it. The speaker said, "Who can be a disciple?" I said, "Anyone who wants to be." He said, "Can Miguel be a disciple?" (Miguel is the meanest, nastiest one of the bunch). I said, "Miguel can. If Miguel wants to give his life to Jesus and be born again and wants to learn how to follow Jesus, Miguel would make a great disciple."

Now Raven started coming alive: "Well, Pops, what about these guys wearing those 'dresses' and those fancy crowns on their heads. You mean they don't have to do it?" Raven was really smiling. He hates the establishment, government, and what he knows of the church.

A group of five were sitting at a table. The youngest, about twenty-one years old with eleven years of prison ahead of him came over to me. "Hey Pops, the guys have a question. They're not trying to poke fun, but they really want to know. Will you come?" I walked over. This group has never been in our Bible study. The spokesman spoke up, "Pops, is it a sin to masturbate?" This is a big question around here with both Christians and non-Christians. I said, "Yes, guys, it is a sin. It is a sin because it shows you are not controlling your mind. They responded, "So when you are a Christian, you don't do that anymore?" I said, "Guys, Christians are still sinners. Every man must work on his own mind, and a Christian asks God to help him with that. But, guys, don't let that keep you from becoming a Christian. God can help you deal with that."

6/14/10

We got four new people in our pod this week. One was Monty; he was threatened, and they moved him. One was J.T. We were all locked down because they always lock us all down when they introduce new people to the pod. Through the window of my cell, I saw this somewhat handsome black man with a shaved head, possibly a body builder, who seemed very confident. Men were greeting him from their locked down cells. I prayed that if God would give me favor in his eyes, I would like to talk to him. From his stature and demeanor I thought he could be influential in the prison if he would become a Christian. Wednesday, I tried to make contact just to greet him, but he always just looked straight ahead. He sat with the gamblers, and that is not a good sign for me. They are a hard crew and stay very busy with that, which makes it hard to develop relationships. Thursday came and went with no contact. Friday morning, I signed up for gym. I got in the wrong gym (I thought). I usually go with the volleyball group. I ended up with the basketball group, which really doesn't make any difference because I ride a stationary bike anyway. I'm on the bike, and I saw J.T. He was shooting baskets, and he is really pretty good. I finished my 40 minutes on the bike then sat down on the gym floor as I always do to cool down. J.T. came over and sat right beside me. I offered my hand and introduced myself. We talked about his basketball playing which led to high school talk and his childhood. He said he grew up in Detroit. He never knew his dad, and his mom was a heroin addict. His grandmother raised him. I asked him why he's here. He said for bank robbing. I said, "Well how many banks have you robbed?" He said, "Only one." I said, "And you didn't get away with even that one." We laughed. He said, "Actually, I didn't even plan to rob the bank. They gave me $1,300, but I wasn't after the money." I asked him why he would rob a bank if he didn't want money. He said, "I knew there was an armed policeman in the bank. I figured he would pull his gun and tell me to get down on the floor; I didn't even have a gun. My plan was I wasn't going to get down, and he would shoot me. I really wanted to die." I asked, "Did you get away?" He said, "I got all the way to the crack house." Ends up the crack house was only two blocks away. He lived in the crack house. I asked if he sold drugs. He said, "No, only a little crack. Just enough to pay for my own." He said he pled guilty to the bank robbing charge and was hoping to get help (treatment) in prison, but they are only going to give him two years. He is concerned that it isn't enough. I told him I might be able to help him. I said, "Look me up. I'm in 121."

I watched him the rest of the day. He kept playing cards. I decided to walk on the catwalk. He left his table to come and see me. I said, "I'm going to walk. You want to join me?" He said, "Yes." We walked. The catwalk is up above the cells so everyone sees who is walking and talking with whom, and everyone was as surprised as I was that J.T. was walking with me.

I had told him in the gym that I was interested in meeting him because he seemed like a very confident person, that he seemed like a person who others would follow either for good or for bad. This is when he really unloaded his story on me. He said, "I am not confident at all." He said, "I get so depressed. I smoke crack to get relief, and when I come down I go so low I get suicidal." He showed me his arms full of cut marks. He said, "My whole body is all cut up. I'm so embarrassed. I'll never take my shirt off in front of anybody."

I didn't really know how to proceed, so I decided to do what I always do when I feel undone. I told my personal story, only this time I jumped in at the middle of it where I start selling life insurance. I didn't know how, but I just figured it out and bought my own policy at age fourteen. After twelve years of selling, I felt God's purpose for me was to work with young men, showing them how to develop their lives with the four Fs: faith, family, fitness, and finance. I said, "I'm a Christian. I want to help others become Christians." He asked how long it took me to learn that. Then I went to the beginning where I had a Christian father. As a boy, age seven to nine, I wanted to help people become Christians, but I didn't know how. I prayed that God would show me how. That's why I think I'm here right now." When I saw you walk into the pod Wednesday morning, I told God I would like to meet you. He was amazed. I said, "I have 150 prayer partners, and tonight I am going to call my son to e-mail them to pray for you. " He was more amazed. We set up to meet again the next morning so I could give him a reading assignment. Through the night, I wondered if he would show. He did.

I left the fellowship meeting Saturday night so encouraged. On my way back to my cell with everyone out in the day room, right in front of me, a big fight broke out. It looked like one guy attacking another but ended up being much more. The guards started hollering, "Code orange lockdown! Down on the floor; on your stomachs!" I was right there almost on top of it when I realized I could be in this thing. It was so surreal. Guys all stood for a minute wondering who should be helping whom. It finally dawned on me and others that the command "lock down" was for us.

Through the next two days, I realized that what looked like a fight between two guys was really a small battle of a much larger war. The guys were pinned on the floor face down, handcuffed, and taken to the hole. All night long guards went back and forth reviewing videos from the camera. All day Sunday we were locked in. They brought our food to our cells at 8:00 a.m. The guys with black suits and knuckle gloves came by; handcuffed us, took us out of our cells, and searched everything. I saw them go from cell to cell and do the same at each cell. I was amazed at the huge pile of stuff they removed. After that they took us out one at a time to the gym where we sat on folding chairs; they wanted to know what we knew about what was going on: any racial wars, drug wars, gambling wars. It was all very interesting.

They came back again during the night. I kept watching as they removed eight guys from the pod, some for extorting the sex offenders and some for carrying debt books from gambling. (It's unlawful to give credit or carry debt). Dale, my neighbor in the next cell, was taken. Dale takes eighteen meds per day, and he also has a gambling addiction. When we take meds, we always have to take them and drink water; they open our mouth so that both the nurse and the guard can see that the meds are gone. Somehow, in spite of all that, Dale hid his meds in his mouth and was selling them to work off his gambling debts. As a "greenie" (new guy), I live here in this jail, and it looks like a pretty peaceful place. I don't realize all the underground fighting and aggression that's going on.

6/19/10

Tuesday morning at 4:30 a.m., I got the knock on the door and was told to pack up my stuff and go to booking. Three of us were placed in a cell and joined by a fourth, Jim, who has since become a good friend. At 6:30 a.m. we were removed from the cell, taken to a room where we were told to take off our prison orange suits and given back our street clothes.

We were all cuffed and shackled and placed in a van along with three others in orange suits. We had no confirmation of where we were going. We came to Anoka, stopped at Anoka County Jail, and picked up two more guys in orange suits. After Anoka we ended up at St. Paul Federal Court house where the prisoners in orange suits got out. The rest of us went to Minneapolis where we were delivered back to the US marshals.

At 9:30 a.m. they removed the four of us from our cells, replaced the shackles and cuffs, and loaded us back into the van; we headed east. We got our first look at Duluth Federal Prison Camp at 2:00 p.m. on Tuesday. We couldn't see any fences. There was no guardhouse and no gate. It was a dark, overcast, and rainy day. It seemed like we were just at a campus of some kind, which is what it is. It was originally built as an Air Force base, and I'm sure it had more security at that time than it has now.

The bus pulled around behind some buildings, and we were unloaded. It was amazing for us to be standing outside with no cuffs, shackles, or chains. Even though it was raining, it was the first time we stood in daylight in seven weeks. We never saw a gun, taser, or handcuff. We were about to enter a world of big change, the first to be negative.

6/20/10

As the bus pulled up to the booking office, it was raining, and the place looked bleak. We saw a lot of men walking on the compound dressed in army green suits. The booking officer came out and was taking our names. A man (I presumed an inmate) walked up like he was going into the booking office. The booking officer screamed at the man, told him to get out of here, and said he didn't want to see him again. It reminded me of how we might run off a stray dog on the farm when we didn't want to see him on the farm again.

The door opened, and we were marched in. Two officers were doing the booking. Now, the correctional officers (CO) at this place are beyond constructive discipline. They are people who hate their jobs; they hate inmates, they are lazy, and they see people like us as obstacles to mess up their quiet, self-centered lives. Inside, we were all placed in two cells, and they took us out one at a time. We were taken to another cell and strip searched. We were given some temporary, surgical-type suits and slippers just to last us to the next day, but they also easily identified us as new prisoners. We were passed from psychologist to nurse to counselor. The interview with the CO, Duke, was him basically telling me to get the [expletive] out of his office.

I was waiting with Jim, a young farmer from Southern, MN. Jim is in for buying cocaine on the phone. Jim likes to talk way too much; he talks dirty and claims to know everything but comes across as really foolish to anyone who is a little older. Duke asked Jim if he was a member of a gang. Jim said, "No." Duke checked "Gang Associates." Duke couldn't find his pen and accused Jim of stealing it. I happened to know that another CO didn't have a pencil and took it. They seemed to believe me when I told them.

We were waiting in line until around 9:00 p.m. Then we were escorted to our dorm. The dorms are Air Force barracks that were built in the 1950s. I finally arrived at my building, 208, which has 150 inmates in it and is an old two-story wooden structure. We walked in out of the rain, and the inmates had just finished "cooking" their after-dinner meal, which was beans, rice, curry, and a lot of seasonings I have never smelled before. Men were all over, peering at me, and wanting to get a look at the new guy. My room had four bunks and three men: Bert is a thirty-eight-year-old serving ten years for selling cocaine; Ace is twenty-two years old; and Jose is twenty-six.

Bert is a barber in prison; he sold drugs on the outside. Bert has two children but no wife. He seems very level headed but was caught in a robbery when he was fifteen and served time in juvenile detention. He came very close to being involved in an armed robbery where someone was killed. He has been here five years and has fifteen months to go.

Ace has been in business since he was twelve. His businesses were landscaping, T-shirt spraying, and tennis shoe painting. He found out he could buy really good T-shirts that normally sell for twenty-five dollars for five if he bought them in volume. He would buy them for five dollars, spray them, and sell them for twenty-five. He had four people on the pay roll in his dad's garage working full time. He paid them $250 per week. One day in school, the teacher was using him as a bad example in an economics class. He always wore expensive clothes. The teacher asked him how much his shirt cost, his pants, his shoes, etc. When she added it up, she had almost $2,000 worth of clothes. She went on to say that his dad's income is probably $45,000 and proceeded to tell the class how foolish that was. Ace felt humiliated so he went to the front of the room and told his business story. He pulled out a roll of $100 bills and counted out in front of the class a stack totaling $1,000. Then he did it a second time and a third time until he had $10,000 out of his pocket. He said, "My father didn't pay for any of this. I have my own business, and this is my money." The teacher said, "Oh, we need to go to the principal's office with this." The principal came in because they were all sure he was selling drugs. He said, "No, I'll prove it." He took them to his locker. He kept all his records in his school locker because he didn't have a safe place anywhere else. He showed them the dates and the times of the landscaping work he had done, all the T-shirts sales he made, and all the tennis shoes he painted. He explained his business.

The teacher thought he was a business genius after that. But then they started thinking about his income tax reporting. He didn't know anything about that. They said we better call the IRS. They did. The guy came over and wanted to see his garage where he did the work. It was well equipped. They asked his dad why he did this for his son, but his dad said he didn't know anything about it. Ace had all his money in a shoebox in the house. He said he never spent any of it other than his business expenses. The fancy clothes he had were always given to him by girls. He always took his cash from sales and had it turned into $100 bills and put tape around them. Ace said he didn't really know how much money he had in the box because he never bothered to count it. The IRS guy started counting, and it came to $150,000 in $100 bills. The IRS took $100,000 and returned the rest to him. His dad told him he couldn't have more than $250 in his possession again. Ace had to lay off his employees and close his business. He gave them each $2,500 severance pay. He was fifteen.

At sixteen, Ace had gotten used to the higher lifestyle, and since he couldn't work, he got into selling drugs and then really made a lot of money. He bought his mother a house to get her out of the ghetto, bought cars for people, spent a lot of money, and then got caught on a drug charge. And now has five years to serve.

Jose got confirmed last night in the Catholic church. I went to his confirmation. A bishop was here to do mass, hear confessions, and do the confirmation. It was a big deal to some. Jose thinks it's pretty good because now he can get married as a Catholic if he ever wants to. Jose describes himself as a womanizer and a partier. He likes marijuana and ecstasy and lots of women. I slept but woke repeatedly; I survived the first day.

Bob, age 8, with his dad, age 46

5

I finally have a job, and it is in the recreation room. I don't really have anything to do there, but it's the place to which I report. I found favor in someone's eyes and got appointed there. I keep telling the people that I don't mind work. I like something to do, but I also want to show them I'm not lazy. That small amount of effort gets attention, partly because it's unusual here and partly because of my age. Nobody expects me to have any energy. But we have been praying that God would give me favor in their eyes.

It's really kind of strange how life is here. It really isn't boring, yet it's not exciting. A lot of time is wasted waiting in lines for food, phones, washing machines, mail, typewriters, pills, and more things than you can imagine. Very small things are much bigger here: trying to keep rules that aren't written or explained and trying not to put energy into rules that are written but never expected to be kept. In a way, that makes life simple.

Today, I got a call to the dorm and learned my room had been changed. I am now in a room with three very nice, quiet guys who are all in their fifties.

7/10/10

The chapel is a nice looking building. It's hard to get a job there, but I am told they like to give those jobs to those who participate. Makes sense to me. The downside is that the chapel is the chapel for twelve religions, some I have never heard of. The Native Americans have their sweat lodge on the chapel grounds. The pagans have their service that has something to do with Wicca or something like that. I couldn't tell if any of the staff are Christians or not. The chaplain spoke at our orientation. He weighs about 350 pounds, didn't introduce himself to the group, and said if you want to see him his hours were 11-2 on Wednesday and Thursday and two hours on Wednesday night. He didn't strike me as a guy who would be very interested in any ideas that would even remotely make more work for him.

I went to the service on Sunday. The minister was from the street and was exceptionally good. He was a retired Presbyterian minister. Unfortunately, he needs to have surgery and won't be back for quite a long time. Most of the guys say the speakers are pretty bad. I went to a Wednesday night gospel meeting put on by inmates. It was okay for me but not something I could take new believers to and expect them to get anything out of. It was mostly nice emotional stuff. Saturday night they had a good movie. I'm looking at it through the eyes of evangelizing, but I don't know if it's the right tool for me. I think I could get a job there if I worked at it, but the guys in the barracks are really resistant to church. Most of them have never been inside a church and are afraid something freaky will happen to them if they go there.

The spiritual environment here is so different from Elk River. The Bibles in the rooms are not used at all. The only Bible studies are done in the church, and only a few churched people go there, maybe twenty guys or so. I'm praying about direction on what to do with that.

The environment in our barracks is more pagan than I have ever experienced. It starts with the staff who are typical government employees with mindsets that go along with that. They don't want to be talked to for fear it might give them more work. But I think God is watching out for me because guys are amazed that I got in a four-man room and not a six and that I got a bottom bunk. The first night guys came with things I needed like shaving cream, a razor, a tooth brush, tooth paste, shower shoes, shorts, tennis shoes, and everything I would need for a while. I was just amazed.

7/11/10

Five of us guys who came up together get together every night and make jokes about the system. There are those who know how to get everything they want. They know how to work the system. We all have decided that we are not going to do that though because it really nurtures a gangster mentality. It sucks you into it without even thinking about it. As we were discussing it, then, we all realized that the shoes we were given by inmates when we checked in, the haircut we bought with stamps, the alarm clock that was given to me, and the shower shoes loaned to us by inmates were illegal. It is illegal to accept things from other inmates or exchange anything between inmates.

We are going to work at finding some positive story of someone who really learned something here. While it's a source of a lot of humor at night, it really is sad. It's sad because these younger men come in and spend five to twenty years of their life here like this, and they are released with no positive connections on the street and a felony on their record to boot. It's going to be hard. I'm confused about connecting with the church. It is such a hodgepodge of everything. You might get a sincere prayer, then a humanistic message, and then a new age poem. You just don't know what it will be. The singing has been so pathetic too. This week I thought I would go to choir practice and see what it is like. They seem to like the old songs that still have a base to them, but the singers don't know how to harmonize, and I don't know if they can carry a tune. Well, the two songs they picked for today were "He Touched Me" and "I'll Fly Away." Both have a strong bass moving part, and they didn't have a bass. After we sang through it once, they identified me as their bass, gave me my own microphone, and turned the volume way up. We sang it in church this morning, and I sang bass like I never sang bass before. It went over big in the service because I don't think they have had a song that was even partially musical before. Next week, the quartet sings, and I'll be the bass.

7/12/10

I have developed a good relationship with a young Puerto Rican named Chas. Chas has taken a liking to me and has really taken care of me. He has given me all kinds of things I needed, tells me the things to watch out for, and is very protective of anyone he sees talking to me. He told my room-mates they better clean up their language (not that it's done any good) and introduces me to people all the time, and telling me if they are good people or people I need to watch out for. While Chas tells others to watch their language, his own language is just out of the park, stuff I would never put up with on the outside. I put up with a lot of this kind of thing because I want to see these guys as what they will be rather than what they are now. Chas is a key help for me, and I am hoping that Chas is going to be my main leader. Chas runs interference for me with Duke to the point now that Duke thinks I'm a pretty good guy. Chas walks with me every day, and Duke is so curious that Chas and I are so close. He calls me "Chas's Dad." Today he said to Chas, "What's the old man indoctrinating you in when you walk with him every day." When I walk with Chas, he talks about his dad taking him out selling drugs with him when he was twelve years old. Chas got half the money. He joined a gang when he was twelve. He said his son is now twelve, and he wants to be with his son so that he doesn't follow in his tracks. Chas's dad just got out of prison this week. His dad was a very tough guy, always lifted a lot of weights as does Chas. He talks a lot about how tough his dad is. His dad has now apologized for how he treated him. Chas lifts weights and has a very hard body. He always wears very loose fitting clothes. I said at home guys that work out wear very form fitting clothes to show it off. He said he never did that. He said he wanted to hide his build so that guys wouldn't know what they were getting into.

From Jan

The drive to Duluth became routine. I would leave my apartment at 6:30 AM on Saturday, arrive at "the camp" at 9:00 AM, and visit Bob till 3:00 PM when visiting hours ended. I knew every land mark and exactly how many minutes it would take before I would get there. I could bring nothing in the visiting room except my driver's license and cash for the vending machines. (The hamburgers and sandwiches in the vending machines were such a big deal for the guys. It was such an improvement over the regular prison food.) Often, I had a slip of paper in my pocket with questions or information for Bob.

At first, our visits were awkward. I would wonder, "Who are all these men? What was their crime? Is this a safe place? How long can I keep doing this?"

As the weeks passed, I met more women, and Bob introduced me to men he was getting to know. The men in the visiting room were more or less the cream of the crop. Only a small portion of the men get visits. This was to become our new community of friends.

I met many women from various backgrounds: Russian, Latino, African-American, and Asian. They were kind, generous, and loving people, all helping each other survive this prison experience.

My weekend visits were not just to see Bob but also to meet up with friends.

Sometimes, we stayed in a hotel, several of us in a room, and brought crock pots of food to cut down on expenses. We would sit by the pool at night and watch children swim and play with their new friends. I was thankful the children could look forward to this after long visits with little to do at the camp.

Sometimes people on the outside gave me gifts to give to the children of inmates. I could not bring anything into the visiting center so I kept them in the back of my car. When visiting hours were over, I would open my trunk and let them choose something to take home. It brought a smile to their faces and mine as well.

Bob and I have friends from our church in Willmar that spend summers at their quaint cottage on a lake near the prison. I was blessed by their warm hospitality, comfort, meals, and company while playing games on many summer weekends

From Amy, My Daughter

When Dad went to prison, we were very open with our children about what was happening. We decided to be open and honest about it, and while it was painful seeing Dad in prison, we decided to make the best of it. We drove from Kansas City to Duluth four or five times a year. We enjoyed seeing Dad, but we enjoyed the trip as well. Our family has fond memories of Duluth, the North Shore, Gooseberry Falls, and just being on Lake Superior. The visits in the visiting center were very special, and I think Dad had more contact and input with our children than most grandparents do on the outside.

7/16/10

The guys who came up with me on the bus are Jim, Tony, and Peter. Jim and Peter are really funny and have us laughing a lot. I am convinced that Jim and Peter are here only because of bad attorney work, and I think their cases will be overturned. It is gut wrenching for those guys to be living with the injustice of that every day and fighting their cases from in here when the communication is so limited. In a strange way, I feel I am better off just being resigned to the fact that I have lost everything. I don't feel good about all the happenings but really believing and understanding God's sovereignty makes a big difference. Even the injustice in the justice system is under God's control. At the same time, I think it is right for Peter and Jim to be fighting to overturn their cases. Most of the frustrations for these guys are from their attorneys who won't respond to their phone calls and letters. Jim and I have been meeting together, fasting, and praying for his case. Jim is really growing in his faith through it all. He is a great guy. He has been divorced three times and is interested in going through *First Principles* with me.

Another guy is known as X. That's the only name I know him as. He is Mexican and from Chicago. He told me he really wants to change his life. I take that as God at work. I told him about my prayer partners, and I told him I would have my partners pray for him. He said, "Would they do that?" I said, "Yes, they will."

The movie *Fire Proof* was on in the chapel last night. I had invited five of the hardcore guys to go to the movie with me. Three went, and two stood me up. Heavy went. Heavy has two children with a girl who is not his wife. In the past as I encouraged him to think about "being with" her, he resisted. He said he didn't care about her. After the movie he said two things. He said, "Bob, don't take me to any more of these movies. They are too hard on my heart." As he hit his chest, he then said, "I'm going to call my girl and have her see that movie." That's the first time he has called her his girl. Now, he is agreeing to be in my first principles class.

This afternoon the Duluth Air Show was on. I sat by another inmate named Bert. Bert is a hog farmer who came in last week. We have seen him crying and hanging around the chapel a lot. He said he hasn't been to church in twelve years but now has been five times in one week. Bert has just started a five-year sentence. His wife of twenty-two years has had three strokes, is mostly blind, and needs him very badly. He feels very bad for her, his dad who knows nothing about his offense, and his twenty-one-year-old son who he is real close with. Bert is Catholic, swears like a trooper, and he says he really wants to change. He says he still loves drugs but knows that he needs to be with his wife and needs to change. I have an appointment to walk with him tomorrow at 9:00 a.m.

7/30/10

Jim and I meet at 6:00 a.m. almost every day. We skip breakfast (we call it a fast) and pray through that time. It is really amazing to us how we can identify answered prayer. For Jim, it is about his case and the mismanagement of his businesses. Jim had no idea he was coming here and has a lot of unfinished business. His attorney told him he would only get probation if he pled guilty. He pled and got four years; they took him into custody from the sentencing. Jim is really growing spiritually and wants to support me in getting some ministry established here. Tom has sent me two copies of *First Principles*, and Jim loves them. Jim works in education and thinks we might get the curriculum approved. The first time around we are just going to do it on our own.

Yesterday, walking to the dorm, I found myself walking with Joe. Joe is grey-haired, has a ponytail, comes to choir, and sings badly. I asked him if his faith has been an important part of his life very long. He said, "No, only since prison." He said he accepted Christ in his prison cell and got baptized by the chaplain.

Midweek, I came in the dorm, and Chas was standing by Duke's office. He hollered, "Bob, come in here." I went in, and he said, "Tell Duke about that Bible study you want to do here. Maybe we could do it for the dorm orderlies." Duke said, "Well, Bob is kind of an inspirer. He inspires me." I know I have never been inspirational around Duke. It was God working. I was just greatly encouraged.

This morning I got a beautifully illustrated Bible story book in the mail. Security tore off the wrapper so I don't know who sent it to me. I showed the Bible to Sam first because Sam seems to have softness in his heart, and he said he was baptized a few years ago in prison but doesn't seem to know anything about the Word.

When I was with X today I showed it to him. He really wanted to know where I got it, and I had to say I didn't know and that someone just sent it to me. I told him, "There are people praying for you, and I don't even know all of them because there are way more prayer partners than I know. There is quite an opportunity for ministry here.

6

I have been putting most of my energy into making contacts that will lead into Bible studies. I now have eleven people on my list. The guys range from two that are Christians and seem quite well established to some who might be Christians but are not established and some who are definitely not Christians.

There is another group of guys who are Mexican and Puerto Rican; they who prefer to have their own group. These guys are going to be more challenging and mostly know nothing about the gospel, the church, or even family life. They have not known their dads, but now they are dads. The biggest hot button for them I have found is that it will help them be better dads.

I am amazed how God has placed me in a work situation where I have nothing to do or to tie me down but still have the freedom to go anywhere on the compound. That means I can walk into these guys' work sites and talk to them on the job. They have nothing to do anyway, and they are extremely approachable.

8/18/10

There are thoughts that have been rolling around in my head that I have never dared to attempt to put on paper. It has been interesting, almost strange, how experiences and thoughts from my childhood and early adult life revisit me here. When I was seventeen, I had just begun driving a livestock truck for Gerald Zylstra. It was a tractor-trailer configuration, and I was excited that he trusted me with his new rig, along with the challenge of driving a load of cattle through the twin city traffic to deliver livestock to South St. Paul. I was to drop off the cattle at the stockyards then spend the night and pick up a load of twine at the Minnesota State Penitentiary.

I brought my load to the stockyard at about 10:00 p.m. I then proceeded to the wash rack where I scooped out the truck and then washed it out with a high-powered water hose. I slept in the Shippers Club, which was a large second floor dorm where one would check in at the desk and for three dollars a night they gave you a bedroll and the right to pick a bunk where you could spend the night. I would guess the room held about one hundred bunks. I went to sleep that night in the strange environment, excited that the next day I would see what a prison was all about.

By 7:00 a.m. I was on my way to Stillwater with my freshly cleaned truck to get my load of twine. I was excited and a little nervous about maneuvering my long truck inside the walls of a prison. I was excited to see what these kinds of people would be like who had done the kinds of things that lead them to life in prison. I was wondering if it would be safe. Would I be threatened? Would these be dangerous guys?

I checked in at the prison office and took care of the paperwork. They told me to bring the truck around to the side where there were some large steel doors. I was to pull up to the doors and wait for the guards. As I pulled up to the doors, four guards came out. They inspected the truck inside and out, underneath and on top. I didn't know what they were looking for but, for me, it added to the drama.

The big doors opened, and I followed the instructions and backed up to the loading dock as they walked in and out of my truck. I watched as though some real drama could break out at almost any time. I thought I must be surrounded by gangsters and killers.

My truck was finally loaded. Two guards hopped in the back of the truck, and I drove over to the big steel doors as instructed. I stopped while two more guards came and inspected in, under, over, under the hood, and every inch of the truck. The doors opened, and I was free to go.

I drove the four-hour drive home thinking about those convicts who were prisoners in Stillwater. Who were they? What had they done? Were they terrible people who were haters and killers? What all goes on behind those walls?

I was intrigued by prison life ever since, and I find it so ironic that I am here today, probably thought of in much the same way I thought of those guys when I was seventeen years old in 1955. The thoughts of that have come back to me many times.

I have been really busy recruiting for my *First Principles* classes that begin Tuesday. I've had a challenge getting the books in here. I was told I could receive five books at a time. When they arrived in the mailroom, the man called me and asked what I was doing with all these books. I said I'm giving them to guys for a study, which the chaplain has approved. He said, "You really don't want me to know that; I could put you in the hole for that. I'll send them back and let you go this time, but I don't want to see any more of this." I told him there were more already on the way. Next day, the same thing happened. Turns out I need to send the donor the specific name and address of the recipient, and they need to go directly to that person. I have been surprised with the enthusiasm some of the inmates have for the illustrated Bible and also for their enthusiasm to be part of the *First Principles* studies. It's really rewarding for me.

One example is a young Puerto Rican named Beni. Next year, he will be thirty-two years old and will have spent half of his life in prison. I told him I would like to walk with him and talk. He lit up and was eager for it. He had no idea what it was about. He had seen me walking and talking with some of the other guys. During the first two miles, I got his story. He grew up bouncing around between Puerto Rico, New York, and Philadelphia. He has never known his dad and was raised mostly by his grandmother. Beni was in jail the first time at age fourteen. He said he has been in jail so many times it doesn't mean anything anymore, but this time when he gets out he wants to make sure he supports himself and is not dependent on family. He is taking carpentry, truck driving, and he is really good at cutting hair.

I asked Beni if he has ever had an older man speak to him about life. He said, "Never. I have never had an older man talk to me." I told him a little about my life. Then I told him about life development and my four Fs: faith, family, fitness, and finance. (That's my standard presentation.) I told him I would like to meet with him more, and I invited him to my class. He was so happy to be invited. Since that talk he has seen me three times. Yesterday, he said he has another guy he would like me to talk to. He had told him about our conversation, and he said he wants that also. I can see now where there is going to be a challenge just keeping up with this.

Another example is James, who is African-American and just over six feet; he has gold-plated teeth and a tear tattooed under his left eye. He has been a gang member. James has looked after me since the first day I came here, always asking me if I'm doing okay. Last night, I asked James how long he has been down. He said, "Ten years with ten more to go." I asked him how often he gets visits, and he said he has never had one. I asked him if he gets mail ,and he said he didn't. I asked if he would like someone to write to him, and he said he would really like that. I said it would not be romantic writing. He said, "No, a pen pal." James claims to know Christ, and he said he was baptized two years ago. I don't think he knows what that means. His language around the guys is really tough. I hadn't invited him into the class because he seems a little slow, and I didn't think he'd get it. I decided to invite him. He said, "Bob, I see you with a lot of different guys, and I respect you for that. I should have done that. When I got here, I just stayed with my own tight little circle." He has a soft heart with a very hard shell on the outside.

I met a new inmate this week by the name of Plato. He has been down six years and became a Christian six years ago. He is so zealous for the gospel and is going to be in our group. He is in a few separate Spanish Bible studies. He is a singer, and he says he sings falsetto and plays the guitar. We are going to try to work on a few songs together. He might be in both of my *First Principles* groups because of his Spanish. I will also try to get him to come to my Mexican and Puerto Rican group. I would like to have at least one Christian in the group. It might become a little challenging for me.

7

My mind is constantly on evangelism, the Gospel, and how to communicate. I read it, sleep it, and work at it all day long. I am learning a lot. I feel I have excellent resources with *Alive at Last*, a book by John Piper, my Bible, and the constant exposure to the men. I am learning a lot. It's rewarding at times and frustrating at times. It's impossible to tell you how I feel; any description would be right for moments and wrong for moments. It's all over the place in the same day.

My phone, e-mails, and postage run almost $150 per month. It's my biggest expense. It's a challenge because if I end up paying restitution, they won't allow more than $400 per quarter coming in or else they will take it out of my account here. I just have to live on as little as I can. A candy bar is a real luxury. I have to learn to live like this. This is how most of the world lives.

Exercising is going really well. I have a personal trainer, a young black guy from Kansas City. He has me on pushups, pull-ups, sit-ups and a real prescription. He works with me three days a week. I only work out twenty minutes at this time. Then I walk on my own. He is in my *First Principles* class.

I eat well, and my trainer is coaching me on that too. I don't behave as well on that. Sleeping is pretty good, but I am up a couple times per night and sleep about seven hours. I think that's about as good as I can expect. My roommates sleep a lot more.

As far as loneliness is concerned, it's hard to describe. Someone sent me two books on loneliness. I identify with all of it, but it's not even interesting for me to read about it because I feel I know all that. I never consider loneliness my enemy. It hurts sometimes. Yes, there are tears sometimes, but in the same day, like this morning, I might sneak to chow early to get in the dining hall before the crowd. I will just pick a table so I can sit all by myself. So, I guess what I'm saying is that it's always hard to say how I feel and have it be accurate because it's all over the place. The most important thing is purpose, and most of the time I feel purpose.

Since my incarceration I have listened to many stories. Obviously, the stories are not all the same. In fact, everyone is different. There are, however, feelings and emotions that can be identified in most all of them.

For some reason I knew that four to five years was a possibility. I don't know if I was in the denial stage or the last stage where I thought there may be a reprieve and that "probation only" could be a likely possibility. That was what I was thinking when I went to the courthouse that last morning. I didn't know what to expect. I was told earlier that the sentencing process is short. Although I had been told to be prepared for the possibility of going into custody that day, I really was thinking that I would probably have thirty days to get my affairs in order and then do a "self surrender" by having someone drive to wherever I was going to be incarcerated. It was another moment of shock and awe when as I was standing facing the judge a man in uniform came alongside of me and said, "I am a federal marshal. I am taking you into custody. Please remove your watch, necktie, belt, and coat. I did. He placed the handcuffs on me and walked me out the side door. I heard some of my family crying behind me and heard them call to me, "We love you, Dad." To this day I cannot sort out my feelings as they placed me in a cell.

They talk about great rehabilitation available through education. But what I hear about almost all the classes is that when the instructors walk into the room, they say, "Sign here!" and hand out the papers. The paper says that you have taken the class. If you sign the paper, you can leave. It would be very difficult to learn a trade here. It is sad because that is what these guys need. When they get out of here with a felony, it will be almost impossible for them to get a job where they can support a family. They have tasted the easy money of drug dealing before and that is why the recidivism rate is so high. Most do not intend to get in trouble again but most are so ill-equipped when they get out.

As far as white-collar inmates go, most that have had and lost a business, are broke, and are also unemployable. They have to have enough creativity to be self-employed so that their felony won't be a problem. One man who was a physician's assistant is taking a truck-driving course. They do the class work, and then they are given some toy trucks which they pull around on a road laid out on a table. They pull the truck with a string. An inmate has written a good curriculum for the class. A truck-driving school wants to use the curriculum and has offered two tractor-trailer rigs in exchange for the curriculum. The warden says "no" to that. There are so many things that could be done, but they get rejected.

Today is Saturday, and we had choir practice. The choir director came to me before practice and said, "I'm resigning as choir director, and you need to do it." The choir is so bad, and the quartet is not good. But the director said that the guys say the service is so much better since we now have a choir and quartet. It is so dry with just listening to the chaplain. The sad part is that some guys come so broken with so much sorrow that they are just looking for some relief. Even if it is bad, we need to be doing something for them. These untalented energetic microphone grabbers who are thinking mostly about themselves having a chance to be on the stage are what we have to work with. Strangely enough, God seems to be using this crazy thing to meet some needs. At first I didn't want to be associated with it but now I see it is so desperately needed that I can't say no.

9/7/10

It is starting to feel like Fall. One thing I've learned about the weather is that it is really either the best or the worst. On Wednesday it was fifty-five degrees with rain all day and winds twenty-five to thirty miles per hour. We were all wearing parkas with hoods, and standing in line in the rain makes me wonder about winter here. The last two days have been cool. Even so, the sun has been out, and there isn't a prettier place when the sun shines.

I worked hard to get one class of ten recruited for my *First Principles* class. Jim is a real promoter. He had open houses where we gave away a can of Pepsi so we could tell the guys about the class. Jim was a real blessing the whole time with the administration side of the classes. He used his influence to get us a room, made sure tables were set up, and really added a professional touch to it all. I am so thankful for that help. It seems like in the last week, the word got out about the class and all at once I have two classes of twelve each. It is a lot of work. I meet with every man individually for at least one hour to get their story and to check out to see that they have motivation and understanding of what this is about. They all really like the idea of something that will help them develop their lives. If they are new, they are scared about their time here. If they are thinking about getting out, they are often scared about what that means. They know they need change in their lives. Most say they believe in God and in Jesus, but they really don't know what that means. It is such a privilege to be able to be with them during this part of their lives.

I could go on forever with stories of the experiences. Even how we get together is interesting. I do feel that God is really at work in bringing this together. I feel very challenged, and I am learning so much. I never have been satisfied with my own presentation of the gospel. I have really been in the Word, working on my presentation, which is my story, and I have been presenting it so frequently. I seem to be getting it down to where it makes sense and is attractive to others.

I have a man named Flip in a class who is fifty-two years old. He has used drugs for twenty-five years, and toward the end it was all methamphetamine. Flip said he was high on meth continuously for the last eight months before he was arrested. He has been down for five years, and he said it took two years to get over the meth. When we talked about eternity, he said he believes in heaven, and he thinks he's in pretty good shape there. I asked why. He said, "I've done a number of pretty good things in my life, and I think I'm all right." I said, "If you are wrong would you want to know it?" He asked what I meant. I said, "If you're wrong about getting to heaven on the good things you've done, if it doesn't have anything to do with that, would you want to know it now?"

He met me the next morning, and I briefly shared the gospel. He is coming to class just based on that.

9/12/10

I realized from the start that I am not well-equipped to lay out the gospel in a very effective way. This is the story of my life. I have not had a lot of formal education. Most of what I've done in my entire life has been from seeing it and watching it done, internalizing it, and seeing how it works for me. Then I pass it along in story form to someone else. This is what I did in the life insurance business. I really didn't have any teacher. I was fortunate to have bought my own policy when I was fourteen years old. When I was twenty-two years old, that policy gave me the money to buy my first piece of real estate.

My next phase in business was as a recruiter and trainer. I didn't have any formal training in recruiting and training either. I just thought through how I survived in the business. I taught people how to think through their lives and then connect it to their own financial experience or what they found to be solutions to their own problems. Then they would formulate that into a story, and it became a major part of their presentation. It worked well for us. Many became leaders in the company.

When BILD asked me to work in development, there was no one to educate me. The idea was just to talk to men of wealth in local churches across the U.S. and talk to them about how they might spend their time, talent, and treasure. The outcome, hopefully, would be that they would rethink their life goals and see their wealth as having a greater purpose in God's kingdom. I was intimidated by this. I found myself always talking to people much more educated and wealthier than I was, with greater success than I had. As I would pray about upcoming interviews with these guys, it always seemed that God's desire for me was just to tell what I knew and not try to talk about what I didn't know. The only thing I knew was my own personal story so that's what I talked about. It seemed to work quite well. I am reminded of this repeatedly when I feel unequipped for a task before me now.

As I meet with inmates, I feel unequipped and inadequate. But when I talk to guys I always ask them about their childhood, their family, and their dad. Almost always, their dad was absent, or if he was present, they didn't have good memories of him. At first, I felt guilty because I had a good childhood experience with home life and with my dad. I have done a lot of thinking about that. I have developed my personal story from my memories, and I see how God has used it even to shape my theology about God. I have come to an understanding that it is possible for my story to be used as an encouragement and that it doesn't discourage the men when they think about their own lives.

9/13/10

Yesterday, I was coming out of the chow hall, and a young man called out, "Mr. Goris, can I talk to you?" I walked over, and he said, "I heard about your class. Can I join?" I said, "We are full, but I'm willing to overfill it. Usually someone needs to drop out." We set up the time and met in the chapel.

His name is Miguel, but he likes to be called B.J. He was born in Chicago. His mother went to prison when he was eleven years old. His dad went to live in the Philippines for a while because he was attached to a crime, and he knew he would be indicted. He later died in the Philippines, never returning to the U.S.

B.J. lived with different brothers and sisters. He was the youngest of seven children. He never got into drugs and never joined a gang. It just never interested him. He wanted to try to make something of himself. He attended three different high schools. He became very depressed because he was searching for the meaning to life.

He wrote in his journal every day and what he wrote in his journal was a cry out to whatever god would hear him. He bought a Bible and read it completely through. He didn't understand much of it, but he did gain some understanding. He became more depressed. One Sunday, he stopped into a neighborhood church. He sat down, and when the preacher began to preach, he just began crying uncontrollably. He had never been in that church before. No one knew him, and nobody talked to him. He just left.

At the age of nineteen, he decided to move to San Diego. He had $700 in cash and bought a bus ticket for $300. When he got to San Diego, he stayed in a youth hostel for a week for $150. He couldn't afford that anymore so he found a hotel advertised for $125 per week. It was a horrible hotel, and he said even though he had lived in Chicago most of his life he had never met such strange people and goings-on as he saw in that hotel.

There were three questions that had gone through his mind for a long time. They were: 1) Who am I?; 2) What am I here for; and 3) What's the meaning of life? One night, he had decided there were no answers to the questions, and he decided to kill himself. During the night he got up to go to the bathroom. It was a communal bathroom at the end of a long hall. Walking down the hall, he found a table with a few books on it that people were throwing away. A book was lying on the table, and the subtitle of the book was the three questions, exactly the way he had been asking. He read it and believed. He stayed in California for two years and found some churches and attended them.

When he was twenty-three, he moved back to Chicago. His oldest brother picked him up at the airport and told him he should work and hang out with him because he needed a place to live. He did for six months. During that time he found out his brother was dealing drugs so he left to go Honduras on a mission trip. He was gone two years.

When he came back, his brother had moved to the Philippians to avoid an indictment. The FBI came to B.J. because their names are very similar. When they found out he didn't know where his brother was, they indicted him as he was named as a conspirator along with twenty-five people who were involved with his brother. He plead guilty and got five years. He served one year somewhere else so we will have four years together. He is such a nice, committed Christian and so eager to learn more and grow. He has never had an older man to lead him, and he is so happy about this. I am, too.

9/19/10

The studies are going well. We are losing some men, of course. That's the way it happens even in the church. Some have conflicts that come up, some just don't want to do the work, and some are in Satan's grasp and he just won't let them participate. Nonetheless, our Tuesday night class has a net of eight right now. At the end of the second lesson, which is on baptism, four of the men wanted to be baptized. I just finished helping X write a letter to the donor who got him an illustrated Bible.

8

10/2/10

The lost has been found, or rather the stolen has been returned! My Bible was taken from the activity center. The guys I hang with were sure that it wasn't for value but revenge. One suspicion is that the word is that I don't like drug dealers. About six weeks ago the guys were saying that at least drug dealers are honest because they give people something for their money. I made the remark that they give young people and children ruined lives for their money. That got the idea out that I don't like drug dealers.

In any event, Jim suggested that I hang posters around the compound, saying that my bag was missing and what was in it. I did that. The response to it was amazing. I have been careful not to be flaunting my Bible. When I carry it around the compound, I always have it in a bag, not to be ashamed, because I don't want to be known as a Bible thumper. I think someone felt some pressure with all the talk about it. This morning it showed up in the activity center. It was in a different bag, my typing cartridge and stamps were missing, but my Bible and files with the article on my dad were all there. God has answered our prayers. It is so good to have it back.

I went to a movie last night. It is always revealing to me because I think of myself, after losing so much, to be positive about the opportunity to experience life with less material possessions to distract me. It is easy to think that in here, when the distractions are not here. When I see a movie, I see homes on the lake, boats, houses, restaurants, and lifestyles that I know will never be part of my life again. It's a big emotional experience for me to see that. It's not just a sad emotion. It is much bigger than that, and I find it necessary to remind myself that this is a good thing. I will depend on God, let him be my provider, and lay my burden down before him.

I don't think much about life after prison. It is too far away. In my own way, though, I identify with the drug dealers and the cocaine addicts who really want to turn over a new leaf. They don't want to return here again and are desperate to do the right things to help them change while they are here.

They know that living a Christian life here isn't that hard. It is when they get out, and the kids need shoes, friends are driving new cars, and they can't get a job because of a felony that the pressure will be on.

10/7/10

My father, Amos, was a farmer. He started working with his father as a boy and never quite finished elementary school. His mother died when he was seventeen years old, and his father was so grief-stricken that Amos had to take over most of the farming responsibilities at that time. Dad only knew hard work in his life, and there never was time for much relaxation or games. Dad and Mom had five girls, and while they were considered to be real blessings, Dad was really hoping for a boy. I suppose that was because of all the natural reasons that men like to have sons, but there was an additional reason—Dad really wanted to farm more land. He had trained the girls to do a lot of the work that men normally do, such as milking cows, driving tractors, and other outside work. But Dad really wanted to have a son.

Then Mom became pregnant with me. The doctor came out to the farm, and I was born in the farmhouse at home, right in my parents' bedroom. I don't know what conversations Dad had with God about me while Mom was pregnant, but when I was born Dad did a very unusual thing. When I was old enough to understand, I was told that the minute I was born, when I came out of my mother's womb and before I was even cleaned up, Dad took me in his arms, knelt by the bed, and dedicated me to the Lord. As I grew up I was told this story many times, and it had a great impact on me. I knew this was not a customary thing. I knew it meant something important for me, but Dad never told me for certain what he had in mind when he did that.

Dad was a spiritual man, and he took his faith very seriously. Sundays for Dad, and for the family, were mostly about going to church, twice. We practiced very strict Sabbath observance. We would never start a tractor on Sunday or ride a bicycle. We never did any more work than was absolutely necessary such as feeding the livestock, gathering eggs, and milking the cows. The rest of the day would be spent in resting, visiting around the dinner table, and, if we were lucky, on Sunday evening our family might visit another family from the church. The kids would play games while the parents visited.

Being the youngest of six, my parents were older and visited people who didn't have any children. Even when I was very young, the host would get out a few toys for me to play with. I might sit behind the big chair of the man of the house, play with the toy, and listen to the men talk. The conversation usually would be first about the crops and then would turn to Bible doctrine and discussions about the Heidelberg Catechism. I would listen to the discussion of the Catechism or Old Testament stories, and I became fond of that kind of conversation. I remember the discussions on the five points of Calvinism, and I could pretty well relate them.

I knew, already as a boy, that Dad was very proud of me and that I was important to him. I knew that, in addition to dedicating me to the Lord at birth, he and Mom also baptized me at church. That was the custom, but as I grew older I knew it was much more than a custom. I knew there was responsibility in that for my parents and for me as I got older. I pondered my baptism as I saw other families baptizing their children. I wondered about the covenant they were making with God.

I was with Dad a lot. I was very hurt if he ever told me I couldn't go along. As a five-year-old, I watched every move he made. When he hooked up the trailer, I ran to put the bolt in before he did. On the tractor, I watched closely, and when he got off the tractor to open a gate or chase a cow, I would always hop onto the seat and watch for his head to nod, which meant I could drive through the gate or to wherever he wanted. I was with him when he was working on machinery. I watched him like a puppy, to be quick to notice if he needed a wrench or tool, and I would run as hard as I could to get it so that he wouldn't have to wait. He would brag about me to the men at the grain elevator in town. The elevator man would say, "Well, I see you've got your hired man with you today." Dad would say, "Yes, he's the best hired man I've got." It really made me feel good.

When I was six, I hauled every load of grain out of the field that year. I loved taking Dad's note and giving it to the teacher in school. The note said, "Bob won't be in school next week. I need him to help me in the field."

Dad was my hero. I wanted to be like him. When Mom dished up food at the table and was filling my plate, she would ask, "Bob, do you want corn?" I'd say, "Is Dad going to eat corn?" If the answer was yes, I would eat corn too.

By the time I was ten, I took pride in the fact that I knew how to operate every machine on the farm except for the corn picker because corn pickers were just too dangerous. Before I was age ten, Dad would run the combine around the field, and I would haul grain. When Dad stopped for lunch, I would take the grease gun and grease the machine so he could get going again as soon as possible. I knew he liked that and it made him proud of me.

After the combining was finished, we started plowing, each of us on a tractor with a plow. We would start early and work late, only stopping for lunch mid-morning, dinner at noon, and lunch mid-afternoon. I really looked forward to those lunch times. Dad and I would sit in the shade of the tractor wheel and drink coffee and eat a cookie. I would pepper him with questions about tractors, farming, crops, cattle, horses, and all the things I was thinking about when we were going around and around the field with the plows. I would see our neighbor Ben go by with a team of horses. I liked horses. I would say, "Dad, we should have some horses to mow with." He'd say, "No, that's old-fashioned. Progressive farmers don't farm with horses."

Dad never talked to me about what I should be when I grew up. Going back and forth through the field, I thought a lot about that. I knew how Dad gave me, as a baby, to the Lord. I knew that had meaning, and I thought maybe that meant I should be a preacher or a missionary. I just didn't know how that could ever be. Our oat field in Erickson Township, Sacred Heart, Minnesota, seemed a long way from any place where anything like that could happen. I had heard a missionary from Japan speak in our church. That sounded awfully good to me, but I just didn't know how anybody could become a Christian who didn't already know how to be one. In church we sang songs that made me feel very convicted that I would do something important for the Lord, but I was puzzled. At the age of eleven, I sang one song over and over while on the tractor. It went like this: "Must I go up empty-handed? Must I meet my Savior so?

Not one soul with which to greet Him. Must I empty-handed go?"

I didn't want that to be me. I would get tears in my eyes when I sang it. It embarrassed me because being in the dust, tears left a real telltale sign across a dirty face, and I didn't want Dad to know I had been crying. I just knew that real men didn't cry. So it was in the field, riding the tractor, eating lunch behind the wheel, or hauling grain to town with the tractor or car that I was pumping my dad with questions and getting my education. I wanted to be like him, and I was becoming that way more and more each day. I remember the elevator man saying to me, "Well, little boy, what are you going to be when you grow up?" I said, "A preacher." I think I surprised myself when I said it because I had never told anybody that.

10/9/10

My sisters and I went to catechism class in church on Saturday morning. We were required to memorize answers to questions. There was one question and answer that I pondered on a lot. The question was, "What must we know in order to live and die happily?" The answer was, "To know that we are not our own. We have been bought with a price." Dad used that answer, and I thought it had a special meaning for me since he gave me to the Lord as a baby.

I knew when I got old enough I should make public profession of my faith in front of church. I understood that this was a serious event because after that my sins would be on my own head. I lived carefully because I didn't want Dad to suffer for my sins. My main reason for living carefully and obediently was that I didn't want to disappoint Dad. I asked Dad about movies. My friends went to a movie, and I really would like to have gone with them. Dad said, "We don't go to movies. Remember, son, we are not our own. We have been bought with a price."

Dad raised me with a great sense of trust. He trusted me with a lot of things, and I heard him tell other people how much he trusted me. He trusted me with the machinery and that I would operate it just the way I should. He trusted me with the jeep, letting me drive it to the neighbors to visit. When I was in the fifth grade, he trusted me to drive to school every day, a twenty-mile round trip. (He wanted me to go to a Christian school and there was no bus service. I even picked up neighbor kids on the way, never going over his twenty-five mile per hour speed limit.)

I don't think people used the word "love" in those days. I never told Dad I loved him, and I never heard him say it to me. I don't think I missed anything by it. I think I felt love but didn't even think in those terms. I don't think Dad ever hugged me. I don't know what I would have done if he had hugged me. I never saw men hug, and I don't think I would have liked it. I do remember looking at his big hands and wondering what they felt like. I would like to have touched his face, but I never did. Even at age seven, I was much too much of a man to do that.

It was a custom in our church that when kids reached the age of eighteen, if they were responsible and showed their commitment to their faith, that they would go before the elders and make a public profession of their faith. They would be asked catechism questions and, in most cases, were asked to give a reason why they wanted to profess their faith. Then, if the elders made no objections, they would make a profession before the congregation. After that, it was understood that they stood before God as an accountable person and it was their own faith that confirmed that they were in agreement with their baptism.

Those were my experiences growing up. My father had so much passion and love for God. Everything about God was important to him. He trusted God with everything, and Dad trusted me with everything. I learned to trust God so early that I can't remember not trusting him. I didn't want to break Dad's trust, and I didn't want to break God's trust. I wanted to and was striving to please Dad as I am striving to please God today. I find it amazing that it is God's nature that he would even take pleasure in a sinner such as I am, but I know he does and that excites me. When I serve him, I sense God's pleasure, and it energizes me.

I don't think Dad ever thought of the word "commend." It is a word that I have added after thinking about the way Dad raised me. As a boy I was in a hurry to become a man. Dad liked to see me do manly things. For Christmas, when I was ten years old, Dad gave me a Hereford calf. I wasn't too excited about that since we had a whole barn full. I was really thinking of something a little more exciting than a calf. I do believe Dad had a vision for my own development as he gave me that present. The feed for the calf is what I would earn by doing the chores and the field work all year long.

It really worked out well. The calf grew into a steer of about 1,200 pounds. When it sold I was able to buy two to replace it. When I was fourteen, I had sold my steers and went with Dad to Clara City to buy a feedlot of feeder cattle. Walt, the cattleman, said to me, "Bob, come out here in the yard. I've got seven head you really ought to own. They will do real good for you." They were seven big Holstein steers that weighed 700 pounds each. I said, "I don't have enough money to buy seven head." Walt said, "You give me what you have, and I'll take your note for the rest." I agreed that I would like to do that. Walt said, "Well, we'd better ask your dad." We did, and I heard Dad say something I was to hear him say many times after that day. He said, "The kid makes his own decisions." I bought the steers, and they were a good investment.

When I was twelve, the Christian school was building a new grade school. The men from the school came around visiting all the families for a pledge for the school. They sat at one end of the living room and visited with Dad. Dad wrote out a check, and then he said to them, "Now, you'd better talk to Bob." They moved over to my end of the room. I was so honored and proud that these guys would actually talk to me.

That year Dad had allowed me, after the work at home was done, to work for the neighbor, Ray. Ray paid me fifty cents an hour, and for a ten-hour day I could make five dollars. With those earnings, and a little I had before, I had

$250 in my checking account. When the men talked to me about the school, I took my checkbook and emptied it for the school. I wrote out the biggest check I had ever written. It was for $250. That was never such a remarkable thing for me until I became a father and watched my children earn money. I thought back to that day and thought it through from Dad's perspective. As a father myself, I know I would have had a strong tendency to interfere with my son emptying his checkbook. I might have said, "No, you don't need to give that much." But Dad never said that. He didn't interfere. I'm glad that he didn't, because I look at that day as the day I learned how to give. It was important to Dad that "the kid makes his own decisions."

The year of that gift was also the year I decided to make profession of faith at the church. I think that was the time of "commending" for Dad, and I think that was the event that really cemented it for him. I think he really saw me as a man right then and there.

Another important event for me that same year was that I bought a life insurance policy. It was not because I needed life insurance. It was rather that I heard through my sister Marcy about some policies they bought for their boys. They were policies of a savings nature. So I called up the agent and told him I would like one like that. He didn't come. I'm sure that in his mind I was too young to be talking business of that nature with him. One day, I saw his white car coming down the road, and I went out and stopped him. I convinced him to come into the house and show me the policy. He wanted my dad to come and join the meeting at the table. Dad said, "No, the kid makes his own decisions." I started that policy that night, and it ended up being a very important event, one that would lead to my lifetime career.

What is happening in the ministry is amazing. While our class size has reduced because of a lot of confusion of the moving of the classes and having to cancel some, the quality of the classes has increased so much.

This week in our class, we had one particular individual who came saying he needed to investigate and pick a religion. I'll call him Bret. Bret is very opinionated and very financially secure. He said he has the first dollar he has ever earned and is set for life. He just wants to be left alone and not be bothered by anybody. At the same time, he spoke of great anxiety, trying to make sense out of life. I walked with him, and he did all the talking but didn't take much time to listen to answers. This week was his fourth week in class. He said, "So, when we believe this and get this then we deserve to go to heaven?" We spent the next twenty minutes talking about grace. Bret didn't want to receive it as a free gift. It didn't seem right that we could never deserve it. He has never wanted anything in life that he did not deserve, and he didn't want to start now. At the end of the night, Bret was starting to understand that grace is unmerited favor. It was fun seeing his "lights come on." We prayed a prayer of salvation at the end. I believe Bret prayed it in faith, but only God knows.

10/15/10

My friend, Todd, from Minneapolis has shown signs of brokenness ever since I met him. He is in the class and is very attentive. He is here for three years. Two days ago an investigator came and questioned him about some new issues, not connected with his original offense. It was and is very alarming to Todd. Todd and his wife, Jane, have three children, one is a fifteen-year-old who has special needs. Todd is desperately afraid of losing his visiting privileges with his family. Last night we spent time with Todd after the meeting. He is so appreciative. We invited him to our 6:00 AM prayer time, and he came. He says he has totally committed his life to Christ. We spent the whole time talking about Psalm 51 and what God wants to do inside of him. We didn't talk about Todd's case. We prayed together at length. He seems totally broken and contrite. He is confessing Christ. His wife, Jane, is having a hard time living in the community with the publicity of their case.

My roommate, Leroy, is Jewish. I have been careful not to offend him with the gospel, being in the same room. He opened up a little before, but two days ago we spent about thirty minutes just talking about God. He wants to hear more because he really has no religious faith.

Gordon, from California, is doing so well. His wife made an emergency visit from California last weekend. Gordon is fighting for his marriage. His wife didn't think she could survive another year and wanted to compromise their marriage. We have been praying for Gordon. This last weekend was a big victory. It is not all over yet, but God is showing him how to love his wife and fight for his marriage.

My friend Jim had a challenging week. His challenge is the difficulty of living with the understanding that public opinion against someone who is a convict isn't easily overcome. Jim is growing so much and is really drawn to the Word. He is feasting on it and has changed a great deal.

Lloyd, from Topeka, is an amazing guy. His life was so totally overrun and controlled by Satan. Lloyd was involved in every type of crime one could imagine. He had a profound conversion, but after three years had a relapse back into his old, dirty life. He picked up his crime and received a ten-year sentence, which is nearly over. His family has come to faith in a very dogmatic way, thinking of things as either black or white. His son doesn't know if he can trust his dad in his home. His brother-in-law feels the same way. Lloyd is wondering where he will go but is also being courted by the old life. It is amazing that women from his old life know when he is getting out and are courting his attention and making offers. Lloyd is incredibly strong in his faith and knows he cannot return to his old environment. He has been a high roller, lived in luxury, and now must be content with none of that though Satan is offering it back to him on a platter.

The prison has a parenting class, and a friend has suggested that I teach a class on marriage. It would be about how to emotionally support a woman. What I hear these men say about their wives and how they talk to them on the phone is pathetic. A class like that is needed. Most of these wives live terrible lives. If their husbands just talked to them decently it would make such a difference. I'm sure they would be encouraged with even a little effort on the husband's part.

Today Chas asked me what I wanted to talk about. I said, "I want to talk about you and God." He said," I'm waiting till I get out, and then I plan to go to Mass because I'm Catholic." I said, "I don't care if you are Catholic, Presbyterian, Baptist or what you are, because none of that makes any difference. What you need is new life. You are dead, Chas, and God needs to give you new life."

He said, "I'm a real tough guy. I don't think God wants anything to do with anybody as tough as me." I said, "The Apostle Paul killed way more people than you ever have." We talked some more and then he said, "When I was five, my dad shot a man right in front of me. I saw the blood gushing out of his mouth, and I knew I would never be the same. When I was twelve, my dad had me stand outside a bar with a gun. If certain people came for drug money, I was supposed to kill them. I can be better, but I need to do it on my own."

I kept talking to him, and I said, "I think one of the reasons I'm here is for you, Chas. God has a message for you that I need to bring." He said, "Let's hear it." I said, "No, we are going to sit down, and we are going to read it in the Bible. It is Jesus talking to a man, and everything he says to that man is for you." We talked about the fact that Chas is important to God and that God knows him and is a personal God. Chas didn't say much, but he didn't blow me off. We left, both of us expecting to continue the conversation.

This is such an amazing place. I feel as if the house is on fire, and I'm carrying the water from a block away with a bucket. The bucket has holes, and it is leaking. I go to my room and read the Gospels and try to find better ways to present it. Then I read Piper's book. I think I have it down and go to "the street" to use it. I'm making progress, and this seventy-two-year-old mind is learning so much. I have a tremendous practice field right here. I get more experience here in a week than I would in a year on the outside. If I don't get better at presenting the gospel here, there is really something wrong. The real deal, though, is that the Holy Spirit is really working here. I'm just the water boy. God is so faithful, and he is giving faith where there wasn't enough before and strength where there was only weakness. He is giving favor and belief among a bunch of thieves and drug peddlers, and I have a front row seat.

10/19/10

I met with Fred, a guy from Fargo, and we had a good time. I told him my story today and told him I know God has a purpose for me here in the camp. I told Fred that I really think talking to him is part of God's purpose for me. He was in tears the whole time. He appreciates the visits so much and wants to meet more often. The next time we meet we will talk about the nature of God, what he is really like, and what God wants us to know about him. Fred is open.

10/29/10

I walked the track with Fred, and we sat down on a bench to talk more deeply and with greater intensity. Fred was crying, overwhelmed with his lot in life. He had been raising his nine-year-old son by himself and didn't even have a chance to say good-bye to him or explain to him what was going on. Fred had just told me he doesn't know why God would allow these things to happen along with all the other pain in the world. We sat down so I could tell Fred that what he was thinking about God is not the way God is. I told him my story. I asked Fred if I could pray with him and ask God to open his heart, his eyes, and his understanding to God. He said, "Yes." We prayed only for that. We didn't pray the sinner's prayer or anything like that. We just prayed that God would teach Fred's heart how to be open to him.

On Sunday during the chapel service when they asked for prayer requests this a man who is Native American came down from the balcony and spoke from the back of the chapel. He was shy but seemed very sincere. After church

I motioned to him that I would like to meet him. I have met with him three times now. He comes to our 6:00 a.m. prayer time. Thomas Red Feather is his full name, and he is from the Lakota tribe in Pine Ridge, South Dakota. He is thirty-nine and was given a sixteen-year sentence. He has seven years left. He has four daughters ranging from four to nineteen. Each daughter is from a different woman, and he never married any of them. When Tom was twelve, he was introduced to sweat lodge worship, the dances, the pipe, and all the things that Native Americans do to pacify the spirits. Tom didn't like any of it even at that age. He always felt that there was something greater than the gods they were worshiping.

When he was thirteen, he was molested by an older woman, which went on for some time. He was a very angry person and grew to hate women, even the mothers of his children. He longed for a relationship with a father. His own father was an alcoholic, and he was shamed by that. His mother had boyfriends, and he would get along with them. Every time he got close to an older man, they died, and he grew to hate men too because of his dad's failure. He was very troubled and would cry out to God, but he didn't know God or even whether he existed for sure. He got arrested for drugs.

One day, he asked another prisoner if he had another Bible and if he could have it. He gave it to him, and he started reading Genesis. He said he knew immediately that this was the key to life. He read the first seventeen chapters and knew this was the way. He wanted to know more. He cried out to God to show him more. A voice behind him said "Deuteronomy." He thought it was his cellmate, but his cellmate said he didn't say anything. He turned toward the wall and cried. He read Deuteronomy for the next two days. He saw the laws and traditions of the people, and he connected it to the laws and traditions of his own people. He understood God was a god of the laws like the Native Americans' gods, but he knew it was different. He was so happy to find God, but he still didn't know grace. It was a year later when another man introduced him to the New Testament, and he read about Jesus being hung on a tree—hanging on a tree is part of the Native American traditional religion, and he recognized the piercing of Jesus's side and the cross as important. He became a Christian, pretty much just on his own with his Bible. He knows the word in a very sound way

We have met twice now, and he wants to take the *First Principles* class. When Tom talks you can tell he comes from a long line of storytelling. Tom wants to be a regular part of all that we do in hopes that it will prepare him for ministry when he gets out. He wants to be a church planter amongst the Native Americans of South Dakota. It's amazing the way God has just reached out and touched him. Tom has appealed his sentence once against his attorney's advice. He said God told him to do it. He got four years off his sentence. He is appealing again in order to get more time off.

10/30/10

My memories of my school days are not good: not liking school, not being a good student, and feeling that the teacher who got me in her class was an unfortunate soul. I never got the feeling of satisfaction from a job well done because there were no jobs well done by me. When Miss Henrietta recruited me to sing in her quartet at Western Christian High, it was a significant event in my life. For two years, I had this person in my life who was not my dad but who believed in me and told me I was doing well.

Throughout my life I clearly remember the people who believed in me and trusted me. I was raised with belief and trust, and I wanted to raise my children with belief and trust. When I began recruiting men into the insurance business, I loved to study people. I loved finding people I could believe in. In some cases I believed in them more than they believed in themselves. I always felt it was strength. Sometimes I was wrong. Sometimes I believed in people who weren't worthy of my belief. Even after more than twenty years of trusting and believing in people and sometimes making mistakes at it, I still feel I would rather make a mistake in believing in a few people who aren't worthy of my trust than to make the mistake of not believing in someone whom I should.

I had dropped out of college and joined the Navy in hopes of finding a vocation I liked and in which I could be successful. Upon discharge, I still didn't know, but when I arrived at home there was a message by the phone. The message was that I should call Al Mohler, the man who sold me my life insurance policy when I was fourteen years old. The minute I heard his message, I was convinced that this is what I should do. I was saving money in the policy during school, and while I was in the Navy I was sending fifty dollars to my policy frequently. All the other guys I knew were spending their money. I knew I could do this and built my sales talk around my own experience in saving money this way. When we bought our first home, we borrowed from the policy and used it for the down payment. When I was twenty-one years old I had already replaced the money I borrowed and used the policy again to buy my first rental property. So it was my personal story that helped me be successful in my career. This is how I learned the value of my personal story.

In the early days of my life insurance career, the sales were few and far between, and I was hanging onto a thin thread of believing I could ever make it in the business. Sometimes, I would come home, and Jan would say in somewhat of a joking manner, "Don't worry, honey, I believe in you." Jan had no idea how much it meant to me that she would say such a thing. It was so meaningful that today, almost fifty years later, I still get tears in my eyes as I write about it. Belief and trust are such a deep part of my life. This is the background that makes my faith in God so important to me. It has always been important but has become even more so in here.

10/31/10

My mind came back to prison. Todd was losing his home to a sheriff's auction, and his family was going to have to move. The auction was to be on Wednesday. We prayed. On Tuesday, the bank cancelled the auction, and they are working out a way to continue the mortgage. Todd is so amazed by God, and he is learning to walk with and trust God.

9

11/1/10

Jim has a vision for when he gets out—that we will have a ministry helping inmates and their families connect to other people and to services that can help them through their incarceration and release. Teaching *First Principles* would be at the heart of it, and getting the teachings to their families would be another important part. It would be a ministry that would exist both inside and outside the prison. We are thinking of a name, something like "Life's Principles Guidance." The idea is too big for an old guy like me. I am glad there are younger men who seem energized for that kind of venture. The idea has come partly from realizing that it will be very difficult for anyone who has a prison record, especially a felony, to be accepted in most churches. We think the ones who understand that the best are the ones who have been in prison.

11/14/10

Tonight we had a memorial service. An inmate from Colorado, a very nice man in his fifties who was a lawyer who had graduated from Harvard Law School, became very sick about three weeks ago. He went to the medical center, and they gave him some medication. He worsened, but he couldn't get any more treatment. Friday, he could hardly walk and was bleeding from his body cavities. They took him to the hospital, and Saturday morning they said he was brain dead. They said they were keeping him on life-support until they could get a family member's permission to take him off. The family had not been notified prior to that. He has two daughters and a son, and they were very close. The chapel was packed. The other inmates said lots of good things were said about him.

Jim has been working very hard on getting *First Principles* approved as a regular prison course that gives inmates credit when they have their exit interview. Tonight, after the service, we saw the chaplain and told him what we have been doing. We needed his approval because it is religious; he gave us his approval, and it is finalized. This has huge significance on getting us what we need, including space, a copy machine, mailings, etc.

Tomorrow and Wednesday are the open house. We think we might have up to fifty people there. We believe God is moving in far greater ways than we ever imagined.

The big event, our *First Principles* open house, is past. It was fun and funny. Jim really did the whole promotion, and the guys did the recruiting. We had about twenty come. It's getting much easier to get guys to come because we are getting better known. Notice, we are now calling this the Campus because we have our school registered and approved through the educational department. It's going to really change how we work. We will be on the list of offered courses for each quarter's sign up. The graduates will get credits placed in their files that should make a difference when it comes to their exit interviews with counselor. Everyone is required to have at least one religious class and up until now there has been only one, so now we have two. When this is announced the demand will increase.

Jim donated pop and chips, and someone from the kitchen donated cookies. It's a big deal here to have refreshments. When the guys saw how hard he was working and that he was donating all this stuff, they could see how serious he was about it all. It made an impression.

We want to have another class for those who aren't able to grasp or aren't attracted to our *First Principles* class. The plan is to use the illustrated Bibles. We will use them for a Bible walk-through class. Because we are approved through the education department, we can get all the Bibles and books we need sent right to the education department. This is a big plus for us.

11/17/10

There is a lot I could say about my life after leaving home before my junior year of high school. However, this is really not my story but rather the story of my relationship with my father. After the tenth grade, I was gone most of the time, but Dad still remained very much on my mind because I didn't want to let him down. I wanted to be sure that he could be proud of anything he heard about me. I never got into trouble or did mean things because I didn't want to let him down. I was in school 150 miles from home, and we just didn't use the phone in those days for anything other than a serious emergency, which I never had. We didn't write letters so my dad really just lived in my memory.

During the summers I was at home, but I always worked two jobs so I only saw Dad for about an hour in the living room when he sat with his Bible.

I don't remember our conversations in those days. I only remember that Dad really loved his Bible.

In 1957 I joined the Navy and saw Dad even less. I didn't think of writing home. At that time there was no war, but there was the crisis in Lebanon. I was stationed in Washington, D.C. Most of the guys I was with were sent to Lebanon, but I was never sent there. Never getting a letter from me, my folks finally contacted the Red Cross to find out where I was.

I mention the separation from Dad because it was also a time when I felt separated from God. I went to a church faithfully, but although it was the same denomination I was raised in, the church life was very different from the way I was raised. They had dances, and an elder's wife would treat the young men to slow dancing and things that went along with it. I became very confused by it all. Later, I found out there were a lot of divorces in that church and even between that elder and his wife.

I didn't know any Christians in my Navy squadron. I did know some really neat guys who befriended me. I really liked them, and although they were atheists, I respected them as men and began respecting their atheism. They were having a lot of fun, even immoral fun, and I was fighting desperately against sin. I came to the point that I didn't think Christianity was real. I remembered my father's faith, which I had adopted as my faith, but I wasn't seeing any working models around me. I decided to become an atheist and have the same kind of fun the atheists were having. This only made my confusion increase. The "fun" I thought I would open myself to just never seemed to work out. The atheism, which had looked attractive to me as I watched these men, was not attractive, not real, and way more out of reach for me than Christianity was. I couldn't explain any of this even to myself. I was nearing the end of my tour of duty with the Navy. I felt confused, separated from God, and embarrassed by my failures. With my discharge coming up, I felt I just needed to get back into relationship with God—to do that I figured I had better move back to Minnesota.

One of the first nights I was back at home I had been out; when I came home I found Dad sitting up reading his Bible as he usually was. I can't remember what we talked about, but he was tired and said, "I'm going to bed." My parents' bedroom was just off the living room. When he went to bed the door was left ajar, and I could see through the opening. I saw Dad kneel down by the bed, praying. It was at that moment that the realization of God's grace and keeping came over me in a powerful and emotional way. As I saw Dad pray, I realized that he had done that for me every night while I was away. At once, I understood why I couldn't be an atheist. I understood why, when I had opened myself up to Satan's playground, things hadn't worked out. I was overwhelmed with the understanding that I had gained as a child of the covenant. Dad and Mom's prayers, through the power of the Holy Spirit, kept me from falling when I was too weak to stand on my own.

That night started my quest for a deeper walk with God, and it took me still another two years to have total peace and assurance. The memory of my father and the feeling of separation from home, then returning again, has been important to my understanding of how little I had to do with my own salvation. My salvation is by grace alone. God was with me even when I didn't want him to be with me. That time of being home for two years, seeking after God, and finally coming to peace with Him was a very definite and powerful time. It was so transformational for me that for the next ten years I testified to it as my conversion experience. After ten years of saying that and listening to a lot of other people's testimonies, I realized that what I perceived as my conversion was not really when I was saved. I realized that I was born again at such a young age that I couldn't really remember not loving God and wanting to serve him. God used a man with less than an eighth-grade education, who loved God and who entered into a covenant with God about me, to show me and lead me to my heavenly father. By being a man that I could love and respect so much, Dad made it easy to love and respect God in a personal way.

Dad was not perfect, but my parents were faithful with all that they knew and understood. Dad always spoke to me as if I was the Lord's. He did that by faith. He believed that the faith of a parent can act on behalf of his child, and I believe that also. I was raised on, "We are not our own. We've been bought with a price." There were times as a young man that I felt cheated as though I would like to have had something to say about that. I was never given the option to not follow God. I always thought that God and Dad had expectations of me, and I didn't want to let them down.

I'm sorry to say that over the next fourteen years as Dad got older and I got busy with starting a business and raising a family, I didn't get with Dad as much as he wanted nor as much as I should have. Dad talked about dying a great deal. He loved talking about going to heaven. I didn't like talking about that. In 1972 Dad's health slowly began to fail. In 1974, at the age of seventy-four, Dad was in his last days. He was living at home with Mom in Willmar. As Dad was failing, there were a lot of things I still wanted to tell him. I wanted to tell him how much he meant to me, but I just couldn't do that. I would get emotional, and I wasn't comfortable being emotional in front of him. One day, I had a lengthy road trip for business so I took a hand held tape recorder along in the car. I recorded all the things I wanted to say. I'm so glad I did that because it meant a great deal to both Dad and Mom.

The day before Dad died he became very sick. My sisters all came home to say good-bye to him, and I remember that night well. The next day they were going to take Dad to the hospital just to keep him comfortable and let him die. Dad always told us and his doctor that he didn't want to be kept alive artificially. The last night at home the girls all took turns going by his bed, talking to him, and they kissed him good-bye. I couldn't do that although I wanted to very much. I left that night, tormented by not having done it. The next morning I went to the hospital early, hoping that if Dad was still alive I could do what the girls had done.

It was the day before Thanksgiving, and it was very dark and dreary with heavy overcast skies that made the town look dirty. It had just started to rain and was wet and sloppy. I arrived at the hospital room and the nurse said, "Would you like to feed your dad his cereal?" I was surprised because I didn't think Dad would be eating that morning. I said I would like that, and the nurse had me sit on his bed. We lifted Dad up so that he was lying in my arms, and I fed him a little cereal. He didn't eat much, but I was so overwhelmed with what God had provided me with that morning. There I was, holding my father in my arms for the first time in my life. I told him that I loved him. I'm not certain that he understood. We sat there like that for moments. Then the nurse said that I should leave the room because they were going to change Dad's linens. I left the room, but they called me back quite quickly. Dad was taking his last breaths. I was very occupied with Dad and not conscious of anything else going on around me. Dad had a very bad case of emphysema, and he labored to take every breath. When he took his last breath, it was as though peace settled over his whole body. I knew Dad was with the Lord.

I held his hand, and I remembered Dad talking so much about his sin, even more as he got older. When he talked about heaven, he talked about there being no more sin there. We sang the song, "Whiter than snow, yes, whiter than snow. Just wash me, and I shall be whiter than snow." I remembered that song as I was bent over Dad that morning. Holding Dad's hand and looking out the window, I saw that it had started snowing, the first snow of the season. The ground had turned from dark and dreary to absolutely white with snow.

Everything was covered. It was so amazing. I accepted that as God's special gift that morning. I also took it as God's affirmation that what Dad had talked about and longed for was happening right in front of my eyes.

I was sorry the family wasn't there to share in this. It all happened so fast. Once the nurse asked me if I wanted to feed him his cereal, I thought, "Well, he's not going to die today." I think God kept him alive for me, knowing what I needed to do. I was so thankful that I could finally do it. I am sorry it did not occur to me to call the rest of the family, but being caught up in the moment, I just didn't think Dad was going to die. I still have that regret today that my sisters and my mother didn't have the opportunity to be there.

11/20/10

We had the first class on God Tuesday night. I thought I was prepared, but Tuesday night did not go well. In my opinion it flopped. Others didn't think it was that bad, but I was disappointed.

Wednesday night went much better. In fact it was an awesome time. I decided to talk about children understanding God through their parents. I started out by telling about growing up with a Christian father whom I loved and respected. With parents who stayed married, I grew up thinking it was this way for everyone. I was sheltered and naive, but my experience made it easy for me to trust and love God.

I shared our experience when Jan and I adopted Joe, who is Korean. He was eleven at the time. I compared my experience growing up in the love and belief of my father to the experience Joe must have had coming into our family. We met Joe at the Minneapolis airport. He came in on a flight with about twenty other orphans. All the others were infants; Joe had been helping care for them on the flight over. Joe was one of the last ones off the plane. It took me years to begin to comprehend what was going through Joe's mind. The Korean attendant introduced us to one another. We couldn't speak his language, and he couldn't speak English. Joe had just met his new father. I now realize how much I minimized that. Joe was supposed to love and respect me as a father. The only father he knew anything about dropped him off at an orphanage when he was about four years old, and he never saw him again. He was angry at him. What a great difference there was in the concept of my fatherhood to him and his concept of the same.

I decided I wanted to share that experience with the inmates because maybe it would communicate something about God. God is a God of relationships.

He loves, he grieves, he understands pleasure, and he created us for his pleasure. He has created much of creation for our pleasure. In the best parts of our relationships with our children, we can find aspects of the relationship God wants to have with us. The men responded well. Some came up with their own stories about their children; some were good but most were bad.

We have two new men in the group who are Mormon. David, a cowboy from Wyoming who contracted out his services to large 100,000 plus acre ranches with 6,000 head of cattle that grazed in the foot hills of the mountains. David was raised Catholic, and became Mormon when he married his wife. He had an affair five years ago, and his wife could never forgive him for that. They got divorced last year. He told us what happened, and he said, "I am living with so much guilt I can hardly live with myself."

He cried hard and couldn't continue talking. I have never seen this happen before in prison. Inmates are way too guarded for that. It did wonderful things for the meeting, and others shared things they had never shared before. The guys are so eager for the next meeting; I think it was a giant step forward. That kind of conversation never happens in groups in prison.

Tom is growing so much. He thinks deeply on his own while he works and while he lies in his bunk. It shows when he speaks. So far, he has not joined our classes, only our early morning prayer time. He said he is waiting for God to speak to him about that. This morning he spoke of God leading him to Deuteronomy where you are to teach your children and grandchildren. He was confused at first, but now he feels that God wants him to teach his children here in prison. I told him that's what I have been hoping for and also that he would join us in the classes. When he prayed he thanked God for giving him an answer. I think that means he will be part of our group. He will be good. He is very credible and sincere. He uses a lot of Scriptures when he expresses himself. It's amazing for the short time he has been a believer.

11/22/10

I walked with Tom yesterday, and he told me his story. I asked him to write it out for my grandchildren. The next morning, he gave me his story:

"My name is Thomas Red Feather. I am named after my grandfather whom I never met. My name, I believe, was given by the finding of a man or woman many generations in the past. I was born on the Pine Ridge Indian Reservation in the state of South Dakota; it is in the southwestern part of the state and borders Nebraska and Wyoming.

I will speak of some childhood adventures, hurts, and joys, at a time when the American Indian Movement of the 1970s was slowly winding down. It was a time of turmoil and confusion of identity. I was born in 1971 to my parents, both of the Oglala Sioux Tribe of the Lakota nation. I was born in an old hospital in Pine Ridge in the winter month of Christmas. Know, too, my life as a child as I best remember. I remember my very youngest years of a new world to explore. As I look back I will tell you of thoughts of long ago as a child. I remember when my mother did little drinking. There was a time we lived on the Arapaho Indian Reservation in the state of Wyoming, at my grandfather and grandmother's. We lived in a home that had three bedrooms, two closets, a living room, and a small kitchen. We lived as an extended family, including aunts and uncles. We didn't have running water inside. We had to haul water from outside. We used propane gas to warm the home. We had electricity, but we had no indoor restroom. We had an outhouse at least 100 feet from the house. We lived up from the river where I spent much time as a child fishing, swimming, and exploring. The home and land belonged to my grandfather.

I remember a time when alcohol was not a part of our lives. I don't know exactly when it came to be a burden and destruction of my family. But I do remember my grandfather being a very, very hard working man, and I liked that. My grandmother and aunts as well as my mother would do all of the house work and cooking. They took care of us. They were always busy making star quilts with many designs. Those were wonderful times. My cousins and I would be exploring warriors. We didn't have men to teach us how to make shields, arrows, and bows or spears so we learned on our own. Our family wasn't too traditional at the time.

I will tell of a few adventures my cousins and I had as children. We had a creek that ran through our land. It wasn't too far away from our house. We would be like fish to water during the summer season. We would run around with no shirts or shoes, and we always wore our hair out like wild Indian boys. Many times we would play cowboys and Indians, and other times we went on hunting parties in search of tutanlia (buffalo) like our ancestors, only in our small world we never saw buffalo up close like our ancestors did. Still, we would prepare our bows, arrows, and decide who would hunt with whom. We climbed trees, hid in camouflage, and learned to be silent. I truly believed we were just like our ancestors. We swam in the shallow creek day after day, and we became dark from the sun. We never spoke our native language because we weren't taught it. We were very superstitious. We believed in spirits, both good and bad. We never lived in tepees. We had cars, seldom rode horses, and we didn't use buckskin or moccasins or beaded clothes. We had slacks, jeans, and bell bottoms.

I remember our grandparents drove us to many places and told us stories of our people. But we also went to places like the trash dump and rummaged for things people threw away. To be honest, those were times I looked forward to because then we talked and had time with our grandparents. We would go to town—the town was prejudiced towards us. The nearest town was Riverton, Wyoming. My cousins and I would go to town to see all the buildings and stores, and we especially liked to go to places like the dumpsters at Dunkin' Donuts. We kids would be hoisted into them, and we would fetch all the different kinds of pastries. Then we would dumpster dive for vegetables and other edibles at Safeway. We liked to go to the parks with slides, swings, and other such fun inventions. We didn't have any on the reservation. We liked the green, cut soft grass. All we had were weeds, sage brush, and wild plants and dirt.

We didn't have toys like other kids so we made our own out of anything, such as spare car parts, etc. Our sisters didn't have dresses or dolls. We learned of our traditional ways and formed a kid's opinion. Such things were left up to the adults and were sacred. We weren't interested in the adult stuff. We wanted to be kids. We had pow-wows. We gathered together as a people, and there was singing and dancing. We made outfits that mimicked creation, such as ravens, chickens, or the grass. The girls did likewise. The drummers beat a big drum with drumsticks and sang songs in our language. I liked that we ate and took home watecha (extra food). Seeing all our friends and making new friends, as boys flirting with girls and just for fun, made the pow-wows great. I had so much fun as a kid until I started into my teens. Somewhere along the journey of life, it changed.

Somehow, unknown to me, alcohol became part of our way of life . . . then separation. When alcohol and drinking came so did the authorities and the welfare workers. It got to the point that our parents would lose us to welfare, and the welfare would take us away from our family. They would place us with foster families.

I remember this one family I was placed with. When I was very young, I was taken from my mother and placed with this man and his wife. They were older, white people. Out of all the white people I've come to know over the years, they seemed to be the only ones who had hearts. Well, I got so attached to them that when my mother finally sobered up so she could fight for me, she came for me, but I didn't know her. I truly believed the man and his wife were my father and mother.

But this was my way of life. I only knew my mother to ever say that she loved me or my brothers and sisters when she was drunk, crying, and hanging all over me, always saying, "I love you son." But when she was sober or hung over, she never acknowledged me. I was confused. What was this new way of life? Is this how it has always been? Or when did it start? The child I once was disappeared slowly and steadily each day.

I remember a time that my family (the adults) were ready to start their ritual of drinking until they were broke, without food, fighting, and hung over. It was the first of the month, and the adults got their annuity or SSI or welfare checks. They got ready early in the morning and checked the mail until they got their checks. The adults were happy and asked us kids what we wanted from the store, promising to bring it back. As they left us, we were excited to get stuff. We waited, waited, waited, and were so anxious. It got later and later toward late afternoon and early evening, and we noticed the cars coming. We were so excited and happy as the cars got closer. We ran to the road to meet the cars, and we noticed the people were drunk. We ran to the house in hopes that at least we would get our stuff. As the adults got out of the cars, drunk, all that they remembered to bring was food plus more alcohol and more partiers. This would mark the first of many broken promises and lies and drunkenness.

That night my three cousins and I were mad and sad and didn't want to be there. We decided, as mere teenagers, to hitchhike from Arapaho, Wyoming, all the way to Pine Ridge, South Dakota, to get away from all the drinking and deceit. We started to go through the house and get the younger kids together. We put them into a room with food, and we packed clothes, food, rucksacks, and water. We took extra clothes, jackets, etc., and we got all our stuff in bags and put it by the creek. We returned to the party house and took care of the younger kids until we put them to sleep and knew they were safe. Then we made our great escape—a long journey to another camp.

As we walked, talked, laughed, and envisioned what we would do and who we would see, we started to get hungry and thirsty and tired from carrying all the stuff. When we reached a town fifteen miles away, all we left was stuff that fit in our pockets and what we had on. As we came into town, there was a bridge, and as we crossed the bridge, we saw a drive-in theatre. We decided to sneak in. It was about 7:00 PM, dark, and getting cold. We found an opening in the fence and made our way in. There was a playground so we sat on the swings and watched the movie. I can't remember what was playing. We were excited about the movie, and when it was over we went to the hole in the fence and crawled back out before anyone saw us. We wandered around and wondered what to do. We walked up to this tire shop and found cardboard boxes for tires. We crawled into them. It was dark, lonely, and we were hungry and tired after a long journey. We planned to continue the next morning.

We fell asleep, cold, hungry, and confused. Early the next morning we were woken up by the owner. He told us to leave, or he would call the cops. We left, but my cousin was gone. We left hoping to find him. As we came around the building, so did the cops, and my cousin was in the back of their car. The cop put us in the back. I was so scared. We went to the jail that morning, not knowing what was going to happen to us. As we got to the jail, we were put into a cell. We must have looked so scared. For Indians off the reservation, it was scary. We were fed and given blankets and mats. We fell asleep, but before we did, the cops asked where we were from. We said we lived down the road from a sheriff. We told the cops to call him and to tell our parents. Then we fell asleep, scared, alone, hungry, and in jail.

The cops got us up about 9:00 a.m. and told us the sheriff was there for us. We were released to him but not to our parents. He drove us home and asked what we were doing. We told him about our great adventure and that we were tired of the drinking. As we got closer to our home we were nervous and scared. We thought we were in trouble. As we pulled in to the house, no one came out. The sheriff said, "Sorry, boys. You have to get off." As we did he pulled away. We watched him drive away. We turned and walked to the house, opened the door, and our family was still drinking, not even knowing we were gone. It was sad, and it was our life."

10

Tom is growing in the Lord so fast. This is a continuation of the story of his life:

"There are great memories I have of my grandfather growing up. He was a very hard worker and he loved us dearly. This was at a time of turmoil and loss of identity in a new world. Tunhushilu (Grandfather) knew he needed to teach us to live in this new world, as well as hold to our way of life as Natives of the Americas. He knew we needed to assimilate to this new world. I remember when he worked, at a time of no drinking, in construction. He was a heavy equipment operator. He drove dump trucks, backhoes, road graders, and Bobcats. He would always bring a new vehicle home after work. We loved this because we got to see new things the white people would use. As Indian kids we didn't see much of these big monster mechanical things. Plus, we didn't always have a lot of food, and since he would be the one working, he got the best lunches and would always give us what he didn't eat. The best things were the pies; they were the best. We never got them . . . just Tunhushilu. We would take turns to get the dessert.

"We would make our own things out of scraps . . . like when we would make our own boats to go out on the ponds or float down the river. We would make sharp spears and arrows with fishing string as we went fishing, or we would use old blankets as nets. We never had fishing poles, but we always had string. We did a lot of fishing. We would learn so much about God's creation. We studied hands-on about different insects and animals. They fascinated us. We played with and chased many different kinds of snakes. We would see who could catch the biggest snakes, but we were careful with rattlesnakes or poisonous snakes. We were told that if we played with snakes they would come and get us since snakes traveled in pairs.

"I was comfortable as an Indian child with long hair and dark skin. I was so innocent about the world around me, and the encounter with white people was always a hard one.

"We were looked down on or just misunderstood. We never had white friends. We would act like warriors hunting yet stayed prepared if we came upon our enemies. We would try to cross the river. It was great. We would find wild berries and red or yellow buffalo berries. They would be our sweets. And we would carry sage because all warriors would carry sage. It was fun. We were young Indian warriors, and we taught each other new things. We didn't have dads to teach us how to do these things so we learned from one another. We were strong together, a group of modern-day hunters. But when we came to a bridge or good swimming hole, we were kids again. We always had rope with us so if we crossed the river we could use it to guide each other. We would make swings on the bottom of the bridges and swing off the bridge and dive into the river.

"We had so much fun together. We were just us four Indian boys against the world, exploring a new world. We never saw an airplane close up, but we would see them way up in the sky like eagles gliding and leaving a trail of white behind them. We knew all the places and walked four miles a day, exploring our world. We saw deer, antelope, rabbits, owls, snakes, ravens, eagles, skunks, and many insects. We set traps, never catching them.

"We got good with bows, arrows, and spears. We made sling shots and clubs out of willows and rocks and string, or the bark of the willows if we didn't have string. We loved the winter and frozen creeks, ponds, and river. We never went to the river during winter though. We knew better. We made forts and followed tracks in the snow. We loved when it would snow hard and a lot. We would jump off cars and the house into the snow, and many times it was so frozen we could walk on top of the frozen snow. It was so fun."

12/15/10

Another Jim showed up in the chapel. I call him Little Jim because he is really short. Little Jim got here about four months ago. He is a person I have tried to avoid because he has such a fowl mouth and is so negative. He has a huge Napoleon complex, and no matter what comes up, he's always done it bigger and better. The most offensive thing about him though is his mouth.

We have noticed Little Jim in the chapel every morning. He has a second wife who I met in visitation. She is a really cute little Mexican girl who has a lot of Botox and silicon in all the places they put Botox and silicon. When she walks into the visitation room even the most sanctified of men (of which there are very few here) can't help but turn their heads, even a little bit, to take a quick peek. It turns out that Jim's wife has been going to bars a great deal. She likes to drink and enjoys the attention of men. Of course, Little Jim met her in a bar and married her because of her cute looks; however, he seems to have fallen in love with her and really does love her and their three-year-old daughter who is cute as a button. Jim also has two children from a first marriage who he says he loves dearly.

Last night I went to the theater to watch the Vikings play the Giants. I lost interest in the game and went to the phone room to call Jan. Little Jim was there and asked me to go for a walk with him. We walked, and he talked. His life is a mess. His wife is likely going to leave him. One time she was drinking and left their daughter alone. He is afraid she might lose the little girl. He then stopped for an e-mail. He said his wife is saying that she doesn't like her life; she doesn't like who Jim has become and who she has become. Jim was in tears.

I said, "Jim, we need to read John 3. It's about a man who asks Jesus how to be saved. Would you like that?" He said, "I want that. I don't like the way I am. My parents were drug dealers, and nobody ever went to church. I've tried to make something of myself. I was the biggest mortgage loan officer in Minnesota. I wanted to make something of myself. I never went to college. I've tried my best, but here I am. I can't do anything about my wife, my daughters, or my business. I don't know why this is happening to me." I said, "Jim, do you want to meet tomorrow?" He said he did. We set an appointment for right after count.

I went to the dorm just in time to get razzed by some young guys about dirty books, dirty toys, and that all their friends need to go to church with me. Then others said, "No, all these jailbirds that go to church are just hypocrites. As soon as they get out and some nice booty goes down the street, they'll be gone." I said, "Why do you guys need to be judging these guys? Don't they all deserve a clean break?"

I spent time with Little Jim. He is a tough cookie but very broken at the moment; he even seems contrite. We went to John 3. He prayed a sinner's prayer, confessed, repented, yielded, and received. I prayed for him at night. I worry about him, and I still see him with bad company, of course these are his friends and can't just leave them so quickly.

12/25/10

I get to do the message in the chapel for the Christmas Eve service. I hear guys say they wish Christmas were over. They don't want to hear Christmas carols. They don't want to hear people say, "Merry Christmas." This will be the background for my Christmas message. Some Christmas seasons are better than others. Some aren't all they are cracked up to be, because we take our eyes off the main thing. Having a truly great Christmas really has nothing to do with our circumstances. It has everything to do with who it is that was in that manger. That's my Christmas Eve message.

12/29/10

It truly is a Merry Christmas for us here. Like so many things in life, to make Christmas a "merry Christmas" takes interpretation.

Yesterday we had the afternoon off. We were all called to the dorm, and the warden had them come by with large bags of candy, snacks, and all kinds of things. Each guy got a big plastic bag full. It really was very generous. It was interesting watching the response. From some there were complaints that they weren't as good as last year. Others were eager to receive them. Then there was a feeding frenzy of trading for stamps. The first bags went for one book of stamp (twenty stamps to a book). Later, they went for one-and-a-half. Some are still holding out for two books.

We were invited to the dining hall for eggnog and a small bag of cookies. The warden was there along with the COs to wish us "Happy Holidays," but the warden did say "Merry Christmas." It was noticeable that the warden was smiling and was doing her best for us.

It was a good day. Jim had traded half his bag for some packages of smoked oysters; he and I celebrated by going to the chapel. We ate smoked oysters on crackers and checked out the movie *Hanged on a Twisted Cross*— the Dietrich Bonheoffer story.

11

1/2/11

This week Little Jim asked me to meet with him again. He said he wants to change. I asked him if his prayer of commitment meant anything to him, and he said it did. I said, "Your mouth is so filthy and your words so profane. You sit in church and pray, but I don't think God listens to prayers that come from such an awful mouth." He said he is trying to change and wants to change. I said I would commit to meeting with him every day if he wants to. I said, "You have a baby inside you; it's the new man. Old Jim has to die, and you need to feed the new Baby Jim. And we need to feed him very frequently. We met three days ago. We read Jude and about the punishment of the wicked. Then yesterday we read Psalm 51, which is David's prayer of confession. He hardly knows the story of David; we will have to go over that later. We worked through Psalm 51 verse by verse. I asked him if he understood it, and he said yes. He wouldn't have if we hadn't gone through it like that. We prayed together. He didn't want to pray, because he said he doesn't know if he prays right. He will pray soon. He ordered an ESV study Bible like mine; I told him he needs that to grow so he was willing to spend the money for it. People think I'm a martyr in spending the time with him because he has been such a miserable guy. I'm just doing it out of obedience, but I think I can see that he is really changing. I know only God can do it, and God can do it with or without me. I see myself as privileged if he will see fit to use my feeble efforts in this way. Guys here are praying for him.

It's an icy morning. We were only let out of the dorm for breakfast (most skipped) and had to return right away. The chapel was closed so I actually had breakfast, which I am not used to eating. I have decided the most animal-like thing about being here is standing in line for chow. I decided to stay in my room for lunch and enjoy a packet of mackerel on crackers by myself. It was good, a nice treat. I enjoy the solitude with roommates out.

1/12/11

I have done okay until recently. The doctor says my blood is low, and they need to find out why that is. They have drawn blood twice but have not done the right test according to the doctor. I have asked them to hurry up and do it again. They are sending me downtown for a sleep apnea test, but the doctor said it might be Christmas before that all gets done. My sleeping has gotten worse, and I fight staying awake during the day. If I sit down, I fall asleep; thus, the blood test. I thought I might be dehydrated so I am drinking more water. I thought that helped for a day, but now it is not helping. Maybe it's all emotional and from lack of activity.

The education department shut down for six weeks over the holidays so we could not have our classes. I have missed that a lot, and I think it took away some of the purpose I feel in being here. We still meet every morning with the four of us and that is very rewarding. It seems I have a pretty big appetite for ministry, and when that slows down things get harder.

This week we start classes again. Tonight we start a Bible overview class. We haven't gotten the proper approval yet so it isn't publicized. We will have an open house for it next week. That seems to really work to get guys out.

We had class last night. We had only three people show up. We had so much excitement about this when we had our open house but that was four weeks ago. Guys have a hard time remembering that long. It is hard keeping track of putting something new in my own schedule. It's something strange about an institution. When you don't have a routine, life is miserable, but once you have a routine, it's hard to break it.

We did have two guys come in late that really came to mess us up. They wanted to argue that the Bible is written by men; therefore, anyone who believes it is stupid. When asked about his belief, he said that God is in him and that he is the manifestation of God. I have been exposed to most beliefs in prison. One of the guys is seventy-five years old but doesn't look over sixty and seems quite intelligent. He is very personable, but I find him very opinionated. The ESV Bible has been such a great resource for me; I was prepared to answer these guys. I have learned to turn the conversation from the defensive to the offensive. I asked them about their belief and then asked what they based it on. It surprising that they ran out of gas so quickly. I told them this is a Bible class and that we do believe in the Bible. I told the older guy that if he had something else to teach he should go get himself a room and teach that. He said he really didn't have anything he thought he should be teaching. Then he said that he could tell I was a good minister and that he wished he had faith like that. I told him that faith is a gift of God and that we could pray for his faith if he would like. He didn't want that and left.

We received our twenty-four copies of the illustrated Bible, *Good and Evil*, and they came with a promotional DVD. Our idea is to get with the inmate who runs the Saturday night movies in the chapel and run a three minute clip of it between movies. Then in the back we will have free Pepsi for everyone at the movie, compliments of "Life's Principles" (that's what we call ourselves) and advertise our open house the next week. We think it will be a good promotion.

Physically, I had a good night's sleep last night and am feeling much better today. It seems that I can get about two nights of good sleep per week, and last night was one of them.

1/25/11

Gifts have come in, and we have been able to do ministry that could not have been done. We have enough now to carry us for quite some time. Fathers are being joined together with their children by providing money for gas and hotel; illustrated Bibles have been furnished with money to buy more when needed. We are ordering fifty ESV paperback Bibles that are not study Bibles so we can all be reading out of the same Bibles when we do the studies. We have given a number of the ESV study Bibles away. The guys appreciate them so much, and it is fun to see them get them. Soon we will have special classes on how to use them.

Another man who is Native American has joined us for our 6:00 a.m. Bible study and prayer time. He is about sixty years old. It ends up he has been a Christian for some time. He knows the Bible quite well too. He is from South Dakota and belongs to the Dakota tribe. Now, we have five of us meeting.

1/27/11

I was reading a book in the activity center and X came up behind me and put his face right down by mine and said, "What are you doing, Mr. Goris?" X is one of only a few who call me Mr. Goris. I said, "I'm reading." I asked him if he missed his girls, and he said, "I haven't seen them in two months." (He usually doesn't give direct answers.) I said, "Are you writing to them and telling them you miss them?" He said, "Yes." I said, "How is your wife doing?" (They are not married but have two children. I call her his wife, trying to encourage him to commit to her.) He said, "Good. I don't know if she will wait for me." The rest of our conversation was as follows:

"Why do you think that?"

"She is only 30. Young women need men."

"She is a Christian, X. If you would give her some hope; if you would commit yourself to God and to her, she would wait."

"I don't think she would."

"X, you are not giving her any reason to wait for her. If you won't be responsible to her, she would be foolish to wait."

"Well, she can go, but she better never bring a man in the house that my kids can see."

"That's not realistic. If you aren't willing to be a man for her, the best thing she can do is to bring a man into the house who can be a husband to her and a father to your children."

"I don't like that."

"You are self-centered and selfish. You are only thinking about yourself and unwilling to yield yourself to God and to your family."

(We gave him a Bible, and he has read the whole thing. He has committed to coming to class, but so far he hasn't shown up.)

"Do you think there is a heaven?"

"I know there is, X. Your wife is a Christian, and she is going there. She will bring up your children to love the Lord, and they will be there too. There is also a hell, and that is where Satan is going, as well as the millions of people who he is deceiving into thinking they are more important than God." "When are you meeting again with the *Good and Evil* book?"

"Monday night. X, What you need is a new heart. Your heart is full of sin and self, and you can't begin to help yourself. You need to ask God to give you a new heart. Nothing short of that will ever change your life. Your wife and your daughters are just waiting for signs of encouragement and hope from you. You need to be a man and step up and give them the commitment, hope, and encouragement that they need.

X changed the conversation and soon walked off. X saw his family early in December due to the generosity of our prayer partners. He was very appreciative of that and does hang around me more because of that. He works in the hobby craft shop and made me a little leather card case to carry my ID cards in. He is a really nice guy to me, but I know he has another side as well when he's with his guys. He is a gang member, and I pray that he will denounce that.

12

2/2/11

I was given my job in the activity center and told very vaguely what to do. I was told to walk through the bathroom twice a day, and if I saw paper to sweep it up. If the floor was in bad shape I was to mop it. That's what I have been doing. Saturday night, I was in a movie in the chapel. I was told my name was called to go to the activity center. I did not hear the call so I did not go. On Monday morning an inmate told me the bathroom smelled like urine, and I should take care of it. I sprayed down the floor with disinfectant and mopped it. I had a visitor in the visiting center so I left. When my visit was over I went back to do the bathroom a second time. Someone else was cleaning the bathroom. I asked the clerk if the counselor still wanted to see me from my Saturday call. He said he didn't know, but if the counselor was in, I should knock on the door and ask him. I knocked on his door, but there was no answer. I opened the door two inches and saw him on the phone. He saw me and shook his head no.

I closed the door and waited a while longer. I finally left since he hadn't actually called me. I brought my books to the dorm. As soon as I got to the dorm, there was an announcement through the intercom, "Goris, report to the activity center immediately." I went there, and the counselor's door was open. I reported in, and he tore into me for opening his door. He seemed to know I was a businessman on the outside. He said, "What would you do if someone opened your door?" I said I had an open door policy and anyone was welcome in. He went on a long time about how rude I was to open his door without knocking. When I said I did knock, he said, "What did you do on the outside?" I said, "I was in the life insurance business." Our conversation went like this:

"Where do you think you are?"

"In prison, sir."

"What do you think your job is?"

"To clean the bathroom floor, sir."

"What are your expectations?"

"To meet and exceed your expectations, sir."

"Did you have employees?"

"Yes."

"What did you do when employees didn't meet your expectations?"

"I met with them to be sure they understood what my expectations were."

(He seemed puzzled and was asking me the questions in somewhat of a thoughtful way. I really couldn't figure out what was happening. He wasn't friendly, yet he wasn't swearing at me like he usually would. There was no sign of emotion or expression on his face.)

"What is your job description?"

"I never received a job description, sir."

"You never signed a written job description?"

(I thought he was joking.)

"I've never seen a job description, sir. I do my job, sir. I'm not a slacker."

"That's not what I heard."

"What have you heard, sir? If you have heard differently, I should know."

(He ignored my question.)

"Do you know about the brushes and soap in the counter?"

"No, sir."

Evidently his expectation was that I was cleaning the urinals and the toilets. I told him nobody had told me to do so but I would be happy to do that if that is what he wanted. I left that meeting, rattled, disappointed, embarrassed, and very puzzled over what was happening. I was puzzled over his interest in my thoughts but his lack of warmth or concern about my thoughts.

Hours later, I began to put things together. Jim and I have drawn a lot of attention from the COs in education. Our classes are the only classes that are well-attended. They walk by our class window and look in to see guys intently interested in the classes. Word is getting around. I think this CO really wanted to see what kind of a guy I really am. I think that he is wanting to know if I'm a real guy and how I feel about work and responsibility. I see that he is watching me as this man of God (as some call me). It motivated me to really clean that bathroom. I'm cleaning that bathroom as God's representative. I clean toilets to the glory of God. I'm going to more than satisfy him. I can do this, and I will to the glory of God.

2/4/11

Just when I thought I was finished with the CO regarding cleaning the latrine, I got a call over the intercom, "Goris, report to the activity center at once." I was in the gym and went immediately. He said the bathroom was not cleaned. I said, "I understood it was to be cleaned after the count clears." He said, "No, I want it cleaned first thing." (Someone cleans it last thing the night before so if I clean it "first thing" it hasn't had a chance to get dirty yet). I said, "Okay, sir. I'll do it." Then I said, "Can I tell you what my thought was on doing it after count?" He said, "I'm not interested in what your thought was." That was it.

That wasn't so bad, because he didn't swear at me and didn't use the "F word," but I was disappointed. There are so few ways here to prove yourself, that you are something more than a dirt ball. I wanted to do a job well, even if it's cleaning the latrine. I wished that I had known what his expectation was all before I started so I could please him. They don't do that here. That would take too much planning. I think it's like the guys must have experienced in the prisoner of war camps. It's such total lack of respect; you look for the opportunity to prove that you could be responsible, even if it's cleaning a latrine well. There is nothing here where you can do that. If you ever think you have won favor or respect from one of them, you're mistaken, and you will soon find out.

I do still think, though, that the watchful eye is on Jim and me because of the success of the classes. Our numbers are growing, people are standing on the outside of the windows looking in, and they are asking about the classes and saying they want to join the next quarter. The success is not because of us. It is because God is showing Himself through the classes. We do have a curriculum as well, and the guys know what is going to happen in each class. This is the only class that works with a curriculum.

2/5/11

The law library where we do our e-mailing is pretty much in the center of the compound. We all check our e-mails many times per day. Many of the guys I hang out with love to fish. So as we go by the library I will say, "I have to check my lines to see if I have any fish on them." When I open it up and see something, I'll holler "fish on." If I haven't had any for a while I say, "I need to put on some fresh bait".I feel like I need to write something so people have something to respond to. It helps me get more e-mails. We all think that's funny.

The morning of the latrine story, I was really stressed. I was shook. If I seemed calm, I wasn't. I felt offended, violated, and a bunch of other things.

It took me a while afterward to come to the peace that I found in doing the latrine for God's sake. I had to think through what was going on. I sensed there was a greater purpose for this than I was seeing. When it came to me that I was really being watched and examined because of what I was doing and who I claim to be serving, it gave me peace and even satisfaction that it is all worthwhile. Now that I know what they want, what they expect, and I clean the latrines with more purpose than anyone can know as they watch me do it. It's not because of my quality or integrity. It is because I know to whom I belong and what He has done for me. The shame he bore meant nothing to him because he was focused on the greater purpose.

I have been able to use the latrine story as an illustration twice since it happened. One was in our class on Thursday night. We were studying Ephesians 6 where Paul says, "Slaves obey your masters with fear and trembling, with a sincere heart, as you would Christ, not by eye service, as people pleasers, but as servants of Christ doing the will of God from the heart."

I explained that in today's world the slaves would be employees, and as employees and employers, we should read these verses as though they are talking about us. Bob really bristled about that. I then used the story about my latrine experience to express how I felt and related that Ephesians 6 was speaking to how I should think about the guards and COs. I know one thing for sure: I will never walk through a hotel, or any public restroom again, and see cleaning people without thanking them for the clean restroom. Also, I will never feel ashamed or undone by someone lording it over me, thinking that I am a loser. In Christ, I am not a loser. I believe, and I want others to see Christ in how I clean the latrine. I pray that day will come.

I didn't always feel this way. In my early days in my sales career, I had such a fear of failure. Without a college degree, I didn't think I had a lot of options in life especially as far as being an employee was concerned. I knew I couldn't afford to fail. When I was struggling in business, it was so personal to me. I had mistakenly attached my personal value to whether I could succeed or fail in business. As I watch, coach, and advise young men entering business today, or even struggling through school, my heart goes out to them so much because of the pain I feel for someone who struggles with failure. I really feel I have overcome that. I think I have learned to trust God a lot more than ever before. I know he will provide for me and my family, although I must say I can easily become anxious whether he will provide for my needs close enough to my perception of what my need is. I trust him more, though, because I know he has changed my perception so much and because there is still so much more room for change.

2/8/11

They call the prison gossip line "inmate.com." There are a lot of stories about the warden, and some of it can be observed to be true, and some . . . who knows. We can see that the warden is a real micromanager of inmates but also staff. She gives out orders to the lowliest of the lowly even if she has five staff people between them in the chain of command. She loves to tell guys to take off their hats, tuck their shirts in, how to run the salad bar, etc. It's funny for guys when they do even the smallest thing and somehow the warden just happens to be there.

The warden has been gone for a while and "inmate.com" said that she had cancer or she was on a trip or a lot of things. Everyone was kind of enjoying her being gone for whatever reason. Guys like going off the compound to go to the medical facility downtown or on other errands, just to get a few minutes or hours away from the warden and the system. The other day an inmate was taken downtown by the "town driver" in the "town car." The drivers are inmates. So this guy goes to the clinic, and in the waiting room they have a coffee pot for complimentary coffee. The nurse offers him a cup, and he accepts. While he is sitting there enjoying this brewed coffee (we never get brewed coffee), the door pushes open and someone is pushing a lady in a wheel chair into the room. It's the warden, and she apparently had foot surgery. The warden said, "What are you doing with that coffee?" He said, "They gave it to me. It's for the public." She said, "You're not the public. You're an inmate. Get rid of it." We just thought it's funny how she is everywhere, almost omnipresent.

Another interesting character here is a lieutenant who looks kind of like Bob Poe with hair. He has bleached blond hair and wears it shaved on the sides and spiked down the middle, always waxed and standing up straight. He sprays himself with tanning spray (or has himself sprayed). The guys call him "Johnny Bravo." It didn't make any sense to me, but I guess if you know cartoons, it's funny. The other name they have for him is Agent Orange because his tan is usually orange. He also just shows up all over, when you least expect it. When I first got here I saved some seats in the theater, before I knew you weren't supposed to do that. The way he got on me . . . I never did it again.

A fight broke out in the theater Friday night. A guy was saving a seat with a piece of paper on it. Another guy came and sat in it. The first guy came back and said, "That's my seat." The second guy said, "I'm sitting here." The first guy punched him in the face and broke his nose. Blood was all over. The guy with the broken nose stood up and was a really big guy. He followed the other guy out of the theater and beat his face into the sidewalk. It was dark, and there was a lot of excitement, but by the time the cops got there it was all over.

That night we were called to the dorms early. We were told to stay in our rooms. Then they announced that we were to stand up and remove our shirts. They came around, and we had to show them our knuckles, our chests, and our eyes to see if we had been hitting or had been hit. It's the most respect that I've gotten since I got here, to think that this seventy-two-year-old body could do that much damage to someone's nose.

The food goes in cycles. Somehow, they must have gotten a large shipment of blueberries. They are individually frozen. We are having blueberries in everything that is baked. Saturday morning we had sugar-coated corn flakes with a large cup of blueberries on the side. Boy, was that good. We have a cup of blueberries for dessert now quite often, sometimes served over cake. Some of the best foods here are hamburgers and fries (Wednesday), fish on Friday, this great meat loaf they make every other week, and corned beef and cabbage (every other week). They also make awesome cinnamon rolls every Monday morning, which I have given up, and a great tuna salad. It's interesting, though, how things change after having had it for six months. I'm sure at the end of four years, it won't look as good. The first night here we had chicken fried rice. We thought it was awesome, just having come from Sherburne. Now, it's the meal nobody likes. We liked it because we could actually recognize the pieces of chicken. For the seven weeks in Sherburne, we couldn't recognize anything. Overall, the food is good; it's more carbs than I want, but nobody goes hungry.

2/11/11

On Monday, a friend of mine who is a pastor mailed me about a large mission, church planting movement they have started on the East Coast, with a view of including the whole U.S. He has asked if we would like to be the ones praying for South Dakota. I think he asks that because of our activity with Tom and the Native Americans.

I printed the e-mail and took it to Tom. My question for him was, "Should we do this, and if so, should we do it for the Indian Nation in South

Dakota? Should it be for just the Native Americans or the whole state of South Dakota?" He didn't really address the question. Instead, he talked about how difficult it is for the Native Americans to trust the white man, that they see the Bible as the white man's book. He expressed appreciation for the way we have worked with him and the other Native Americans that I have mentioned.

I have a sincere interest in learning the value of the Native American traditions because I think many of the traditions came from very good values. They really do teach respect for each other, and for creation. When they pray they sometimes pray to the "Great Spirit," and we talk about whether that is God or not. I plan in my head conversations that we might have with others.

Midmorning, I was in the library, and Tom came through. I motioned for him to sit down with me. He did. I said, "Am I being too aggressive with you about ministering to the Native Americans?"

He said, "No. I am very passionate about this. When you said the other day that your dad prayed for you and that you have sisters praying for you now, I thought, who has ever prayed for me? I know my dad never prayed, my mother never prayed, and my grandmother never prayed. How did I ever come to faith with nobody praying for me?" "Now," he said, "I realize, Jesus was praying for me. He prays for me all the time and that's how I found him in the Scriptures."

He said, "Now, I met you. You didn't come down on me to tell me I had to do certain things. I appreciate that. My world used to be so small." He made a fist and a small hole with his thumb and forefinger. "My world was this big (small hole). Now I have people praying for me all over the world. I had a need in my account. I had no money. I didn't tell anybody. I didn't even tell God, but He knew. Then a lady put money in my account, a lady that I didn't even know. My world has gotten so big." He threw his arms apart as he said that. He said, "She didn't even know me. She didn't love me, but she loves God. I love God, and I just thank Him. He met my need. I really needed that money badly, but I didn't ask anyone for it. God took care of me."

"So," he said, "I want to do this." I had said that I saw the outreach to the Native Americans would be only with Native Americans leading it. I explained that wherever we have gone in India, where 100,000 pastors are being trained, and in Cambodia, where 12,000 pastors are being trained, we go in only by invitation. We don't believe in Americans moving in and staying. I explained I saw us as back up support, supporting Native Americans who God calls to join him.

Tom said, "Why? The way you are doing it you are trying to understand the Natives. I want to help you understand the Natives. If you understand them you can do it. The reason the Natives hate the Bible and Christians is because it was forced on them. They took the children, cut off their hair and put them in schools." He said, "I went to one of those schools. I wasn't taught anything about a relationship with God. It was all religion, rule, and liturgy. Other than that, it was like any other school. When the Natives think of 'Christianity,' they think of that. Whites think we are just savages. They don't know us any different. They don't know of all the treaties that were made with our forefathers and how they broke every one of them. We were given land, whole regions of land. Then they took it back and kept taking it back until most reservations are only about a section of land." He said, "I don't feel that way, but that's what they feel. If you talk to them without knowing that, it won't be pleasant."

2/22/11

Growing up in the church, I always thought the church was the right place for me to be and to do all I could to help further the ministry of the church. The church was not an easy place for me to do ministry though. It often seemed I would become passionate about some idea, some ministry opportunities, a teaching curriculum, or ideas in general, but then I needed to funnel ideas through other people because the leadership would rather not hear it from me. During those times, I thought to myself, maybe someday when I retire I will move someplace and minister to the down and outers. They might be people who live under bridges, in shelters, or on the streets. I will find people who want to hear. I seriously had those thoughts.

I found great gratification in going to developing countries where there was great hunger for leadership development, where they didn't care who you are or where you were in business or in your social life. They wanted truth and help, and they wanted to be resourced to bring the gospel to their people.

Saturday, as we walked on the track, Tom said he wanted to talk with me, but he wanted to sit down with me. He had a book with him, *The Wolf at Twilight* by Ken Nerburn. He said, "You need to buy this book. I can't give you this one, because it's not mine. You need to get this book." He was both earnest and serious. It is rather strong and straightforward about how the Native Americans feel about white people. As he read he got choked up. As he read more and came to the place where he talks about the children in the Indian schools, he began to sob and had to stop reading for a while. He said, "Board-ing school wasn't that bad for me, but in boarding school I was so lost. When I read about this boy, I felt just like he felt. I was so confused. I had no identity. I didn't like who I was. On the reservation there just was no hope. There was nothing to make you think you had a future. You knew that the white people just thought we were a bunch of savages. We didn't feel that they saw us as people."

I told him about my own prejudices and bias as I encountered Indians. I remember going to Kenora, Canada, and seeing that most of the Indians were drunk. None of them seemed to work. I didn't care for them. I saw them as outcasts. The same was true in South Dakota. I never knew any Native Ameri-cans personally. I never met one who I knew to be honest and respectable. I told Tom that meeting him and the others had changed my view. I'm begin-ning to get a new vision of what God must think about all this.

Tom said, "I don't know how God decided to save me." He said, "I always had the mentality to work and try to improve myself." He said, "I've done some dumb things and some bad things. I did care about it. It bothered me that I had done wrong." As he closed Tom said, "I've shared a lot with you today, and this means a lot to me. When your family writes to me and tells me they love you, that says something to me. That's what I want my family to say some day. I want them to love me and to love God. I know that Jesus is pray-ing for them just as He prayed for me. It gives me the feeling there is a greater purpose in this, and that's why they are helping me."

2/24/11

A friend went to a class the other day that all inmates have to take before they are released. He was quite shaken by the class. He said, "They want us to know that when we leave here we are felons for life. They said, 'You cannot vote, and you may not have a gun or be near anyone who has a gun. If you are riding in a pickup with a friend who is a hunter and even if he has emptied all the guns out of his pickup but there is a bullet in the truck, if you are stopped for any reason, they will arrest you. They will tell you that the minimum guideline sentence for that is five years in prison. You can then go to trial or plead guilty and take a sentence of two years. You will take the sentence of two years. It happens all the time.'"

They informed the class that you will file a financial statement every month. You are not allowed to spend $300 or more without your parole officer's permission. You are not considered a citizen of the U.S. and do not have the rights of a citizen. My friend was pretty shaken by this. He is here because of real estate loan fraud. It is for fraud that was encouraged by banks and mortgage companies during the time when the government flooded the market with money because they desperately wanted to get the loans out. The information communicated in his class is alarming for anyone to whom it applies and that is all of us in here. They said you cannot travel outside your region without permission. You will report any income you have and 25 percent of your income must go to the government for restitution for their costs.

When I think of how all this follows us, I think of it most importantly for a young person who must spend the rest of his life with this hanging over his head. I know that most can't care too much. They can't conceive of it ever happening to them or to someone they care about.

I think of Tom and his story. I think how I have seen so many Indians on the road or on the street as I passed by, many of them drunk. I saw them as aimless, hopeless people, and I felt little compassion or concern for them. They were just outcasts.

I think of all this as I think of my friend Tom. I am blessed by him. I am so pleased to meet a couple of guys who have begun to change my image or idea of Native Americans. Studying the Scriptures together, praying together, and walking many miles together, I want to have hope for them and for their people. My desire for Tom's people is very strong. While I know that the history of evangelizing Native Americans proves it is very difficult, I pray that God is in this. By "this" I guess I mean an idea or a vision that these people could be helped.

Unlike most of the outcasts I am living with, I have people praying for me and a great family who believe in me and who don't see me as an outcast. That is a huge blessing to me. Very few of the men I am with have that. Every day since before they were indicted, the system has been doing the best to get them to feel and understand that they are outcasts. They will deal with the label for the rest of their lives.

I think of that every time I mail a letter. I am forced to have Duluth Federal Prison Camp spelled out on the return address. I think of that every time I talk to my family on the telephone. A recording breaks into our conversation every three minutes that says, "You are talking to an inmate in a federal prison." It continues on the outside. You cannot have any contact with another felon. If one is in the room or house you must leave. All these restrictions for me, a seventy-five-year-old-man (that is what I will be when I get out), but for a young man needing to support himself and his family it is a lot of baggage to carry. They carry it whether they are a murderer and a rapist finishing a thirty-year sentence or if they got caught with marijuana and someone named them in a conspiracy, and they had only ninety days. Once a person is logged into this system, it is a lifetime stigma. They are outcasts.

I'm not any more soft on crime than I have ever been. However, I see these people now more as real people. These are real problems for people in our country. Locking people up for long prison terms is a convenient thing to do, but is it the right thing to do? Is turning our backs on the Native Americans as I have done in the past okay for me to do? Does God have a better plan? Is he preparing hearts of men who could be leaders to reach out to his people? I pray this would be the case. I don't have the answer right now, but I will pray.

If we who pray are willing to follow God in whatever he gives as an answer and be sensitive to him, maybe we can be part of His will being carried out for people that we sometimes ignore. We ignore because we don't see ourselves in them.

13

Yesterday afternoon as I was walking back from the medical building, I met Ron. He is about seventy years of age. He is very distinguished looking. He got here the same time as I did. He is from Chicago, and I believe his case had to do with real estate loans. His son was involved as well, and he is in a different prison.

Ron has a full head of silver white hair and is a very nice man. He was so sad when he came; it seemed he was fighting severe depression. His wife, Betty, would come and visit him. We met in the visiting center. Jan and Betty got to know each other quite well. When I asked her how she was doing, she said, "Well, I'm doing a lot better than Ron." She would drive up about every three weeks from Chicago to be with Ron because Ron needed the encouragement. I always tried to include Ron in our walks on the track, etc., just to keep him moving. Ron improved from that time and seemed to be doing better. When I met Ron, he was walking extremely slowly, barely walking. After he passed I turned around and called to him and said, "Ron, are you okay?" He hesitated and said, "I'm all right." We both kept going. I found out that he was just coming from the phone, where he learned that Betty had passed away. It is such a shock. She seemed so healthy and so alert. She reminded me somewhat of Jan. I tried to get Ron to join our groups, but he didn't pick up on the conversations.

At noon I met Ron coming from the dining hall. I told Ron how sorry I am and that I am praying for him. He was crying. He said, "Just pray for her." It's so very difficult. Inmates aren't supposed to go into one another's rooms, but I did go to his this afternoon to talk. He was not in.

This is something that most of us are not prepared for. The husband is supposed to die first, not the wife. Little did he know the last time they visited he would never see her again. The warden has full authority to allow or deny a furlough for a man to go to his wife's funeral. It's not been the custom of this warden to do that. The only case where it has happened, it has taken a senator or a judge to force the issues. It can be done that way. Ron had voluntarily surrendered when he came. He drove up here and turned himself in. There is not lock on the gate here. He is certainly not a dangerous man. It would be fitting for him to be released for it.

I feel like there has been a seasoning process here in the camp with the inmates. It's rather interesting for me to see some of the inmates that I purposely have not had much contact with because they seem very hard and coarse. My roommates who were very dubious of me at first have really warmed up. Dave, the hippie, is now friendly but very unbending.

I never talk to the inmates in the room across the hall and next door. They seem so hardened and so foul in their talk. They are harsh, brash, and have hollered at me for humming a little in the hallway. I had talked to one for a while, but then he got word that I don't like drug dealers and was passing the word on me. I have been in my room now for seven months, just living and let live. One of them, a man from Lansing, Michigan, sat down with me twice now in the dining hall. He engaged me in conversation and both times seemed to want to talk about his faith. He wanted to tell me that though he has never been much of a man to go to church, only about once a year, he felt he was a man of faith. The mealtime isn't a good time to talk, but since he brings the conversation around to that I told him I had a book I would like him to read. I gave him the book *Twice Pardoned*. He said he would read it. It seems as though just by being around and being steady and consistent, the guys are watching me and reading me. I think barriers are breaking down.

We have all our material approved now, and the guys will get credits for taking our classes. Next quarter we are going to have four English classes and one Spanish class. We will be having classes four nights a week with two classes on Mondays. There is an inmate here who leads Spanish Bible studies, and he is going to come under our " Life's Principles" umbrella and teach our classes in Spanish. It's amazing. God has brought us a long way. At first we couldn't even find a place to have one class. The chaplain still has not helped us out once, but the people in education believe in us and what we are doing. We could have fifty students the next quarter.

Jim has worked tirelessly. He wants to leave this legacy here (he hopes to win his appeal soon and be gone). He wants his legacy here to be these classes, and not only here. We are now approved nationwide. If we have people qualified to teach in other prisons, this can now be taught in every prison in the United States.

3/8/11

The meeting last night went well. I gave my testimony. I must say that while I was giving it, it felt a little strange. I'm talking to these guys about growing up on a farm with a loving family, and I know they cannot relate with any of that. I told them the reason I wanted them to know about that is that each one of them can break a long chain of parent neglect and criminal conduct and start a chain of godly living and godly family relationship. I said, "I am convinced that is what God has in mind once we come to faith in Christ." Many picked up on that and seemed excited about that.

I finished the talk, feeling a little strange, as I said. I was surprised at some of the guys who came. They were really unlikely guys who never come to church. It wasn't a large group, only about thirty guys. The comments were most interesting. One guy stopped me on the compound. He is a guy who manufactured meth and then hired prostitutes to travel a circuit; he paid them in drugs. He said, "Hey, Bob, what's this I hear? You gave your testimony last night, and today the cops are in your dorm." (The cops were in our dorm looking for something.) It was all good-natured fun with him, but I was surprised that he even knew what a testimony is, let alone that it was me giving it. It's interesting how talk gets around here, and what they are interested in talking about.

The leadership staff at education is really getting behind us on the courses. It's not even going under "religion" but under "sharing," which will keep the chaplain from interfering with it. It can be not only taught but also used for credits that are part of how they evaluate inmates upon their release.

3/15/11

Things keep getting more tense around here. The warden keeps tightening the screws on the staff, and the staff hates their jobs even more. Whole rooms of guys get moved, and some get moved out to the least desirable dorm. It could make a book in itself, but one that I don't think I want to write.

We are coming to the end of the first quarter as far as education is concerned. It's so interesting to see how the guys are attaching to the classes. Some real surprises. Some older guys who I never thought would attach. I couldn't figure out why they wanted to take the class; I would never have invited them.

3/18/11

The last week we have had more people in our prayer time in the morning, and it has changed the interaction from Tom. I was a little concerned at his quietness. He does not speak freely until he is really ready. Because some of the other new men want to talk so much, there are not quiet times in our devotion; it is constant talk. Sometimes I would direct a question directly to Tom just to find out what was on his mind. He would answer out of respect, but I knew he did not like that.

This week I was sitting in the pool room reading the book Tom suggested, and a work party came in to work on the heating system. Tom was part of the work party, and he saw I was reading the book. We talked about it, and Red Feather said one of Native Americans said to him, "There is a white guy who is reading the book."

About forty minutes later, I was still reading the book, and I got the sensation that there was someone behind me. I turned around, and there was Tom. He said that when he came here he had made up my mind that he was going to transfer from here as soon as he could. Maybe to be closer to family but, if not, just anywhere to be away from here. He said that he would be coming up on two years and eligible for transfer. I told him I had two-and-a-half to three years left. He said that he thinks God wants him to stay here and learn all he can from me.

3/22/11

It is a strange but interesting time for me as I draw near to the one-year anniversary of my trial. I remember the time before and during the trial being so difficult that I was actually relieved to have it all over, even though it turned out differently than what we hoped and prayed for. It seems like the year has gone quite fast.

There is a new man in our group. He was born in Samoa and lived in Hawaii all his life. He became a Christian early in life, but while in Hawaii he got involved in drugs and served time. When he got out of prison in Hawaii, he worked for a man who was ministering to youth who had been on drugs. He didn't know it at first, but the man was using these young people to sell drugs on the side. He said, "My problem was that at first I didn't know it, but later I did. I didn't stop working there so I was actually condoning it. He got sentenced to twenty-two years. He has been down for some time. He is sixty-two years old, but he is a very committed Christian and has a very sweet spirit. When he prays he does not preach but really prays from the heart. I was so thankful when I heard him pray and speak in class. I had almost come to the point where I didn't want any new people in the class. Some are so legalistic and like to hear themselves talk so much that when they start they don't stop.

14

4/2/11

Tom is now a grandfather. It was interesting to see his response to the birth of his first grandchild, a boy. Tom knows that this would not have been such a big event to him in his old ways. He has said that. Since he has become a Christian and especially since he now understands God's purpose for family, he is so committed to wanting to see his children walk in God's ways. They don't even know about Christ yet. Now he has a grandchild who he really wants to raise up with his daughter.

Ron found out that his wife died because she simply fell down the stairs and broke her neck. Ron was very distraught, and he was blaming himself for not being there and feeling a lot of guilt. I was not able to get with Ron. He had a group of guys he played cards with who stayed around him and tried to help him with things.

This is what is so upsetting. They immediately requested permission from the warden to have a five-day furlough. All day Friday they waited for the approval. Finally, late in the day, she said he could have seventy-two hours. Indianapolis is a fifteen-hour drive so he would need to fly. They found a 6:30 a.m. flight out of Duluth for Monday. The warden said he couldn't go that early. They found an 8:30 a.m. flight, which would be the last flight he could get in order to be there Monday night for the wake, the funeral Tuesday, and be back here Wednesday. She said he could not leave until 9:00 a.m. The only way he could make it was to charter a plane to fly him, leaving here at 9:30 a.m., but it was very expensive. We thought it was taken care of. Usually the prison has what they call town cars and town drivers. The drivers take people downtown, to the hospital, clinic, and also to the bus station when they leave. That is what he was expecting. Then the warden said they could not cost the government any money and that the town car could not go. Ron came asking what to do. No one is allowed to have any money in prison so how could he get a cab? After some thinking they thought of the fact that his wife always stayed at a certain motel when she visited Ron and had become friends with those people. They called the motel and asked them if they would call the taxi, have it stop there first, and then pay the taxi to come and get Ron and take him to the airport. The airport is only one block from the gate, but they wouldn't allow him to walk.

There is so much hate in this place. The attitudes among the staff are so bad. It is hard to think that anyone here cares about anyone. I know it is supposed to be a place of rehabilitation, but it is such a joke. I am quite angry just watching it happen.

4/3/11

Our classes are finally in the catalog, but they have really messed up the schedule so that the times they have listed are not the times we are having the class. Then we were going to fix that by placing posters around the compound a week in advance of the sign up, and now they had the sign up a week early so we didn't get any of that information out.

Also, none of our books have come yet, at least as far as we can tell with the people here. I just don't know if they didn't get ordered, if the orders got lost, or if they are here but can't find them. It seems we go through this with everything. It is just extremely difficult getting anything done. I think this is just an example of how it is when the government runs things. There is no interest, no accountability, and nobody has an interest in seeing things move forward. Right now my biggest concern is finding the books for our class.

I have been having good connections with Eagle Tail. He always comes up to me to talk. Yesterday we talked again. I was talking to him about his traditions. I said, "We should talk more. I'm interested in your concept of the Great Spirit. I would like to talk to you about that and how you see the Great Spirit in connection with God." He said, "Soon it will be warm out. Then we can sit outside and talk. That's where we should be talking about those things anyway, outside and under the sky." We talked again this morning for a short time.

4/5/11

We had a riff in our prayer group. One of the guys took offense to something I said and expressed his offense in prayer rather than coming to me. It is seemingly okay now, but I see the need to be guarded. Men who have become Christians in prison still carry some of their old ways, and one has to remember that. The guys were saying over and over that we have to keep asking forgiveness for our sins. I made the statement that when we come to Christ, God forgives all our sins: past, present, and future. Later, in my prayer I asked God to forgive us for (something). That was one of the offenses.

Last night in the dorm I was in the bathroom brushing my teeth, and two other Christian guys were there, Tim and Ben. We were laughing and having a good time. Then an announcement came over the speakers that those who wanted to watch the rest of the Final Four game could go back to the activity center. Mic, the dorm orderly, walked in, and I said, "Is that right? Are they really going to let us do that?" Mic, said, "They're showing porn movies in the activity center." Just to keep it light, I said to Tim, "Well, there you go." Then Mic said, "The guys that go to the chapel see porn movies all the time." One of the guys said , "What?" I said to Mic, "You ought to go down to the chapel sometime to see what they are watching." Mic said, "They are all a bunch of hypocrites down there. Everybody that goes there is a hypocrite; they are always talking about people."

It was a big blow up, and kind of upsetting, because Mic usually doesn't act like that. None of this, in itself, is that big a deal, but it's just stacking up. Jim works so hard to help get things going, and then the staff just lets everything fall through the cracks. The chaplain still hasn't entered the code into the computer so the guys can get credit. Jim is so tender-hearted toward me; it hurts him to see me get attacked.

4/8/11

I met Virgil Smith shortly after I got here. He works in the library and does a lot of the leadership in the chapel. He is a good speaker and is sincerely born again as a Christian. Virgil is from East St. Louis. If you have ever been to St. Louis, most of the bad things happen east of the river. Virgil was raised by his grandmother who was a godly woman and raised him in the church. When he was about twelve, he got involved in the streets and then got introduced to the gangs by the time he was fourteen. He was in gang wars and always carrying a gun; he shot people and was shot, and he took drugs and sold drugs.

From the age of fourteen, Virgil was involved in a lot of crime but never really was caught. He would get caught and go to jail for a month or two and be released. When he was twenty-two years old, he was caught with fifty-two grams of cocaine and charged with possession with the intent to distribute. He was sentenced to ten years. He has served six years, and with the drug program, he expects to be released in one more year.

Virgil, while once a hardened criminal, is truly a changed man. He has a sweet spirit and loves God with all his heart. He can't stop talking about Jesus. I have talked with him a great deal about his family. Between the ages of eighteen and twenty-two he impregnated five different women and is not married to any of them. He is very broken and repentant about that and wants to be a good father to each of his children. He writes to them all and tries to minister to them.

I asked him what he plans to do when he gets out. He said he would hate to move back to St. Louis because that's where all his old connections are, and they will not want to leave him alone. At the same time, that's where all his children are and so he needs to be there at least for a time. He said, "I want to be responsible to my children. I will be friends with their mothers ,but I tell them I can't have any relationship with them." I've talked to him about staying strong and being pure, and he said, "Yes, that is my biggest concern. I can't be going to bed with them and living that way."

I visit with Virgil a lot. He is very busy with his own studies but has taken the time to be in our class. He does have God's view of fatherhood now and wants to live that out. Obviously, that will be challenging with five children in five different households.

4/16/11

I am not sure of what initiates the hard part of being here, whether it's being in prison or whether it's being totally immersed in a government bureaucratic mentality. We live in a quagmire of not being able to get anything done or accomplished. It finally bogs you down, burns you out, makes things meaningless, and finally it leaves you hopeless. This shows itself in everything, including getting medical issues taken care of—they don't get it done. My roommate is supposed to go home in May, but he can't get his date to leave because the warden won't sign it. The books we ordered in December still aren't here, although through our own investigation we know at least one case of books has been in the postal room since March 16. The officer won't pick it up.

Still, my experience is unlike anyone else because of being able to minister. This week I stood in front of forty guys in four different classes—half have been in studies now for at least one quarter and half are brand new. It is such a privilege and an honor to bring the truth of the gospel to them and to be able to see in their eyes that they are "getting it." I get to see the passion in them for this, and when we have to talk about changing class schedules and times, how they fight to keep it so they can attend. God is truly at work in this, and that is so rewarding.

4/21/11

Every night now we have classes. I do stress out a little preparing for them, wanting them to be not only accepted by the guys but also understood and meaningful. I get apprehensive because this is not light material. We have found it to be too heavy in some churches. People don't like to think this hard. It is not fill-in-the-blanks work. It is thinking through issues and writing. I am finding that although we lose guys in the beginning, the guys who have remained in it are now really getting it and understanding the depths of the Gospels so well. They understand the significance of the family and the church. They understand it and feel called to it. It is so amazing. Every night, walking the half-mile back to the dorm, I feel so blessed and so privileged to be teaching these guys.

4/27/11

My friend George visited me yesterday. We haven't talked for about three months. He asked me how I'm doing. In trying to be honest with someone I haven't seen for a while, I find I have to pause and contemplate. I could give a wide range of answers, and they all would be true. I could say it's terrible, and it is. It's terrible to be so separated from my family and my little grandchildren who I want to see grow up. On the other hand, there is a lot that is good. I am happy serving God. He is giving me more opportunity to serve Him than I have had for a long time, and that's good for a man my age. The distractions in my life are gone. I am thirsty for God, and the other things I might use to satisfy my thirst are not available. I must feed on and drink of him, and he is so good. He satisfies me and my need.

4/30/11

Joel is from California, and he is thirty-eight. Because of his investment business, he lived a very high lifestyle. Joel was gathering money for a high yield hedge fund and knowingly, or unknowingly, was spending too much money. Nonetheless, he and his wife were very spoiled with a lifestyle that most people can only image.

Joel traveled in high circles before his marriage. He liked to pursue high profile women, beauty queen pageants and partying people. Alcohol and drugs were a big part of it. Joel later met his wife. Neither she nor Joel were believers, but she had life values that he admired. She wanted to be a home-maker and have children.

Joel went to prison five years ago, leaving his wife with a three-year-old and a one-year-old. She is a moral person, which is the reason he was attracted to her. She is a humanist to this day. Joel came to faith in prison and has completed many Bible correspondence courses. He said it still left him with some confusion because of the contrasting thoughts and beliefs of the Bible teachers.

By his own admission, Joel was very egotistical, strong headed, wordy, and had very little time to listen to others. Joel came to our first classes even before we were approved in education. I had very little hope for Joel because of his huge ego, and he was very difficult for me to tolerate.

Last summer, Joel was hoping to get into the drug program, which would take a year off his sentence. His wife was telling him that she needed the affection and approval of men in her life, real men who she could see and touch. For four years, Joel was in a facility in California much like Sherburne County where visits are only through monitors. He hadn't touched or held his wife or children in five years, and she was saying she couldn't take it any longer. She didn't want to leave him, but she was on the Internet communicating with men. Joel was wondering what to do.

I encouraged Joel that he needed to be a husband to her, even though he is in prison. He needed to give her leadership and direction, and that if he stayed in the classes, he would learn how to do that. Joel loves to talk about how God is changing his life and his family. Yesterday he said, "My mind used to be consumed with having the highest lifestyle possible. I would dream about having a Rolls-Royce. Then I began to change, and I told myself I would never spend that kind of money for a car. I thought if I could get a real good deal on one for $30,000, maybe I would have one. Now, I don't even think that way anymore. I just don't want that around me, I don't want to be known for that. I just think of moving to Montana and having a little ranch and a garden plot with a little log house on it that we can expand as we have more kids. I am so amazed at how God is changing my heart and desires."

15

5/8/11

Red came to me yesterday and said that he has a new roommate who just got here. He had a letter in his hand from his parents that they had read my e-mails and that he should get in touch with me. He asked Red if he ever heard of Bob Goris. He said, "Yes, I'm in his class." We haven't met yet, but I hope to find him this afternoon.

My sister in Michigan said that she knows someone who has a son in prison in Wisconsin, and he is coming to Duluth. They have received my e-mails, and I told them about our classes.

Today, Virgil told me that our prayers seem to be getting answered in another way (his previous attempts to visit his family failed due to the expense involved). But there is a new male prison opening in Pekan, Illinois, and they are looking for people who want to transfer. Virgil didn't think he would go, but this week he found out he must go to Pekan to take his drug rehabilitation class there. He said he will be one hour and fifteen minutes from home, and his family will be able to come and visit him. That is the closest he has been to home in five years.

5/10/11

God is truly amazing in how he works. I'm supposed to have a sleep test done, but it may take a year to get it, even after they approve it. I was averaging four hours of sleep per night, and it just wasn't working. The guys in my morning prayer time became concerned about me. I decided that just for a couple days I wouldn't set my alarm and had arrangements made in case I didn't show up. I did that and slept seven hours the first night and eight hours the next night. That didn't continue, but my sleeping has improved quite a bit. I really hated to give up the morning prayer time, but I know also that the other guys need to develop into leaders. As long as I am there they will look to me as the leader. I have talked to them about taking over the leadership; I'm sleeping better and using that time for personal Bible study and prayer. It is refreshing, and I'm asking God for what is next. The evening studies are still going strong and will continue until June 17 when we break for the summer.

Yesterday was a great day. We prayed for Tom that he could see his daughter, Jenna. Our prayer partners responded and supplied the financial resources so that the trip was made possible. Then God connected us with a friend from the distant past who lives in Sioux Falls; her name is Ronna. Ronna has worked in Sioux Falls State Prison as the secretary to the warden, and she has been carrying on her own prison ministry for more than twenty years. Ronna made contact with Jenna and has been ministering to her; she drove her to Duluth this weekend to visit her dad. The last time Tom saw Jenna in person was when she was twelve. Jenna just had a baby, Tom's first grandchild. He said when they got together they were both so nervous, he said that they should pray. Jenna had never heard him talk about God or prayer before. He said such good things to her, even though some were very difficult to say.

It is Mother's Day today. I was reading Proverbs 31. One verse that really spoke to me was the one that says, "she keeps her light on through the dark of night." I felt there was a double meaning to that. It had special meaning to me because of the experience we are in. I read "the dark of night" to mean the dark times in life. I felt that when a woman/wife/mother can keep her brightness through dark times it is such a blessing. That's the blessing I am receiving right now from the mother of my children. Her light not only lights my life, but it also lights her world as she passes through it.

5/16/11

Wow! I'm getting birthday e-mails that won't stop. Somebody let the word out that I have a birthday coming. I'm enjoying every minute of it. I am encouraged and empowered.

The prayer time is going along well without me, and new, young leaders are getting a chance to hone their skills. As for me, I am sleeping much better. I am averaging between six and seven hours a night instead of the four to five that I was doing before. Another benefit is that I have more quality time before the world wakes up to have my own personal time with the Lord. I feel a great obligation—a responsibility to use that time to the hilt because the Lord knows I need my batteries charged with new vision and energy for new people and a new routine. It's been almost a year now in this one place doing the same thing, so a change will invigorate me. I find I already have to resist not using that time for watching the news. We only get news in the morning and the evening. With the classes in the evening I don't get to watch the news; I am tempted to go over in the morning to see it, but I know that I need the time with God.

I have a new friend, Dale. He and his wife, Marie, have three daughters, ages eight, eleven, and sixteen. It's a very hard time for them right now. He is sentenced to five years and has had other complications after the trial. I noticed Dale early on because he was in the chapel each morning praying. I made a point to meet him. He has been very busy with legal matters, but this week we connected, walked together several times, and Friday spent a good time in the chapel praying together. We prayed Psalm 51 together, and Dale has committed to memorizing it so that we can pray it together when we walk the track.

It's been a difficult week in the chapel. There is some real tension with the Easter program that one of the inmates put on Sunday night. He used secular music, used Scripture out of context, non-Christian singers. People are offended in various ways, and it has bled into one of our classes.

5/22/11

I have been thinking a great deal about stories, especially life stories. We tend to think of our life as many stories, but when we put a timeline together of our own life, it becomes one story. As Christians, when we see life from an eternal perspective, it becomes God's story; then, even to ourselves, the impact of the story becomes emotionally overwhelming.

In one of our classes, there is a man from Kansas City named Joe. Joe owned and operated seventeen nursing homes throughout the Midwest. Joe has two masters degrees and is working on a Ph.D. Joe has been very quiet in the class, but this week he said, "My success has been very important to me. I have done a lot of good things. My haunting fear is that this one piece of my life, this one snapshot, is what is going to define me the rest of my life."

Some people live their lives in someone else's story, be it a professional athlete or their children's success, even living life without their soul connected to their own story. Sometimes, our own story might be too painful at the time to want to relate with it.

Each one of you has a story. You have probably not developed your story, because you do not think it is interesting. But it is from God's perspective, and God was doing things in your life before you were aware that He even existed. Write about the people, books, places, and circumstances that God used to shape you into the person he wanted you to be. I believe that when you are finished and you read it, it won't be boring. It may just take your breath away. As we live life day by day, there is much that just doesn't make sense. But when we see it put all together and from God's perspective, our lives actually do make sense in every part—the good, the bad, and the ugly. As I talk to guys here, I say, "Don't let this snapshot of your life define you."

I experienced this in 1972. I had finished my twelfth year in business. I was not sure that what I was doing in life was my calling. I wanted a calling, a purpose, and a direction from God. In pondering this, I thought through what aspects of my work had ministry potential. In this process, the thought or idea or dream that came to me was that I should take a strength that I seemed to have been given by God and use it as an outreach tool to engage in the lives of other men. I had learned how to be successful in life insurance sales, and my thought was that if I could pass these skills on to other men, it could be a great way to minister to them and their families.

We had a minister living with us for a weekend because he was holding seminars in our church. His name was Paul Veenstra. One night, after a meeting, we were talking in our family room on the farm. I told Paul of my desire and sense of calling, and I told him of my thought to build an agency that would minister in the lives of men. I asked him if he thought that could be a calling. Paul was excited and said he thought that is exactly the way God calls people. We all knelt down in the family room that night, asked God to bless it, and we gave the business to God.

The next seven months were so exciting. I went to work recruiting men and had great, immediate success. Very soon, I had ten men that I was training. Word got out in the company, and I was asked to speak at a convention in New Mexico. I was honored, scared, and proud all at the same time. I spoke there on how to build an agency.

It was a great experience while it lasted. Unknown to me, while I was away speaking and celebrating, my young agency was getting discouraged and quit. When I got home, I had no agency left. I was so disappointed, discouraged, and embarrassed that I could hardly talk about it. I definitely couldn't pray about it. I was embarrassed before God. I thought I had such a great idea and gave it all to God, and now I really did not have anything at all. Still, I kept working at my dream to build an agency, and God brought it about and made it happen in another way.

The point of the story is that just the picture of that failure by itself is such an ugly picture I couldn't even talk about it to God. When I look back on it from an eternal perspective, God had a greater presence during the failure than later at a time of success. God wants us to come to Him with our failures. We tend to want to come to God only with success.

I am reading a book called *The Gospel According to Job*. The book was sent to me from the employer of my nephew. She has received my e-mails and had this book sent to me. I have never been able to access the book of Job before. It's strange, but it's like I didn't feel I had permission to identify with Job. I have a friend who is a minister from out East. When I told him I was going to trial, he expressed sympathy and concern, and in doing so he quoted God (speaking to Satan in Job), "Consider my servant Job." I'll never forget it. I felt so honored and respected by him, just to be mentioned in the same sentence with Job. At the same time, I felt guilty and unworthy to be compared to Job. The very first page in this book has changed that for me. It's like it unlocked it for me.

The author of the book makes that point that Job was blameless; it doesn't say he was guiltless. Being blameless means that no matter how horrible his offenses may have been, all charges against him have been dropped. Absolutely no blame attaches to him because the very one who he offended exonerated him. Psalm 32:2 says, "Blessed is the man whose sin the Lord does not count against him."

I have thought a lot about, and have written about, pleasing God and seeking his pleasure. The author of the book says we don't sense God's pleasure because we have a lingering suspicion that it is impossible to please God. The real question is not whether God loves us but whether he approves of us and whether we are pleasing to him. For certain, if we are not pleasing to God, he will never be pleasing to us. How can we like someone who is forever condemning us?

I knew what pleased my father, and I loved to please him. I loved to make him smile. I do imagine that I know how to please God. It's not that different than my childhood days, pleasing Dad. I am so thankful for my memories of pleasing Dad. It seems almost seamless, even at this stage of my life, to please God. It even leads me to believe that God loves pleasure, and I can bring him pleasure. I think in the story of the prodigal son, the pleasure that the father had when the younger son returned home is God giving us a glimpse of himself. God loves relationship, pleasure, and joy. He invented it. It was all his idea. That's why he created us; it was for his pleasure. I can hear him say, "You are my beloved son. I like you, and I want to be with you. I want your attention. I don't want you busying yourself with worthless things and allowing them to take all your time. I want your time because I like being with you (see Mark 1:11).

Job desperately resisted the notion that there was still some other step he should take, something else he should do to win God's favor under adverse circumstances. I had to deal with that too. I have dealt with it. I have peace. I am convinced that regardless of my place, hardship, or disappointment, I can please God. He likes being with me, and I like to be with him.

I have a hope that these thoughts might minister to you in the place where you are at right now. If it's a place of dryness and boredom, it can be more exciting. If it's a place of loss of a loved one or possessions, there can still be joy because of God. If it's a time of pain and brokenness because one you love is hurting God or walking away from God, he will turn that into joy. Encourage those you love. Let them see your pleasure in them. Ask God to show them how to sense his pleasure, how to love him more, and how to live deeply with him.

5/29/11

Jim has been playing detective; today he got the assistant warden to take him to a storage building where he was told our missing books might be.

It ended up they weren't there, but they found a shipping slip saying the chaplain had signed for them. The assistant warden went to the chaplain's office and found them there. They have been in his office for six weeks! What a fiasco. We are glad to have them, though.

16

6/2/11

I finally got a sleep test last week. They took me downtown. The hospital has ten really nice sleep lab rooms. They are like a nice hotel room with king sized beds, Sleep Number mattresses, and big, soft, and fluffy pillows; they are completely dark rooms and very, very quiet. They tested me without the machine first, and I slept like a baby. They never put the machine on; they said I didn't need it. I don't know if was a fair test though. I came in with sleep exhaustion and putting me in a bed like that with no noise was so unlike what I experience. Nonetheless, they said I don't need a machine, and they wouldn't recommend any sleep aid. I guess I'll live with it.

I had been looking forward to the trip downtown and to getting off the compound. It wasn't quite like I expected. Because it was overnight, an outside security company took me down. I was placed in the back of a police-like car with the cage in it. It wasn't until the return trip the next morning that I realized the effect the cage had on me again. It was like the first trip here. Being in the camp, I had lost much of the prisoner feeling. The cage is very demeaning and is really hard to handle for me. Many of the guys here have self-surrendered and have never had handcuffs on or been in a cage. The guard had to stay in the hospital with me overnight. He sat outside the door. It just brought back the reality of where I am.

I have been enjoying the benefits of the hour-long workout in the gym every morning. It's been about six months now that I have been doing that. It's gotten fun because the workout I could barely do six months ago I can now do quite well. I am even passing up younger guys who are just starting out. It's the first time in my life I have done that, and it is encouraging to find out I can build this old body back into something less old. I've hit a bump in the road on that as well. Last week I found I'm developing a hernia. It's gotten worse each day so today I had to quit the workout. I'm still walking though. I hope I can keep that up. I will go to the doctor, but they told me they try to postpone all surgery, hoping to postpone it right out to release date. I want it fixed right now so I can get it healed and begin to train again. I hope they will take care of it for me.

I have had two roommates leave so they needed to be replaced. I got Gerry from Iowa, a really nice, quiet guy who is about fifty-five years old. The other guy is Larry, who was picked by my roommate Dave. We didn't want Larry for various reasons; he works in the kitchen, is a little messy, and we had another guy across the hall we wanted. I thought that I could get it done through a dorm clerk, but it didn't turn out that way. Larry showed up in our room one day unannounced and stayed there. I was kind of angry and intended to get it fixed with connections. During one sleepless night, I began to think about Larry, and it came to me that God's sovereignty works through everything. Each day, I ask God to make connections for me and that it is quite possible that God wanted Larry in our room.

Well, Larry is a little strange, but Larry likes me. He tells me that all the guys think I'm "a good old guy." They say, "Are you rooming with old Bob?" They come in the room; we have a lot of traffic, which I thought would be a bad thing. Then I realized that as I pray for connections God brings them. I just didn't expect Him to bring them into my room.

There are also a few benefits in having a cook in the room, some of which can't be put into monitored e-mails. My other roommate complains that his locker smells like onions now. I guess it's all part of the game. We'll see what happens.

6/3/11

Gregory, my workout partner, is really a tough guy. He can press 340 pounds and is well- respected by the other guys in the gym. He has a soft-spoken demeanor, but he can become unwound pretty quickly if someone wants to violate him. He really knows how the muscles of the body work, and I couldn't ask for a better trainer. He seems to really have taken an interest in me. It's a lot of work for him to reserve the spots, set up the equipment, and coach me. I asked him why he chose me to work with. He said he didn't choose me. I just happened to be there when he needed to workout with someone. I don't really believe that. He goes through a lot of work to set things up for me.

Gregory knows I lead a lot of classes, and he has talked to other guys about me. Gregory let me know early on that he thinks the Bible is just a bunch of stories that were passed on verbally for thousands of years, until one day people started writing the stories down and passed them along as truth.

He grew up wild in L.A. Because of his small size, he was very quiet but joined the Marine Corps and there learned to be very tough. When he got out, he ran with a bunch of guys and caused a lot of trouble. They went around violating (not his term) as many young girls as they could. I asked him if that ever bothered him. He said, "No, I was only interested in [expletive], and if the face was pretty that was okay, but not necessary." They used a lot of "weed" and drank a lot of alcohol.

He married a girl and moved to Iowa because her family was there. He joined a cult (not his term) where marijuana was used as a sacrament. This group lived in a commune and studied the Bible strictly. To join you had to confess all the sins of your life to the group and that was your baptism into the group. They lived on a farm, and Gregory grew marijuana. That was his first offense, and he served time for that before. Gregory really knows the Bible, especially all the harsh things in the Old Testament. He uses the killing in the Old Testament as his reason for not believing in God today. I don't enjoy talking to Gregory about it, but listening to these guys is what I do in order to build bridges to them. Gregory asked me some questions about our classes so I proceeded to tell him. That's when he let me know of his disdain for Christian beliefs and beliefs about God. He is also very well versed in why he doesn't believe. He approaches everything from a scientific and technical point of view.

I tell Charles that Christian belief is based on faith, and faith is a gift of God. His belief is also based on belief in something. There is some basis for it and even science requires faith in some point of initiation. I gave him a book that really addresses all the things he is talking about. This morning he said the book is offensive to people like him. It's a book of preaching to the choir and doesn't talk to people like him. I told him, "I don't really enjoy these discussions, because I know you're never going to convince me, and I'm never going to convince you. I am committed to my belief in God and his way of salvation. I know I'll never convince you by argument or debate. I'm just concerned that these discussions will just become something that will come between us."

His criticism is that Christianity causes offenses. I agreed that it does, that even Jesus was offensive. Many times, truth offends. I said my concern is that I may offend him needlessly because of my fallen sinful nature. I may become offensive. I don't like it when I do that. I said, "I would just rather pray for you that God gives you the gift of faith. You're a good friend, and I just want to see you in heaven some day." He said, "Well, if there is a heaven, I'm going to be there, and if I do I'm going to confront God and say you know damn well I was a good person. Why did you screw around with us so much and not give us the evidence that you existed?" I said, "No, Gregory, you won't do that. You will fall on your face before him and plead for mercy; then you will know, but it will be too late." Gregory is still a friend. We both expressed our appreciation and respect for each other and left. It's interesting, though, that he still persists. Actually, for me, I wish he wouldn't, but if God has a purpose in it then it's a good thing.

From Jan

The summer of 2011 was the summer of weddings. I received eleven invitations, two of which were our oldest grandchildren. Bob and I have enjoyed attending weddings together, and I knew it would not be as easy going alone. He wrote very sweet letters to our grandchildren that were getting married, promising them he would be praying for them during the entire ceremony. As I walked down the aisle, I pictured Bob sitting under the big maple tree behind the chapel, lifting these dear ones to our heavenly Father. Once again, his grace was sufficient. These were days to celebrate, not to brood.

It was also the year of our fiftieth wedding anniversary. Several of the family went to Duluth that weekend to celebrate with us. It was a beautiful August day. We sat by a table outside and reminisced. After a while, our daughter said, "We brought a gift for you, Mom." I knew they couldn't take anything into the visitor's center so my eyes glanced around for a clue. I noticed a beautiful, silver bracelet on the wrist of our granddaughter. I asked, "Is that the gift?" She took it off and gave it to me. It was engraved with Ruth 1:16 (the "Song of Ruth" was sung at our wedding fifty years before). It was a sweet celebration.

I often wore a bracelet to the visitor's center called the "Gospel Bracelet." It was made of many colored beads, each one representing the life of Christ from birth to his resurrection. Some children were so fascinated by the story they would ask me to repeat it over and over. One little four-year-old received her own bracelet and started going around to other inmates asking "Can I tell you a story?"

6/6/11

Chapel was a real disappointment today. Our choir accompanist couldn't make it so the regular church pianist played because he does for service every Sunday morning. He doesn't know the hymns and his timing is so bad we couldn't sing with it. He changes the timing so that he can get in all the odd little runs that he wants to do, and it is really hard to follow. I finally said, "Jimmie, Please don't do that. It's hard to sing with." He said, "I've been here for twelve years. I got three months to go. I've always done it this way and so this is the way I'm going to do it." There may be people in the local church like that, but it just more blatant and bold here. It's also like, "If you want to mess with me, you might get hurt." So, this morning, the singing was bad, the sermon was bad, and it was a real downer.

Signs and wonders have been on my mind because we have an older inmate who is close to the end of a twenty-five-year sentence. He is Hawaiian and a really great Christian. He loves to lead the prayer meetings on Friday night, which I don't attend because, as I explained before, there is just too much culture with it that I am better off not engaging in. Well, Al, the Hawaiian, always prays for "signs and wonders."

I pray daily that God will show Himself to me, and I believe He does. Many days, it is two and three times in one day. This is the way I hope to see God. I look for it in people. This is an example of one today.

I came out of chapel disappointed with the service. I had an e-mail in my pocket from Vonna in Sioux Falls. It was concerning Tom and his daughter Jenna. Vonna was concerned that they don't seem to have communicated even though we have a letter that Tom wrote to her. After chapel I talked to Tom right out in the middle of the street. I showed him the e-mail from Vonna. Tom was very silent for a long time.

It came out that Tom had not mailed the letter. He was so ashamed and said, "This is a problem we as a people have: we don't always do what we say. I intended to. I just didn't get around to it." Well, this ended up being a very important time for Tom and me, and it will be for Jenna and Vonna as well. Tom said that Jena does have a hard time reading and writing, and now it ends up that I will e-mail his letters to Vonna, and Vonna will read them with Jenna. Jenna will write back the same way through Vonna.

These are signs and wonders that God is alive, real, and close. He cares, is relational, and is faithful to penetrate some very hardened hearts. I see God revealing Himself to me in short conversations and in the eyes of men when

114

they see a new awareness of God. God encourages me two to three times a day with these signs and wonders. To me, they are important signs and wonders. I have come to see that life's circumstances are not so important to God. The things we might dread the most he uses to change our hearts into the kind of hearts he wants—broken and contrite hearts. It's in broken and contrite hearts that God does his signs and wonders. It is so different from the way I would have ordered it. I am humbled by so often getting it wrong, but in these deeper, quieter, and darker times, God really does show his signs and wonders. I just keep asking him for more of them.

I don't need to see anything more miraculous than that. God is so good. He is willing to come so near. He always wanted to dwell among us. He did in the pillar of cloud, in the pillar of fire, and in the Ark of the Covenant. Today, he dwells with us in a much nearer, personal, and practical way. He dwells within us. The moments of total awareness of His closeness and presence are precious and valuable. I am humbled and saddened that I ever filled my life with things that made him compete with the cheapness of materialism. He is God. He is Lord. Praise His name.

6/9/11

One of my memories as a boy growing up on the farm is that every Saturday afternoon we had to go to church for catechism class. We were required to memorize answers to catechism questions, a chore nobody enjoyed. We would have to recite them to our parents on Friday night. Our catechism teacher was an immigrant farmer named Sam. He spoke with such a Dutch accent that I didn't understand much of what he was saying. Consequently, there are not a lot of fond memories of catechism class.

There is one memory I have, though, that makes it all worthwhile, and that is the answer to the question of, "What is our only comfort in life and in death?" The answer was, "That I am not my own; I've been bought with a price." It may seem odd that this answer should be so meaningful to me, but it really is and is to this day. It clearly states to me that what is of value is not only who I am but also whose I am. The one who owns me is ruler over everything, and everything bows to his will and purpose.

What this means is that he is sovereign, and his sovereignty gives me so much peace. I have trouble submitting to the government investigators and prosecutors who are not agents of truth but agents of evidence. I have trouble submitting to earthly judges who think they know me better than witnesses who witness on my behalf and who make their decisions and statements as though I am only good at getting people to say good things about me and then make decisions that affect the rest of my life according to that opinion. I would have great trouble being at peace if it were not that I know that God is sovereign. He not only rules over them, but he rules over outcomes. What they or Satan or anyone else would ever mean for harm God uses for good. I totally believe that. I believe in him. There is so little peace in prison among inmates. If there is calm, it's mostly because of indifference. It is not peace. Under the indifference, there is anger, and it comes out in so many subtle ways. If one truly believes in God and his sovereignty, there is no reason for anger or violence. If one truly believes he has been bought with a price by a holy and righteous God, there is no room for attitudes of entitlement or being wronged.

It's not easy submitting to the prosecutors who aren't interested in gathering truth but only in gathering evidence. Submitting to a judge is necessary because they are the highest power here on the earth. It's necessary, but not easy, because although they claim to know everything about you, they don't. They are supposed to be unbiased, but they are human, and they make decisions that affect lifetimes for other people. It is not easy to submit, and most don't do so willingly.

You may have your own area where it is hard to submit, be it an employer, employee, friend, or spouse. By contrast, it is easy to submit to God when we know that he cares about us, he delights in us, and he has a plan and a purpose for all things—we are in his plan. I would love to be out of here right now. I would love to be with my grandchildren. I grieve over the times of their lives I am missing, and they grieve as well. God is using these days, and in his grace and mercy, he allows me to see his hand moving.

I want an early release so much, but I want God's perfect will even more. I've read many times of God's secondary or submissive will, where he actually submits to our requests or desires. I am thinking about how Abraham and Sarah had a hard time believing God for the son God had promised them because Sarah had been barren for so long. In their unbelief, Sarah had Abraham father a child with Hagar. God seems to have allowed this, and he even blessed Ishmael to the extent that he made him a great nation. But this great nation caused problems, and the problems exist to this very day. Ishmael's blessing was a permissive will of God, though, not God's perfect will.

I know God has made allowances in my own past and allowed me to have my will and my way when it was not the best way. In my prison sentence and time, I want God's perfect will. I want to be here as long as God has reason and purpose for it. It would be so wonderful to find my time cut short, but as long as God shows and reveals himself here, this will be wonderful too, albeit in a different sort of way. If it is wonderful, it will end up wonderful for my children and grandchildren as well.

I have read books on leaving a legacy. I used to think about that and think that I had a legacy. My legacy is very clouded right now, and there isn't much left. If there will be a legacy, it will be one that rises out of ashes. Anyway, my legacy is no longer important to me. I want only God's legacy. I want God to be in the legacy of my children, grandchildren, and great grandchildren. I pray that God's name will be revered more strongly in each generation, that he will see fit to see them as righteous before him, and that he will take great delight in them.

I was thinking about this idea of legacy but kept all the thoughts to myself. I wondered what my Grandchildren would remember me for. Would I just be the Grandpa who went to prison? I never mentioned this to anyone, and then one day I got an e-mail from Grant, Tom's only son. It couldn't have come at a better time, and it meant so much to me.

Hey Grandpa,

The title of this e-mail may have thrown you for a bit of a loop. You may be thinking, "What is Grant bringing up inheritance for?" Inheritance was the word God laid on my heart tonight.

I just put Grayson down for the night, as Kenzie is working. Tuesdays are my daddy-duty days. I come home early and hang out with my son until bed time. It is a special time. It's time for us to bond. It's time for me to grow and learn to have patience. It's a wonderful time. But after I put Grayson down, I was doing my lesson for the week from George's *God Revealed*. We are in the final session of an eleven-week study. Kenzie and I put together a group of friends to go through the study. The first week we had sixteen people, two of which joined us via Skype from different parts of the country. Most weeks, we number nine to eleven people. This final session was a closing and summary to what we have covered. The book helps us answer these questions: What is the essence of the Bible? Really, who is God? Who is Jesus? What is his significance? and Why am I here? What a journey it has been!

I have been able to read and enjoy working through the Scriptures more than ever before. I have been challenged in my faith and have had to establish and defend why I believe what I do. It is amazing to see how many people (friends) that have grown up in the church know so little. I find myself one of the more educated in the Scriptures. Yet there have been several times where I read something that I have covered, and the Holy Spirit reveals something completely new to me. It's a really cool thing. The Bible isn't boring; rather, it is full of excitement and fascination. I have always admired Brian Gazelkas ability to bring the Bible and its epic stories to life. I am beginning to see some of these things for myself. But I digress.

Anyway, I have been thinking about Grayson and him getting older. I have been thinking about my relationship with my dad. I have been thinking about you. It's a pretty cool thing to have four generations alive at the same time. That doesn't happen all the time. I have also been thinking about generations, legacy, and inheritance.

Generations are of great importance throughout the Scriptures. Generations were a constant reminder of God's faithfulness throughout history to not only the original covenant participants but also to those that would come after. God has been so, so satisfied and honored in your faithfulness and the generational relationship He has had with the Goris family for many generations. This continues even through me and someday to Grayson.

Legacy is your paper trail. It's a very real shadow of the things you were in the past. It's the intangibles you leave behind. It's your life's work carried out in the generations after. Most people, especially businessmen, desire to leave a legacy of success and accomplishment that can range from a plaque on a wall to a building bearing their name, and even an empire or industry in which their name is the first thing you think of when you think of that device. It's Apple to Steve Jobs. It's Microsoft to Bill Gates. To you, your legacy and life work is to honor God in all you do. It's to expand and enable the expansion of the message of Jesus Christ, who he is and what he came to do. It's a legacy that says less about who you are and more about who you serve. It's funny; isn't it? Your legacy that doesn't focus on you. It seems contradictory, when in reality it was God's original intent for a legacy. It's the example Jesus gave. He came to bring glory to his Father in heaven. You have lived that out so well.

Lastly, inheritance. I am so thankful for the inheritance you have left me. It's an inheritance that money often keeps humanity away from. It's an inheritance that is priceless yet can cost you more than you ever imagined if you are left without it. Grandpa, through your faithfulness, prayer, and example, I have inherited a God-fearing father who desired a God-fearing mother. Together, they have raised me to know the Lord. I have inherited a relationship with my Creator.

6/14/11

I'm reading the book *Refined by Fire* by Brian and Mel Ravenwell. Brian was in the Pentagon on 9/11 and was just four doors down from where the plane hit. He had severe burns over 60 percent of his body, and 40 percent of the burns were third degree.

I don't know why I'm so drawn to reading this stuff. I read about guys in prison and now this. Most of the guys here say they don't want to read about prison life and sadness. I'm interested in the process that people go through. This book about Ravenwell, though, was a hard one because of what his wife went through staying in the burn unit every day and every night. While the pain was unbelievable for him, it was very emotionally draining for me to read her part of the story. I think it's because it makes me think about Jan and my family and what they go through, especially the time out of their lives spent coming here to see me. I want their lives to be as normal as possible, and sometimes I think Jan's is quite normal because she is with the children and doing some traveling. But then she reminds me that her life is anything but normal, and I know it is true.

6/16/11

Yesterday was the one-year anniversary of being in Duluth. I would have missed it, but Jim doesn't miss anything. It is one year now that Jim and I have been friends. I remember the day we met. We were brought to a cell waiting to leave Sherburne County jail, and Jim was sitting there by himself, waiting. The lady guard brought in a bunch of papers for us to sign and just said, "Sign these." Jim said, "Well, I want to read these first." She gave him a disgusted look, rolled her eyes, and tapped her fingers on the table as we read. My comment to her was, "The reason I'm here is for not reading and understanding what I signed." My comment didn't change her attitude one bit.

The year has gone reasonably fast for me, and I have been relatively at peace. Not so for Jim. Jim has not been at peace because he has been working constantly at his appeal which means he is constantly trying to communicate with judges and attorneys. He is not getting responses and is constantly trying to make sense out of a system that doesn't seem to operate on common sense. This is the way with most guys here. They spend their time frustrated over not being heard or their rights being violated, and in many cases they really do have a case. Not so with me. I have many of those same thoughts, but by the grace of God I don't think about them. I am so grateful that God has given me an understanding of his sovereignty, and I can depend on that. He works all things for good for those who are called according to his purpose. I don't want to question or challenge something that I know has already passed through his hands.

Tonight, we have a graduation party for the end of the quarter. We should have thirty-five people receiving certificates for completing the work for the quarter. We are celebrating with a can of Pepsi and some chips. We will only be having one class through the summer, and we will be showing American history movies in the theater one night a week. The guys really liked the movie last week, which was about the D-Day invasion. Next Monday night we have a movie on the end of the war in Europe.

Through the summer I hope to have significant, one-on-one visits with guys preparing for the upcoming quarter.

6/24/11

Recently, someone gave me the book *Prodigal God* by Timothy Keller. It's a small book but has a powerful message. This book has stimulated some thoughts.

The book centers around the parable that usually goes by the name of "The Prodigal Son." Keller says the parable should be called the "Parable of The Elder Brother," or, "The Parable of Two Lost Sons." The younger brother is the one we usually do not see as "us." The elder brother we tend to see as "us"; therefore, it is easy to miss the problem with the elder brother.

Living with 950 men on eighty acres of land gives me a great opportunity to see how people think, and it also motivates me to rediscover what I think, and why. The more I talk to people about God and the Bible, the more I see how much confusion there is with what God is like and how we obtain salvation. Most people come into the story of salvation halfway through the story. It's like going to a movie when it's half over and being frustrated the whole time because you are just trying to figure out what's happening. Usually the gospel message is starting with sin, and it's hard to see why God should be so mad about sin. Isn't God all about love?

I started in the usual place when I first shared the gospel here; I talked about sin and how it separates us from God. After hearing about salvation they all wanted to be saved, and they prayed the prayer of salvation. Six months later, I didn't see any signs that they were saved.

Since then I have changed my strategy. I believe the problem for most people, even many Christians, is they don't really know the holiness of God and don't know the fallen nature of man. Now, I begin my gospel presentations in John 1 and talk about how in the beginning was the Word and the Word was with God and the Word was God. Then I go to Genesis 1.Then I give them a *Good and Evil* and recommend they get an ESV Bible.

During the summer we don't have classes, but I have two men who want to get going so I am working with them one-on-one. One of them is Dan, who is from Sioux Falls. Dan moved in across the hall from me about three weeks ago. Dan was told when we were introduced that I do some Bible studies, and I could tell Dan was interested. He seemed to want to hang out with me a little. He said right away he wanted to take my classes. I told him he should get an ESV study Bible, and he did. Since we don't have classes going now, I offered to meet with him one-on-one to give him a head start and also show him how to use his Bible. He really liked that idea.

Dan had his Bible a week before we started. I asked him how he liked it, but he said he didn't know where to begin. He could use some help. We had our first meeting on Tuesday. I gave him a copy of *Good and Evil*. I emphasized why God created the earth and man and that it was for His own good pleasure. I said that God likes pleasure, and he likes man. He wanted relationship with man, and he had it. Then man fell. I told him the relationship was destroyed, and we talked about that separation. We talked about the holiness of God and why God can't tolerate sin. Taking people through this always takes care of the inevitable objection: "How can a holy God send anyone to hell?

We spent an hour-and-a-half together on Tuesday morning and another hour-and-a-half on Tuesday afternoon. We also spent an hour-and-half on Wednesday morning together. Dan was so amazed at salvation, that it is free and that good works are not a part of salvation—that it is effortless. It is all about the heart and the fact that God desires a broken and contrite heart (see Psalm 51). Dan couldn't have been happier to find out his sins were forgiven and that right now God declares him righteous because of Christ. He doesn't see our sin; he sees Jesus's sacrifice. Dan said, "I've been in church all my life. I've been on the board of trustees and taught Sunday School and was the church treasurer." He said, "I've never heard this before." He had gone to some Bible studies but nobody ever taught it right from the Bible. Comments were usually made that you really can't take the Bible literally so it seemed too confusing to get into it.

I was so privileged to be able to be with Dan at such an important time. Since Wednesday, Dan is continuing on his own, spending one-and-a-half hours twice a day in study. He is now up to 1 Kings in the Old Testament. I met with him this morning. He is so grateful. Tonight I will meet with the other guy.

6/26/11

Bullhead is from Fargo. He is a Vietnam War veteran and a drug addict. He blames his drug addiction on Veterans Affairs for giving him too much medication and at the wrong time.

Bullhead does the count in the activity center where I clean at 7:30 a.m. and at 12:00 p.m. We have to sit for about one hour and fifteen minutes waiting until the count clears. I always try to have something to read. Bullhead works on Sudoku. He always wants to talk to me because he claims to know me from my life insurance days. His wife evidently worked for our company, and he came to some of our meetings. He talks nonstop, constantly dancing around if he's standing or shaking his feet and wiggling his legs if he's sitting. He's mad about the way vets are treated, mad at the government and justice system, and really mad at Christians because all the hate and controversy in the world is because of them. Every third word out of his mouth is profanity, and he talks loudly so the whole room hears what he is saying. I usually try to arrange my chair with my back to him and intently read without looking up but even that doesn't work. He claims to be an atheist because he claims his dad would beat him and make him go to church.

About three months ago another atheist, Bob, joined him and now agrees with everything he says and uses the same profanity. I can't even stand to talk to them and don't even want to talk about the Gospels with them. Now a third guy from Mankato has joined him, an elderly man who sits and listens to their talk but seems more gentlemanly than the other two. These men are also in my same dorm. The third guy, who I'll call Monty (forgot his name), engaged me at the dorm and said, "I see you a lot with the Bible." He then told me all about his education, that his dad was a minister and that he has read the Bible eight times. He has two master's degrees and a Ph.D. as well as a business where they move very large, overweight loads (two trucks side-by-side going down the highway while pulling two trailers behind each).

Anyway, after I talked a little, Monty was very pleased to tell me he is an atheist, but he knows the Bible very well. I know he was wanting an argument. I responded, "So you're an atheist like Bullhead. I see you visiting with him." He then said, "I'm an atheist, but not like Bullhead." He wanted to impress me with his intelligence and then with what a good guy he is because of the work he has done volunteering and donating. He then said, "Well, I'm okay either way because if you're right I'm still okay because in John it says everyone who does good works shall be saved." I couldn't recall the text but assured him that this is not what the writer meant. I said I would read it. I then asked him to read Hebrews 11:6, "Without faith it is impossible to please God."

My friend Gregory is also an atheist so I have really had to think through a proper response. This is now my response:

> Look, I'm not 'a salesman for God.' I'm not an arguer or a debater. It's not what I enjoy doing. It's not a favored past time of mine. What we are discussing is like trying to have a discussion on a movie where we came in at the middle of the movie and then debated the issues of the movie. This is the only premise in which we can have a discussion. You must realize that my belief is based on faith. At this point you believe that you do not want faith, although you definitely are basing what you say is your belief or faith on something. That's where we have a difference. I am committed to my faith. Now, if you're interested in my faith, we need to start at the beginning of the story, right in Genesis. We can't talk about God and not know what he is like. He tells us what he is like, but we have to read what he is saying. Let's say we do that? Let's start in the beginning.

They never want to do that. They just want to have what I call a "stand up in the middle of the street argument." I also say that faith is a gift which we cannot attain by ourselves. It's a gift from God. When one does not have that gift, he does not have the freedom to choose the best things about life. If we start in the beginning of the story, you will see why that is true.

Well, I don't have any converts from atheism yet, but at least I have a plan. If nothing else, my plan frees me from the guilt of feeling like a failure every time an atheist wants to argue.

In my mind I'm preparing thoughts on the story of "The Prodigal God." It's speaking to me about the elder brother and his problem. I identified in my past with the elder brother. Now, I see more clearly. Here, I deal mostly with prodigal sons. Sometimes, I get elder brothers in my classes. I have more fear of the elder brothers.

6/29/11

Norman is from Kansas City and had a limousine service. Norman laughs a lot and was always so happy but noisy. Norman is an atheist. Neither he nor his father nor anyone in his family have ever been in a church and don't intend to. He says all that with a big smile on his face. He is one of the nicest guys you might ever meet, and he laughs about everything. Duke has moved him three different times, always putting him in the worst rooms in the dorm because he can't stand his laughing. I've tried talking to Norman twice about faith, Christ, and eternity. He just laughs me off. Well, this all started about a year ago when I got here, and I have been watching Norman with some amazement. How can a person be so happy without God and Christ?

The last three months something has changed with Norman. He is broken down about something. I've tried to talk to him, but he won't talk about it. I saw him one day sitting outside of the education building at night all by himself. I walked over, and he had tears rolling down his cheek. I tried to talk to him, but he wouldn't talk. Then things seemed to get a little better, and he was more normal again. However, today I saw him, and he was really down again. He still won't talk so at this time there isn't any kind of an ending to this other than that happiness for the unsaved can be real, for a season. Norman's season seems to have ended. I expect to hear that Norman is under suicide watch soon. In this place, people who are depressed don't want to let on that they are depressed.

I had a good study last night. It's so good with Steve and Dan. They are open and honest about what they want and about what they don't know. The environment here allows them to be more honest than on the outside, in a church. Dan said he never dared to open up like this in church. They both said in church everyone knows more than them so they didn't like going to Bible studies.

We meet daily. Growth, while a good thing, brings pain. Being unaware in our business of life, we can neglect or hurt people and not know it. It is painful for a man to learn what God's purpose for him is within his family and realize how much of it he hasn't done. Also, their wives continue to feel pain, and they need to learn how to support them emotionally. That is the most difficult thing for us men to learn, but when we understand God's household order, we know we must need to pray to that end.

The weather is so nice, the conversations and classes are so good, and walking outside in this weather with great Christian radio is great. The family has been here, and I am just living in the reality of being so blessed. I know it all the time. I know I'm learning so much, and with this time to do it, I am in the Word so much. I never could be experiencing much of what I experience in any other place. It's so encouraging to me to know that if God is in this, He can be in every circumstance.

I feel strengthened for whatever lies ahead in life, not only for me but for my family as well. Many say that as Americans we have seen our better days, and in many ways we can see that there can be real hardship ahead. What motivation we have to build our lives and the lives of those we love, not on the material things the world offers but on the solid foundation of Christ and his principles, depends on building lives that are deeply rooted, grounded, and fully established in the way of Christ and the way he taught the apostles to teach. There is real strength there and real protection from despondency when circumstances get hard. Life is so rich when it is like the tree planted by the stream of living water, producing Christ's fruit in due season. It makes so much sense. It becomes so clear when the world's things are gone.

6/30/11

A lot of guys here say to me, "I'm not religious. I don't believe in religion or church. I don't like to be called a Christian, but I believe in Jesus. I believe in God." They, obviously. are quite ignorant of the Bible, but it's interesting to me how they come up with this.

Tim Keller, in *Prodigal God*, says, "These people believe moral issues are highly complex and are suspicious of any individuals or institutions that claim moral authority over the lives of others." That really describes the guys here. They want moral values to be situational and individual for each person to choose their own. The guys who have become Christians in prison are quite the opposite and play the part of the elder brother in the parable, "The Prodigal Son." Some of them take a dim view of the "younger brothers" and are quite harsh with them. Human nature is an interesting study.

It's the "elder brother," or "Pharisee syndrome," that is alive and well not only in the local church but anywhere Christians have been around for a while. Keller calls this "religious moralism" and refers to it as a particularly deadly spiritual condition.

In our classes, the guys become very interested in the church being a household of households, a family of families. The idea of them as husbands and fathers being the head and responsible for their nurture is new and interesting to them. We talk about whether they will find that kind of an experience when they get out and about how they must be prepared to form that just as we are doing here. They must do so where they work, at the mall, in homes, or wherever people tend to congregate.

It is amazing how soon a newly confessed sinner saved by grace can become a harsh legalistic Bible teacher, hardcore on "doing" so you will be blessed by God. The pathway from "receiving" to "doing and earning" is very short. Most guys teaching Bible in here are pretty harsh. Jesus was harsh too, but only with religious leaders. He related with and associated with the sinners to the point that this was his most criticized activity.

I've been thinking a lot about deep love, deep passion, deep relationships. I don't know if we ever come to them without weight. A friend has responded to my e-mail about this weight, sometimes not wanting the weight, but always loving the depth of life and thought that comes with weight.

As I work with Steve and Dan almost every night, I carry a weight. I pray constantly that they may really get a picture of God, the gospel, salvation, and a relationship with God. It's amazing to me that they are getting it. They are so honest. Steve is careful to not commit to more of it than he is experiencing, and I appreciate that. As always, going through the first book, I am encouraging them to write their thoughts, not surface answers, but deep thoughts that are authentic. Steve looks at me with bewilderment and keeps telling me that this is so not what he has been like before. I tell him the good thing is that I don't know anything about his "before" life and that I only know him here. I only know what he has told me, but he has been pretty honest. Steve listens to what I say with a big question mark on his face and says to me, "I'm processing."

One thing I emphasize is that we should want and should expect to grow in our communication with God, and the best way to do that is to begin to write. I tell them to do the writing assignments as though they are talking to God. When they say, "But I've never done this before. I feel awkward about it," I just say, "Then write that to God." I tell them how Tom prays. He just says, "God, I don't know how to do this. You're going to have to show me how. You gotta teach me how." That's what God wants to hear. Be honest with God. Don't worry about how literate you are or using proper grammar. Even if your sentences don't make sense, just write. And at the very least, just write words.

As we talk about this, I talk about their conversations with their wives. They all know that communication is often difficult. If they talk on the phone, it shuts off in fifteen minutes. If they visit and have kids, the kids are sitting there all ears and hear details that kids shouldn't. I tell them this is why they need to write. First, they need to learn how to write and be honest with God. Then, they need to write letters and not e-mails to their wives. The e-mails shut off in fifteen minutes too.

They need to be able to sit in the orderly room in the dorm at 4:00 a.m. when there is nobody around and think on paper. This is what wives want and need. We men don't know much about supporting our wives emotionally, and many wives won't express the need they have for that—but they have them. Even with God, we tend to have wayward, wandering hearts, and we are like that between humans too.

When men are gone for a long time, their wives have emotional needs. We need to learn how to support them better than we ever have before. It's not easy for us. Steve told me he wasn't a good husband and dad. He was way too busy with business, and after work he didn't go home. He'd hang out with the guys and just get home in time to say good night to the kids. He said, "I want to change that. I want to be different." He means it and expects to do it, but in order to do that, when he gets out, he has to have some serious changes inside or he'll do it again.

It's all about the heart. We need to ask God to change our hearts because we almost always do what we want to do, and when we are free we will do what we want to do again. The only solution is to ask God on a daily basis to change our hearts about what we want and what we love. We have to change our dreams and our longings. If God changes our hearts about those things, we can do whatever we want the rest of our lives. If God doesn't change our hearts, we have a fight on our hands the rest of our lives. We fight our own wrong desires.

17

7/2/11

It's been a great week! I don't like talking about my health or circumstances other than what I think would be of interest. I only recall the Apostle Paul making a request for his own comfort once and that was when he asked to have a coat sent along with a visitor because it was cold in his cell. I don't think he asked for prayer for a lot of personal comforts or ease of life. He prayed for the hearts and minds of the people, for the church, and for the mission. I'd rather be like Paul, but my little issue does point to how God works in relation to health care. And in case anyone thinks it would be good if the government would take over our health care, this is how it would work.

I was doing well, working out, lifting weights, walking, and really feeling I was gaining strength. It was hard getting started, but after about four months, I really enjoyed it. Then I got a hernia. It started small but grew. I went to the physician assistant, and she said it wasn't anything they would deal with.

Two weeks later it was worse so I went in again, wanting to see the doctor. She said, "They wouldn't do anything for it. There are guys around here with a lot worse." I waited two weeks. I went from workouts to almost no walking. I see guys here with hernias that show through their clothes, some in wheelchairs. I'm told by others I need to be more aggressive with the medical department. I put in another request to see the doctor. This time he gave me an appointment. When I got there, he had no record that I had been in before. He examined me and said he would send me to the surgeon downtown. I asked how long that would be, and he said their committee only meets once a month and had just met so it would be a month before they would call for the appointment. Then it would be up to the clinic when they could get me in. I said, "Then I suppose it will be another 30 days before surgery?" He said it would be three months. When the government does it, they look more at their rules and their own cost than they do at the patient.

I wondered how I would fill my exercise time now that I could no longer work out and walk. The surprising thing is that it is filling. Even with no classes right now, I'm staying busy.

I'm encouraging the guys to pray, but they say it's hard. I encouraged them to write their prayer like a letter to God. Dan did this. At first, he was very shy about it and didn't want to read it to us, and I said that was okay and that he didn't need to. Then he said he would like to, so he did. I was so impressed with his transparency, simplicity, and honesty. I encouraged him that this is exactly the kind of prayer that God wants to hear. He was so pleased.

Tonight I asked Dan if he has ever prayed aloud with his family. He said he hasn't. I said, "So it's going to be quite different for your family when you come home and pray with them." He said, "Yes, and they will like it." He then said he wants to go home and lead his family and be the head of his house the way God wants him to be. That's why it is a good time for me, and there is much more to share.

7/5/11

One answered prayer when all is gone will give you hope. I find this so true even on a daily basis. In the midst of a drab morning, one person's comment, one line in an e-mail, or one small anything that shows me God is in this completely makes my day. The small answers that I might have missed in the light, even just the sparks, I really notice now.

I spent the night worried about someone close to me who is going through some despair. This caused me some despair. This morning I realized how sometimes when I express myself so lifted up above my situation, it could actually cause pain for someone who is dealing with despair. Then this proverb came up this morning: "Like one who takes away a garment on a cold day . . . is one who sings songs to a heavy heart" (Proverbs 25:20). This speaks to me to be careful for those who are downcast, and I experienced a touch of despair through the night as I thought of this person who is struggling.

It seems to me that not all tears are sad, not all discouragement is bad, and not all disappointment is bad. So, I guess what I'm saying is that when men come to prison, at first they are overwhelmed with shock and awe. They are grasping for help like a drowning person grasping for a safety ring. I have learned to be there for them during that time, but I have also realized that there will be a huge fall off of interest in these men when they find out this place isn't as bad as they thought it would be. Or if they file an appeal and think they are going to be released. I consider it like "time in the oven." In here, and in life, in order for distress to serve God's purpose, the distress needs to linger. Quick relief usually doesn't bring results. I have come to this reality. When I am praying for the soul of a person, I get excited when I see them in distress because I believe that God is plowing their soil. Plowing hurts. Breaking up the clods and picking out the rocks is not pleasant, but it creates a perfect seed bed. It's the distressing that leads to yearning, which leads to openness to God. It is what gets us saying to God, "I simply need you, God." Psalm 42:1-2 says, "As the deer pants for the water brooks, so pants my soul for you, O God. My soul thirsts for God, for the living God."

Not all tears are sad, and not all despair is bad. All of it must pass through the hands of our heavenly Father before it reaches us. It's a good kind of despair when a person knows that things are wrong—all wrong—and he cannot live without major change, or he will not go one. This despair is not really despair; it is hope.

I said to a friend only four days ago, a friend who was in despair, "God is in this. He is going to use it for good. The day will come when we will say this is probably the most important part of our lives." He responded, "But it's really dark." I almost apologized for my positive thought, afraid it might have hurt him. In less than four days, God is showing him that he has a vision of what it might be for his life. It's not over. He's not ready to come out of the oven. The baking is just beginning. I hope for all of us that God's will will be done and that his purposes will be fulfilled. I hope that he will bring us out, hungering and thirsting for him more than we ever have before.

Psalm 88 is probably the darkest of all the psalms. It is really dark. Then Psalm 89 starts right out with, "I will sing of the mercies of the Lord forever . . ." It goes on with such joy and peace. It seems that despair and deep passion for God lay so closely side by side. It's just good for me to know that. Not all tears are sad, and not all despair is bad.

7/9/11

We started one new summer class last night. We are on our fourth book so these guys are the most committed of all the classes, and it was really a good time. It's called *Habits of the Heart*, and it is where we really get into pursuing God. We want to work against the idea that Christianity is just about believing and receiving (which it is), but it's so common to think that now that we have Christ and have faith we can stop pursuing. We want to move toward a lifelong pursuing of God.

We also have brand new people coming to us, people we haven't met before and who want to be in a class. We are thinking about starting a new "Book

One" class for the summer, even though we had decided we needed a rest. We have had a rest now for a few weeks and feel quite ready to go back, although just yesterday I was meditating and thinking how good this quiet time is. I don't think I have ever had a time like this in my life when the word is so alive to me. I love to be in it, and I'm learning so much. I even go over old passages and find so much. I relish this time, and God is giving me some meaningful conversations with people whom I really feel are being directed to me.

Ernie is a banker from a small town north of Minneapolis. He is sixty-seven years old. Ernie's bank financed a large real estate development. The developer got cancer, and the deal went bad—and that's how it all started. Anyway, he is new here and still going through the shock and confusion of getting adjusted. I helped a friend of his out last week with a small thing, but Ernie was so appreciative.

This morning he was waiting for me at the law library where we do our e-mailing. He asked me if I could help him. He said he hadn't done much on computers because he had three secretaries who did everything. When he gets on these computers and tries to put in data and something goes wrong, he just starts to sweat and gets very worked up. He said, "I'm sixty-seven years old, and I just can't learn this very fast." I offered to help him, and we did some things for his e-mail account. After that he told me his whole story. It is amazing that he is here because the judge could not find any victims. He has no restitution, but the government spent ten million dollars investigating him. (He and his people spent five million defending themselves). He believes the government had to have something to show for their expenditure so he got four months in prison, but he has lost everything he has.

Ernie said, "So, it's quite an experience." I said, "Even a spiritual experience." And so the conversation turned to that. He said he does believe. He doesn't want to believe, but he's scared not to. At one time, he was the chairman of a church and on boards, but he hasn't been to a church in eighteen years. I told him of the studies we do, and he pushed back. He said the Bible was just mixed up and confusing. I said, "Not really. Let's read a little this afternoon." He agreed to meet. We spent all afternoon talking, and Ernie did read John 3. I had high hopes, but it was a difficult time. Ernie believes the Bible was just put together by people and isn't really reliable, starting right away in Genesis. He believes in Jesus but not that anyone would go to hell. He didn't want to read the Bible and only wanted to talk about it. Well, my own policy on that is that I just don't do that. I just say my opinion isn't worth anything and anybody else's opinion isn't worth anything either. If we can't say the Bible is like a straight edge that we can draw on then there is no straight edge. Personal philosophy is just vain conversation.

We are friends, and we both like to talk. Still, it's clear to me that if the Holy Spirit is talking to him he is not yielding. I need to leave that all to God. It seems like a case where the circumstances are harsh, but he desires different circumstances more than he desires God.

Clearly not everyone here is ready to be serious about God. Even in extreme situations, people do not cry out to God unless the Holy Spirit draws them. It's the Holy Spirit's work and not mine. Although when the prospect looks so good, I must confess that I get so excited and hopeful. And I do feel let down when it doesn't turn out right.

7/13/11

I took a fall Saturday night. I was watching a movie in the chapel. In the balcony there are risers to raise the chairs from front to back. I was sitting in the back row, which is about four feet off the floor. The chair I was on scooted backward (I guess), and the back legs went over the edge. I went over backward and landed on my head and right shoulder. I saw what was coming, and I got my left arm up over my head to protect it. My right shoulder took all my weight. It was a big loud thump that was heard all over the church. I thought I was okay and jumped up (to save embarrassment) and watched the rest of the movie. I even walked a mile on the track afterward and felt no pain. About midnight, I woke up with a lot of pain. I didn't get back to sleep the rest of the night. There is no sick call on weekends so I was preparing to suffer it out.

Jim saw me and immediately went to the captain and told him I needed attention. He told me to go to the lieutenant's office, and so I did. They filled out an accident report, gave me a sling, and told me to wait for a call, which they said would probably be on Tuesday. The pain on the weekend was great, but the sling did help during the daytime. I took ibuprofen at night, and it helped some. I didn't use my arm at all. My left hand had to learn to do a lot of things it hadn't done before. I couldn't even brush my teeth without poking myself in the nose. I typed but only with my left hand. It was not good.

Today, I got called in, and the good news was that because of overload they had a health service officer come in from Rochester. He seemed to really know what he was doing. He determined that the shoulder was not dislocated. The X-ray technician only comes in every other week for four hours, and she happened to be in and was just leaving when they caught her. She did the X-ray. There are no broken bones. He said the thing to do is to take Tylenol 800, throw away the sling, and use the arm more. If I don't, it will freeze up and make the problem is greater.

Next day—I did what he said. I took the pain reliever and worked the arm for an hour. I couldn't tell any immediate benefit, but today it is amazingly better. It still has limitation, but I even tied my own shoes today, which is a big improvement. I know with exercise that it won't be long until it will be completely better.

I think this is just another example of how life requires interpretation. Without interpretation, I thought the pain was bad in my arm, and I shouldn't do anything to inflict pain on it. With the interpretation of the doctor, I took the pain pill and worked the arm. I worked it, and when I felt pain, I considered it good pain that would improve my arm.

That's an example of how there is bad pain and good pain; bad tears and good tears; and bad despair and good despair. It brings us to the end of ourselves and causes us to cry out to God. It's important to interpret it correctly.

7/14/11

It's amazing how my shoulder has healed up. When I took my shirt off at the doctor my back had deep scratches in it from the fall. It was so sore; I was sure it was broken. Now, it's 90 percent better than it was in only one day. God is answering prayers.

Also, the progress with Dan and Steve is great. These guys are so amazed at the Bible, which they have owned all their lives but were never able to read like now.

7/16/11

So many people I talk to here want to shape God and judge God saying "if God does [blank], then I won't have anything to do with a God like that." Man thinks he is more tender, loving, kind, and forgiving than God. Isn't that ridiculous? It comes from man thinking that being a Christian is a religion and that we can choose whatever religion we want. In the religious mind-set, that all works. In the gospel mind-set, it doesn't.

7/21/11

I prepare for the class by doing some reading in the book *In my Place Condemned He Stood* by J.I. Packer. I am reminded how we (I) need to stay so close to the gospel; I simply cannot get beyond it. Whether five weeks into the Christian faith, five years, or seventy years, the tendency is to lean back and rest on our own goodness and that we had to "accept" Christ. It is so easy to become confused in thinking about what we are saved from. In the natural, we say we are saved from our sins. In reality, however, we are saved from the wrath of God that is there because of our sin. When Jesus prayed in the Garden of Gethsemane, he was filled with fear and dreaded what lay before him. The fear was not because of the whipping and the beating or the nails and the dying; it was because he knew he was facing the wrath of God for a whole world of sin. Even now, as we walk as redeemed sinners, we are not redeemed because of our faith, even though it is through faith we are saved. We are redeemed because of the transfer of our sin to Jesus, and the wrath of God toward that sin followed Jesus.

If by God's grace someone says something nice about me or about what I write or about what I say, I take it as a personal credit for me—what a shame. What a sad commentary about me. I have no right, because we have no right to glory in anything except in the cross of Christ. We should bless his holy name forever.

I just finished the class. It is such a good class. The guys are very accustomed to the method of and have matured so much in their thinking. Tonight we worked with an article by Francis Schaeffer. Schaeffer is such a thinker, and he stimulates thinking and processing.

The meat of that quote is so evident all around us. This discussion is so appropriate in a place like this where men want to fashion God into whatever they want him to be with no regard to what he says he is like. When I use the term "place like this" I realize also that this is probably true of the world at-large. I guess I have been pretty sheltered even in the business world because people would be more inclined to try to see things my way. Here, however, they put more energy into trying to see things their own independent way, and it's usually a pretty screwed up way.

7/23/11

Dario is a Mexican from Southern California and has been involved in gangs and crime in the L.A. area. I wouldn't guess that just by talking to him, but he has told me that. I have been watching Dario for about six months now. He was hanging around the chapel a lot; he likes to sing in the choir and sings in the Spanish band. I didn't take him seriously at first because it did seem that he likes to talk a lot—because of that I discounted his faith. In getting to know him better, I began to see that he really did want to grow in his faith, and I invited him to our studies. He started with two classes last spring and wants to participate in all that we do. He always comes thirty minutes early just to talk and ask questions.

7/30/11

I am at the point where every year, really every day, is a gift from God, more realized than in earlier life. I realize my mortality, my fragility, and life's uncertainty more than ever before, and it is a bittersweet thing to live with. It's sweet to know that most of what I have toiled over in my life really doesn't amount to much. That's because even the best things I have done were so far from perfect and were good only in the scale of man. It's sweet because the failures I have had really don't amount to much because all of life is failure except what is ransomed by the blood of Christ. It's sweet because, even though I have had some great experiences in life, great freedoms, great relationships, a great marriage, and a great family, all of it pales in comparison to what lies before us. One day, each of us will walk the path that leads to the better place.

The bitter part comes from the fact that our earthen vessel holds a treasure, and so much of life is spent on the vessel and not the treasure. The treasure is the light of knowledge of the glory of God in the face of Christ. Now that a lot of the provision of the care for the vessel has been stripped away for me, I begin to get a glimpse of the freedom there is in focusing on Christ only.

Prison, as awful and as sinful a place that it is, at the same time is somewhat a place of isolation from the cares and some of the temptations of the world. The removal of opportunity for personal pleasure, wealth accumulation, and career enhancement is somewhat of a reprieve from the cares of this world. If one really wants to focus on God and His Word, it's not a bad place. The temptation to waste time is still here, but it is not as great as on the outside.

My friend Steve has gained such a passion for God, family, and church. We are together five nights a week, and he is so on track. Steve, unlike most here, has not lost all his resources and therefore has a lot of options open for him when he gets out, which is not for several years. He is very sincere and passionate in wanting to use this time in every way to make him a better father, husband, and disciple of Christ. His wife, Mary, is at home with a teenager and two pre-teens. They are a great family, but it is difficult for such a young wife to be alone with her children. She misses Steve a lot, as one can only imagine.

My concern is for my brothers in Christ, not that they lose their salvation but that they lose the total focus of the Christian life: to know God and enjoy Him forever. That's my concern for my grandchildren and for me as well. I don't even trust my own heart. During this time of solitude, I find great blessing in the hours I get to spend in ministry and the Word. How will it be for me when I get out? I don't even trust my own heart. Will the cares and the competition of the cares and things of this world crowd out what I am experiencing now? I find I need to stay grounded in the basics. In my red letter Bible, the very first words of Christ are to repent and believe the good news and to turn away from the things Jesus hates and toward the things he loves. What does Jesus hate? Anything that fills the place in our heart that belongs only to him. That is my goal: to live more in that way, and I cannot do it unless he dwells in me.

I guess that's why the Scriptures say to give me neither poverty nor riches but to be fed with the food that is needful for me so that I do not get full and deny Jesus.

So there is a sweetness to this place. I do not long for death, but I value the race and smell the sweet essence of purpose with the end of the race in sight. I do look forward to being free at last from failure, sin, decay, and death and to being free to look every moment and every day on the face of Jesus as he sits on the right side of the Father, experiencing his joy and his pleasure. The only safe place to keep our treasures is in heaven, and it is safe.

18

8/12/11

I really feel that God has placed in our soul a place that gets hungry. Just like physical hunger, if we are not watching ourselves, we take this feeling of hunger as a bad thing and grab things to satisfy our hunger. And the things we grab are not always the good or right things. When we become health conscious and weight conscious, we learn to recognize hunger as a good thing. When we feel hunger, we either wait until we can get the right food or allow ourselves to be hungry, knowing that it is doing good things to our body. I'm thinking that sometimes the feeling of despair, loneliness, emptiness, and even mild depression may be a hungering of the soul that we may not recognize. God wants us to satisfy that hunger in him, in his Word; instead, we satisfy it with business, entertainment, or anything that occupies ourselves to take our mind off it. Sometimes we feel the hunger because we haven't eaten or drunk from what He has to offer. This is what we have been working on here with the guys. When we are so used to meeting a lot and then miss the meetings for a time, this kind of hunger comes in, and we don't recognize it. We just get into a funk.

I discovered something this week in a word study. I decided to do a word study on the word "satisfies." It was very revealing to me, finding the Scriptures that have to do with "satisfies." It was so good that I had some of our guys do it. God satisfies our soul (Psalm 107:9) and satisfies with good (Psalm 103:5).

I was also reminded of Psalm 23 and how he restores our soul. He really does. I don't feel I have had depression, at least not that I know of, but I respect it a lot. I respect it as I would a grizzly bear in the wild. When I sense its presence, I give it a wide birth. I don't want to be near it. The weapon for me is the Word and ministering to others. When I ask God each day to show himself to me, I just expect him to show himself in the lives of those around me, where through their own words I sense him doing something or wanting to do something. Those times and sightings are so valuable and precious to me.

He does restore me with that on an almost daily basis and some days multiple times. It fills my heart with meaning and purpose, and I come to realize that I have a huge hunger and appetite for that. I can't go long without it.

Last night I was just beginning to teach my class when I was called, which can mean a lot of things from being put in the hole to having bad news about a family member. In this case, it was about going to the hospital. They never let you know anything in advance.

I was sent back to the dorm to get my green uniform on and told to come back. They asked me if I knew what this was about. I said, "I think I'm going to the hospital." They didn't answer, just told me to go with the driver. We went to the hospital. I was sure I was having my hernia surgery. When we got to the hospital, I asked the driver what time we would be going back. He said, "Tomorrow at 6:00 a.m." I said, "Then are they doing the surgery tonight?" He said, "You're not having surgery; you are having a sleep study." This surprised me because I just had one in May, and they said I don't have sleep apnea. Well, it was a sleep study, and it turns out I do have sleep apnea.

The bad news is I still don't have my hernia surgery scheduled. The good news is that I will be getting a sleep machine. In the meantime, the hernia keeps getting bigger. I hold it in with my hand when I walk. I do think, however, that I will be having that surgery soon. When they called me in, it comes over the speakers, and the whole compound hears it. It's pretty amazing how many guys watch out for me and are concerned about me. I always see that as how God is taking care of me. I feel people respect me because of what God is doing in the ministry and also because of my age. It's good to see God's goodness in that.

8/15/11

August 19 is our fiftieth wedding anniversary. In some ways it is not easy to celebrate when we are apart. Yet I won't have a problem with that as there is so much to celebrate. Whether the celebration is done in churches, on cruise ships, or in nice resorts, the place and the circumstances aren't as important as the substance of what is being celebrated, and I thank the Lord that there is so much substance to celebrate.

It's such a blessing to be have been married for fifty years. It's a blessing because it a bond and a mirror of God's faithfulness, grace, and mercy. It's all of that, and he designed it that way. I am so blessed by the gift God has given me in Jan. I have thought through how when we are young, date, fall in love, and choose a wife. How little we know about it all. We experience a feeling of love like we have never felt before, and we experience a feeling of being approved and chosen by our mate in a way we have never been chosen and selected before, at least as we know it in human form. Then we come together loving and thinking we now know all about love, probably more so than anyone has ever known it before, and we live it and celebrate it.

Then come the children, and although expected, the joy and happiness are far more than we could have expected; we are sure that our love for them is more than anyone could have experienced before. Then comes children leaving home, change, others drawing on their hearts; it's all good, but it's an adjustment. This isn't all it's cracked up to be. Are we missing something? But soon grandchildren, and wow! Nobody has ever had grandkids like ours! Being a grandparent is so good—if I had only known!

It's time now for Grandma and Grandpa to be together, to enjoy life together, and to sleep side-by-side, and then like Dinah said to Job, "You know it's a long, long time ago that you held me this way—so long and tight, and without sex, and strong."

Life goes on. We find ourselves apart and say to ourselves, "It wasn't meant to be this way." At the same time, we know that God is sovereign and know that he has a purpose and that his purposes are all good. We already can see some of his blessings, and as we visit week-to-week we hold firmly to what we know about him. He is good, and his ways are good. He will not waste us; he will use us, and that is what matters. While we are apart, we are learning so much of his ways.

There is so much of his kingdom that we can go through life and not be mindful of it. There are broken homes, broken people, broken relationships, broken lives, pain, sorrow, and grief. Yet God, in his grace and mercy, gave us our Savior, who gives all the world an option for a better way, a better life, and a better eternity. What a privilege it is to be used, just to point others to him and to love him and be loved by him.

We visited today and will again tomorrow. We will celebrate by holding hands and walking the little park in the visiting center. We will pray together and thank God for an amazing fifty years, and we will thank him for a future both in this life and the life to come.

Today in chapel, during the prayer request and testimony time, Jim prayed for our fifty years of marriage. It was a much bigger deal to the guys than I expected it to be. One guy said he's been married fifteen years, and he wanted to ask God to give him a marriage like mine. I left the service early to visit Jan, but Jim said that more than a dozen men commented to Jim about our fifty years of marriage. We both grew up in the Christian community and have witnessed so many fiftieth anniversaries that I considered it ordinary. In this place I see how uncommon it is. Most men think it's impossible. In our own flesh, it is impossible. Living in ourselves and for ourselves, it would likely not happen. When we see the world and life from God's perspective, we know it's what he meant for us; that is what makes it so good.

I am so thankful for my wife. In my many dreams of her (while I'm still awake), it's easy for me to see her as that nineteen-year-old vibrant, fun-loving girl that I married. It's easy because she still is that way. When she comes to visit, I think the whole room lights up. Not only is she vibrant and fun-loving, she is also a person of purpose and principle. When I think of her principles and values, I think of her mother, Francis Bonnema, whom I love and respect dearly because of what she has built into her daughters. While she is in heaven, the fruit of her life walks this earth and ministers to many in how to live life skillfully. I am so grateful for those who have gone on before and shown us the way. It gives us great desire and motivation to do the same. We truly rejoice in what God is doing. And we thank him for his grace which allows us to walk that out in a way that the world remarks about, at a time when it seems to them to be impossible.

So we live and still dream of being together again, enjoying our grandchildren who always are glad to see us because their parents keep them engaged with us, saying good things about us and pointing to us as good people. That's what we want to do for our heavenly father; we want to say good things about him, pointing to him in such a way that more will want to know him. He is the Father who cares about his children and loves them and desires to have a relationship with them in even a greater way than we can possibly desire. His desire comes from complete holiness and is without flaw.

Fifty years seems like a long time to a young couple looking forward. It seems so short to an older couple looking back. At the same time, there is so much happiness, so many memories, so much fullness, and so much meaning and purpose. We truly are celebrating. God has given us so much.

As I go to church here on the compound and listen to prayer requests and testimonies and listen to sermons given by inmates, it is so much of what God will do for our situation. Christians so often have the attitude, "What has God done for me lately?"

Yet that is so much of what I hear. I want to point to a different gospel than that. If one believes in the complete sovereignty of God (therein, is the problem for many), then one needs to believe that God uses all circumstances, first for his glory and then to shape us and mold us into the inner person he wants us to become. God is always at work "strengthening the inner man" within us.

8/19/11

The class tonight was on 1 Thessalonians 4:9-12. It's on how to live in the church, but the greater context of the class is seeing all the areas of responsibility that God calls us to in life, seeing it as our "life-work." The passage talks about: living quietly, minding your own affairs, working with your hands, and walking properly before outsiders.

We want to contrast what is usually seen as "life work" (what we do for a living) with a "life work" that is about all that God calls us to do. In most cases that includes husbanding, parenting, neighboring, ministry, managing our own affairs, and all that God lays before us to do. Seeing our life's work in this way really changes how we thinks about life. It rather destroys the idea of retirement, which is seen as the end of work. It moves us from working to build our bank account and becoming financially independent so we can spend the rest of our lives satisfying our every want to using our occupation to meet our need. And when that is met, we can focus more on the other areas.

8/20/11

I have gotten to know some guards who share the duty of listening in on telephone conversations, and they say that Fridays are always a bad day. It's the day when wives and girlfriends say, and it starts like this, "I've got something to tell you." Then comes the news that they aren't waiting. I never imagined something like that happening to me; I knew it wouldn't. Nonetheless, I didn't want a marriage relationship where my wife would come and visit me out of duty or feel deprived or cheated that she had to make so many trips and be deprived of so much time to visit her husband in prison. I prayed about that. I asked God to cause my love for Jan to grow and increase beyond my own ability to love her. I asked for the same for her.

Through our anniversary week, I thought about that a lot and realized that my prayer had become a reality. I think of Jan so much with so much fondness and gratitude for what God has done in our hearts toward each other. That is a lot of what our anniversary was like for me, marveling at a God who hears and answers prayer and is able to work way beyond what our circumstances call for. He picks us up and raises us up way above our earthly circumstances, our lot, and our boundaries. The things of this earth really do grow so strangely dim in the light of his glory and grace. It is wonderfully strange, difficult to explain, and tremendously reassuring. This is why God brings us into the darkness so that we can see his light so much more clearly. I guess that's why we have night. Without night, common man wouldn't know there are stars.

This week I am having my guys read the first five chapters in Deuteronomy. I want them to read it and think through Moses's message to them as they are about to leave the wilderness and enter the promised land. It's also the time of Moses's parting message to them. I love to read and hear parting messages. In Deuteronomy, Moses tells them to remember, remember, and remember. Then he says do not forget, do not forget, and do not forget. The bottom line is, "Do not forget in the light what you have learned in the darkness."

The challenging part with writing about this is telling you of the richness of it. Although it is rich, it is not easy. In fact, I think it is the closeness of the relationship between "potential for despair" and "the joy of the Lord" that makes this all work. There are times when despair is very close, so close that we can see ourselves in it. It is then we realize that we need to get a grip. It's that necessary grip that we might lose out on if things were more normal. We live with the reality that losing our grip is real. It can happen to us. This is a rather unforgiving situation. Losing our grip, or gripping the wrong thing, can be disastrous, and we know it because we can even feel it. Psalm 91 is one of the psalms Jan and I memorized when I was home, and we say it together every visit; we find it so true:

> For he will command his angels concerning you to guard you in all your ways. They will lift you up with their hands so that you do not strike your foot against a stone. Because he loves me, I will deliver him; I will protect him because he acknowledges my name. When he calls upon me I will answer him. I will be with him in trouble. I will rescue him and honor him. With long life I will satisfy him and grant him my salvation.

When I came, I was just a worn out, scared, and humiliated individual, knowing I had nothing to offer to say to anybody. I asked God to not waste my life and to show me his glory. I wanted to see God move in such ways that I would know it was him.

8/26/11

While I was living through my anniversary experience, I was reminded of when I was in the Navy and stationed in Washington, D.C. I was a courier for the Navy, which meant I delivered documents to the various offices of the Department of Defense. I got to know the city pretty well, and it is a very interesting city. On Sundays I would go to a small Christian Reformed Church, and almost every Sunday there would be visitors in church that were visiting the city. I would volunteer to give them a guided tour of the city. It was so much fun to show them all these things they had never seen before. I loved doing that, and it gave me a great deal of satisfaction.

I think about what I might do when I get out. I dream about taking my grandchildren places, especially the Grand Canyon. I would love to be there and see the expression on their face when they look down on the canyon and go, "Wow!"

That's the closest I can come to expressing what it's like to be able to minister to these guys in here. It doesn't make any difference if they were Christians before or not. If they weren't Christians, of course everything is new and salvation itself is so incredible. If they were Christians, none of the ones I met so far ever knew how to use the Bible or really understand that Christianity is not about a set of rules but a relationship. So when we read Genesis, I tell them that we want to be careful not to read this like it's a history lesson. This is God's story for us—his story where he wants us to see that his desire for man is to be in relationship with him. Most of the guys come thinking that God, because of the Old Testament, is a harsh God so they really haven't liked the Old Testament. So we read about creation as God creating the earth and man for his own pleasure. God's intention was that it would always be a father-son or father-daughter relationship. When he finished making man, he was so pleased.

Then when Satan came to Eve and told her that if she ate of the fruit of the tree she would be like God, she should have said, "I already am." That is the way God made her, but Satan convinced Eve that God was holding out on her, holding her back and depriving her. They see that it's a very sad story. A disappointment to God (as much as God can be disappointed). It certainly grieved God. I always pray that at this point they can be drawn into the story in such a way that it's an emotional experience within them and not just a history lesson. I want them to see themselves in the story and that it's not something outside of themselves. When God brings the reality of that story to them, they are so drawn in. It's wonderful and amazing. For many, it is a story they have heard many times, but when the Holy Spirit speaks to them through it, it is as if it is brand new. They get hungry and want more. It's a Grand Canyon experience to think that the God of all power and the God of creation wants them, likes them, and desires fellowship with them. They can give this great God pleasure, and he sees them as valuable, useful, and important to his plan, and he has a purpose for them.

I had the larger group class last night. I wanted the guys to hear about Moses and his leadership and also to see that God doesn't always bless people because of their own goodness but just because he chooses to. I love the power phrases of Moses so I wanted to go through Deuteronomy, yet I feared doing a full study on it because I didn't know if their attention span was long enough to keep them locked in on it. I wanted to do an overview of the book in one night, which would be quite a challenge. I stressed over it and prayed a lot about it all week. We did a fast forward through the book so they could get the background of Moses's life. I wanted them to be impressed by Moses's parting words to his people just before they were to go into the promised land, and he was to go off to die. What God had Moses say to Israel applies so much to us today, that's why I like it.

Deuteronomy 9:4-6 says, "It is because of my righteousness that the Lord has brought me in to possess this land, whereas it is because of the wickedness of these nations that the Lord is driving them out before you. Not because of your righteousness or the uprightness of your heart are you going in to posses their land, but because of the wickedness of these nations the Lord your God is driving them out from before you . . . Know therefore, that the Lord your God is not giving you this good land to possess because of your righteousness, for you are a stubborn people."

Well, I thought it a little odd that I was so drawn to that passage, but I just felt this is the message we needed because I hear so much of, "You need to do this so that God will bless you." God has already blessed us so much so our service to him should be out of nothing but pure gratitude. We have guys leaving prison, and I know they were more motivated to serve God and walk with him in prison. I want them to know and remember these things when they get out. Well, it was an odd message for me to bring, but I prayed about it a lot, and God did bring the message out of it for us. The guys are commenting on it and will go back and read the whole chapter.

This morning I had an interesting thing happen. I had a stomach ache. I don't know if it's connected to the hernia or not, but I get these once in a while. I thought I would try to walk it off on the track. I walked a lap and was in some pain so I sat down on a bench and was just listening to Christian radio music. A guy came up to me and asked if I was okay. I said I had a stomach ache but would be okay. He asked if he could pray for me. He did. He then asked me if I knew what a "Strong's commentary" was and what is it used for. I told him. He said that he had ordered a bunch of books and got one but had no use for it. I said I would like to see it. He went to his dorm and got it and gave it to me. It's amazing. I thought it would be nice to have one, but I never would have asked for one or bought one. And my stomach ache is gone.

8/31/11

I just finished reading the book *The Stolen Life*. It's about a girl that was kidnapped about twenty years ago. She was eleven years old at the time. She was held captive for eighteen years, and I just saw her interviewed a few weeks ago on "60 Minutes." I was very impressed with her maturity in the interview and became very interested in the story. Dan bought the book, and I read it over the weekend.

The first part of the book was so terrible that I don't think I can recommend it. Being a father of three girls and a grandfather makes what happened to her so repulsive. She describes it quite graphically. It's disgusting that one human being can be so degraded to treat another that way. There were several very interesting things to me in her story though, and I think being somewhat of a captive here myself helps me relate with it, even though there is no comparison in the experiences. Even reading about guys in more severe prison situations allows me to relate in just a small way to their loss of freedom and how it brings out different characteristics and traits.

The impressive thing about the girl is that you can see the goodness of God in her and her story, even though she is not a Christian. God certainly had to be protecting her mind because today she speaks with such a well-thought-out philosophy about hate, bitterness, and the lack of forgiveness. The Bible is not appealing to her because her captor used the Bible to justify what he was doing, misusing Scripture and using it out of context. She does not have good thoughts about that. That part is so sad because reading through her experience starting as such a young eleven-year-old girl, suffering and having two children (the first at the age of fourteen), you just can't help loving this little child. She misses her own mother so much and talks about that on almost every page. Her time alone seems to have lead her to some deep thinking and increases her ability to internalize and develop thoughts. That is rather amazing to me. Even after all that, she seems to have a good outlook on life. She had eighteen years of . . . I don't know if one could call it solitude; maybe it was solitude mixed with terror, but she had much time alone with her thoughts.

Prison is a little like that. There is a lot of time, and some just try to fill time with whatever they can find. Initially, that's the best one can do. Filling time and wishing it to pass can be tempting, but I find it rather sad. Living on the lake, I always felt rather sad when fall would come, the end of another summer. In some ways, it's a positive marker now, and it means I only have two summers left in this camp. Every Friday everybody always says, "Well, another week gone." I try not to think that way. Life is still too precious even here. Life and this time of life is a treasure, and I want to use every minute I can. I ask God for that every day.

Sunday morning I awoke and didn't have a plan except to go to chapel. I felt a vacuum so I asked God to show himself to me today; I needed him. Sunday at noon Steve was running on the track, and I was sitting on a big rock listening to my radio and watching the guys. When he finished he came over and sat down, and we spent two-and-a-half hours talking; it was so good. We talked about life, both past, present, and future. Steve has taken a job here in landscaping and works hard all day mowing with a push mower and maintaining yards in the housing area. He was offered a winter job running a very interesting snow removal machine here, one of the most sought after jobs on the compound. I was concerned for him because he is progressing so well, and if he takes that job he will be brooming snow starting at 4:00 a.m. and at night, and I knew it would starve him of his thinking and studying time. He now has decided to turn that job down and take a job where we will have more access to each other during the day. Steve is afraid of having not enough to do, but I think it is good to use this time to slow ourselves down and think through the Scriptures.

With the break from class through the summer (only one going), it's gotten a little quiet for me. In the quietness, I find myself being less patient with the baloney and the nonsense of this place. I feel like I want to be more of a recluse, wearing my headset and listening to radio all the time (especially when standing in line, just to shut everyone out). I want to drown out the cursing, swearing, foul talk, and all the repetitive juvenile nonsense that encompasses almost all the conversation around me. I say I would like to do that, but I feel I need to keep one ear open for the Christian brothers who call out a greeting. I don't want to be aloof from them or others who just want to be friendly.

It's true that the longer one is down the harder it is to think of things to carry on for conversation. Things that used to be interesting and exciting are no longer interesting and exciting. Criminal and drug dealing stories are no longer interesting, and if you get drawn into most of these guys' conversations that's what it's about. Most of the news about the compound is negative and not good to be ruminating on. As I age and see more of life, I need to be careful of cynicism. It seems that experience and wisdom helps one see through things so we can see inherent problems in some things that to others look like opportunities. Then one can see through the next thing and the next thing. Soon it is like looking through glass, and if I continue seeing through everything, soon I won't see anything. That may be how the young sometimes view the old—not seeing anything and getting excited about nothing to the extent that all the joy and fun is gone.

I've been reading parts of Ecclesiastes lately. It's written by Solomon, the only man who has ever had everything the world can offer—money, wisdom, and pleasure. He came to the conclusion that none of these things can satisfy, and this is from a man who had tasted it all. It's like he had seen through it all as though it were glass. He goes through wealth accumulation, discovery of knowledge, and the experiences of pleasure. He didn't do it in moderation but in excess. Solomon wrote cynically at the end of his life, after he had failed and repented. After a good long life of experiencing the maximum of anything that a man can experience, he comes to the conclusion that the only thing that is permanent and satisfying is the fear of the Lord. It seems he went all the way to the bottom and came up with that. It's the fear of the Lord that is the beginning and the end of wisdom.

It's good and reassuring to know that is all there is and that the fear and knowledge of the Lord is everything. I find solace and satisfaction in that.

It's a cool day here. It got down to forty-five degrees last night, and I'm wearing my winter coat today because the wind is strong. It seems that summer might be almost over. Well, that's two summers down and two to go. It sounds like I'm half done, but I'm not. The halfway mark will be in December.

I'm thankful for the guys I'm meeting, and the work that I'm able to do. I am sleeping much better lately, even though I don't have my machine yet. The days get a little long without the one-and-a-half hours of exercise I'm used to.

Bob age 21, the year he started
in business, 1960

Bob and Jan celebrating their 50th wedding anniversary at the Duluth prison camp visiting center

The family together in the visiting center just after the cancer diagnosis

With Tom, Jill, Grant, and Lydia

Bob and Jan with grandchildren in the visiting center

Bob with Matt Tucker with whom he spent much time studying the Bible

19

9/11/11

Ruth 1:16, 17 certainly has been a theme for our marriage, "But Ruth said, 'Do not urge me to leave you or to return from following you. For where you go I will go, and where you lodge I will lodge. Your people shall be my people, and your God my God. Where you die I will die, and there will I be buried. May the Lord do so to me and more also if anything but death parts me from you.' I am sure I took it quite for granted when Jan chose the song based on this passage for our wedding. To be honest, I wasn't thinking much about the song choices for the wedding. I just wanted to be married. To be honest again, during most of our married life, I didn't give much thought to the commitment of marriage. I just knew we both were committed—I was committed, and Jan was committed.

The experiences of the last years has changed all that. Today, I don't take anything for granted. When I first knew I was under investigation by the IRS, I thought, "This can't be." Then I thought, "It can't go any further; this will pass." The day our house was raided I thought "This can't be happening; it has to be a mistake." Waiting and hearing nothing for the next three years, I thought, "It's all over; they found nothing, and nothing is wrong." The days of my indictment and later the trial was more of the same. At each level, I was expecting to find out the next day that it was all called off and that everything would be normal again. I didn't think I could lose my home and all my worldly possessions.

As awful as it was for me, I knew it was even worse for Jan. I no longer took anything for granted. I felt I had lost everything except my marriage, children, and grandchildren. I got to prison and found very few men were still married. I heard that less than 15 percent of the marriages last with sentences of three years or more. Several men here that are married told me that they told their wives just to leave and go their own way. They couldn't blame them for not waiting. I prayed for my marriage, and I prayed for our love for each other because I know that all love comes from God. If ours would last, it would be because of him.

God is answering my prayers. I can say that our love has not only lasted, but I feel it is increasing. I think there was a time when visiting was hard for Jan. She never said it, but at least I couldn't help but feel sorry for her having to make the trip every weekend to see me. I prayed about that with Jan and by myself, every day. Through the last year, I never took the visits of my children and grandchildren for granted. I don't take the love of my grandchildren for granted. I thank God that he keeps that love in their hearts even though there are not exciting things for us to do together when they come. Still, they come, and they write; it's always a big deal. I don't take Jan's visits and love for granted. She is always bright and cheerful, and I think she actually enjoys coming to see me. I know I sure look forward to it. It's a lot like 1960 all over again.

It's been a week of challenges. Not to complain, but it's just how things can go in a crazy place like this.

Steve was at work sitting and waiting for the count to clear. He was listening to President Obama's talk on the radio with his eyes closed and his shoes off. (During count we have to just sit and wait for it to clear). All of a sudden the captain and the warden were there. The captain kicked his chair and hollered at him, swearing, "Is that what we pay you for around here?" He proceeded to really chew him out and sent him to the lieutenant's office. Then he got another chewing out and had to rake the lawn all afternoon. Nothing serious; it's just that nobody works harder at their job than Steve. He really is conscientious.

Second, we are getting ready for the fall classes. We had been having a room each night, four nights a week, and we were expecting that again. We were told we can only have one room one night. Ours is the only real class they have where we take attendance and don't let guys leave until it's over.

Third, tonight we were having our small Bible study outside right beside the chapel. They guys really like that place; there is a picnic table there, or if someone else has it we take chairs out there and study. It's always guys having Bible study, listening to music, or playing on the guitars. Well tonight the cop drove his pickup up on the grass and told us we can't be on that spot by the chapel. He loaded up the picnic table and said we couldn't be there anymore. It's the only place here with any solitude so it's a great loss to us.

On the positive side, my sleep apnea machine came this week. I slept so good the first night; I couldn't believe it was because of the machine. I have had it before where I get one or possibly two nights of sleep. Well, I have now had five nights of good sleep. It's incredible. It makes a huge difference. I don't even have to go to the bathroom at night anymore. Praise the Lord!

9/12/11

Well, today was the day I was waiting for. Dennis was visiting me and had been there thirty minutes when the cop said I had a medical call out if I wanted to take it. Of course I did. An inmate drove me down to the hospital to see the doctor for my final exam before surgery.

The nurse had a student with her and asked if that was all right. Then she said the doc had a student with him and asked if that would that be all right. They left, and this nice young man came in who looked like a doctor but was really young. He examined me, and then I asked him what year of medical school he was in; he said his fourth. He asked me who my personal doc was, and I said the BOP. He looked confused so I said the Federal Prison Camp. He asked if I was in prison, and I said I was. As we talked about him some more, he said, "I never graduated from high school. I'm a high school drop out." I said, "Really, how did you get into college?" He said he got a GED. Then he said, "You're the first one I've told that to, but I figured since you're in prison it doesn't matter." I said, "Well, you're an inspiration; don't be embarrassed about that."

Then the doc came in and asked the same questions about my doc; I told him Duluth FPC. He said, "Are you in prison?" I said, "Yes." He said, "Well where is the guard? Isn't he supposed to be sitting at the door?" I said, "No, I'm on community custody." He was a little surprised.

After my exam they called for the car and driver. I sat outside on a bench waiting for the car to come. While waiting, a really old man pulled up to the curb. He got out of the car and came around to the passenger side, opened the door, and this really little old lady was in there. She was so small I could hardly see her through the windshield. He helped her out. As she was standing there very wobbly, he got back in the car and went to park it. There was a small upgrade there in the sidewalk, and she just stood there shuffling her feet but not moving. I said to her, "Can I help you?" She said, "I need a wheelchair." I ran to the hospital and got a chair, put her in it, and wheeled her into the hospital. I thought it was funny. I wondered what she would have said if she knew a dangerous federal inmate was pushing her up the walk.

Well, it's good. The doc said I need surgery for certain, and he would like to do it right away. I said, "I think we need to get BOP approval first, and then he realized that is right. So, it's good news. One step closer to getting it done.

9/19/11

It is Saturday morning, and I had no visitors today so I stayed in bed an extra long time, just thinking about (stressing over?) and praying about (pick your own category) a situation with one of my best students. Joe (not his real name) has become very passionate about God, deeply committed, and always expressing fear of his own patterns. He says he has been this way before. He goes through seasons of being passionate for God, but then gets busy and spends too much time after work hanging out with the guys, living life, and being far less than he should be. This causes him to doubt his salvation. Joe seems to be hard after God, reading the Bible, praying a lot, and very determined about the classes and doing his work well.

This week, Joe said he just wanted to take a week off from class. He wanted to watch some football games on television. That all seemed reasonable to me; I accept that. Another classmate who is concerned for Joe and prays for him daily, is very concerned for Joe and says he has regressed this week. Of course, that is not easy to determine, yet in this environment and with the newness of faith, one week can be a very long time. One would think that in prison there are no distractions, but there really are. We are so programmed to having time filled that when guys get here they grasp at every opportunity to fill their time. If they are interested in spectator sports that can be it. It can be working out because those who are serious about lifting weights have to get in what they call a "car." A car is five guys that organize their set of weights together, reserve the time, and let nobody get in their way. If you get in a car, it's a commitment, and you don't dare let the group down. There are also card games and even frivolous classes that are just time killers.

I'm just saying that if a guy is going to be serious about his faith and time in the Word here you still have to have a strategy to keep the time open. That's why we get so protective and guarded for our men who are new in their faith. We know the day will come when most of them will "cool off" and get distracted. We hate to see it. Sometimes I feel like an old mother hen watching after her chicks.

So this morning I was lying in my bunk thinking about this, and I would like to say, "God brought this to my mind." The image that came to my mind is that I am just a servant of God, like a table waiter. God is the "master chef." He has prepared a banquet for his people in his Word. When people come to class, it's not for me or to hear me. It's to partake of a feast prepared by a master chef. The tables are set, and the appetizers are on the table. The main course is already prepared and waiting. The guests are out in the outer hall. My table guests haven't come. I see them out in the hall with their drinks, eating nachos and bar food, spoiling their appetites, and neglecting the feast the master chef has prepared. What is my role? I'm just a table waiter. I care as a good waiter would want the guest to see the meal the master chef has prepared at its finest. I can only wait.

I'm reading a book about Bonheoffer. I am so interested in WWII history, particularly how leaders are formed, where they come from, and what drives them. What is interesting with Bonheoffer is that he decided that he should be a theologian at the age of thirteen. He did not decide this because of persuasion from his parents, because they were highly educated, highly positioned people and did not think that being a theologian was a good thing. That is what Bonheoffer wanted to be. I read with great interest how he grew up, how his thinking developed, and how God was bringing him along. Bonheoffer was advanced beyond his years in his education. He had to wait a year before he could minister in the church because they had an age requirement. He took that year and traveled to America, and it was while in America that he became born again. It's interesting that his interest, passion, and calling preceded his complete understanding of salvation and acceptance of Christ as his savior.

While I am deeply thinking about Bonheoffer, I think of my grandchildren. It seems I have a second tier of grandchildren with several at the age of thirteen. I have many young friends at that age. I'm interested in their development and listening to the parents talking about the schedules and activities they are in. I see how busy they are and what considerations they have for their education. Sometimes I hear parents talking about sports and that if their child excels in sports they might qualify for a college scholarship as though that would be the ultimate. I wonder then if the scholarship would dictate their college choice and if that is how their schools will be chosen. I wonder today if some believe that it is a bad thing for a child to be alone, bored, or lonely.

For me, growing up on a farm as an only boy, there was a lot of time to be alone. I don't think I liked it at the time, but today I think it was a good thing for me. It caused me to internalize and think a lot. I know at the age of twelve, I had serious thoughts about what I should do with my life and that it should be ministry; I just didn't know at the time what forms ministry could take.

Moses is one favorite leader I like to study. He was born from a slave into slavery. That certainly is a life of wilderness. He was raised in the house of a king, but then God sent him into the wilderness for forty years more so he could speak to him. God knew he would be a leader and set him apart at a very young age.

I think of Samuel who was born of a woman who was having a very hard life. Hannah was one of two wives of a man named Elkanah. The other wife was having children; Hannah's womb was sealed, and she was in despair. In her despair she cried out to God in such a deep and personal way that Eli, the priest, thought she was drunk. She prayed, and it was her prayer that came from her desperation that God answered. He gave her a son, Samuel. We know that later Samuel was called by God, but one must wonder what Samuel's childhood must have been like. Hannah brought him to the temple and left him there at a very young age because for years she made him a little robe each year and brought it to him in the temple. Samuel's upbringing was so important to Hannah that she was willing to make such a sacrifice for him.

Hannah's prayer is born out of sorrow and despair. We can see that God answered Hannah's prayer in a great way by giving her Samuel, who we still read about today. I wonder what would have happened if Hannah hadn't prayed. If Hannah had not been in despair, would she have prayed? What role did Hannah's despair have in her son being the Samuel of the Bible? What role did Samuel's (boring?) life of growing up in the temple play on his development? Was he lonely? Did he miss his family?

This is why I say not all loneliness is sad and not all despair is bad.

9/24/11

We are between quarters now with no classes going on so it's rather dull. I'll just fill you in on some prison "trivia." Trivia is what goes on when there isn't anything important happening and small things become important.

The biggest trivia is that we all got new mattresses and chairs. The old mattresses were probably twenty years old. There were bad ones and good ones, some with holes, and some all flattened out. Guys were always swapping them around. Once you got to know your way around here and know someone, you would trade your mattress for a little better one. I guess the new warden wanted to put an end to that so they ordered all new ones. Sounds like an upgrade, right? Well it's not. The new mattresses are like a blue oblong bean bag made of plastic. It's a shiny slippery plastic, and when you put it on the bed, it looks good at first. Within twenty minutes, however, all the stuffing is around the outside edges and you're lying on whatever is under that. The slippery mattress makes the bottom sheet all end up in a ball after a couple hours. Our bunk beds, I think, are from WW I, and the springs are so stretched that it's like lying in a hammock. To remedy that, someone has welded two inch pipes underneath the spring to keep it from sagging. In my case the pipes run lengthways. It ends up I am now, after the stuffing works its way to the outside, sleeping on two pipes running lengthways.

I see the guys across the hall working on their beds. One works in welding so he welded a sheet of expanded metal to the frame and sleeps on that. My mind starts working on making a deal. Then I catch myself, and I think God knows what I need. Instead of working out something on the black market, I've been trying to stay off that and do everything completely legal, even to the point of not asking for extra meat in chow line (guys get favors if they work it right). I decide not to do anything to see what happens. I want to practice being satisfied with what God puts on my plate. Last night as I came into the dorm there were six one by three inch boards in the garbage wagon. I thought, thank you Lord, you left these here for me. I took them upstairs, and they fit nicely above the pipes so that now my mattress sets on the boards. It's kind of like sleeping on the floor with a bean bag mattress. Well, I know it's not completely legal, and if they see the boards they will take them away. At least I didn't do anything on the black market. Is that good? I'm halfway proud of myself. It's not black but not completely white. Well anyway, I'm trying not to just take things in my own hands. I don't buy stolen food or any other stolen stuff. I do have someone do my laundry every week for seventy cents of commissary stuff. Every ten weeks he gets seven dollars of commissary. I call that trading. Postage stamps are the currency here, as you know there is no money on the compound. I think I'm doing a good job of staying clean.

This week, because of the frost, the stuff is coming out of the garden like crazy. Again, I haven't bought any vegetables, not wanting to participate in that system. Now there is an abundance, and I got tomatoes for free. I am having tomatoes on bread for the first time in two years! They are serving creamed cucumbers now for the second time. I really load up on those. Today we even had zucchini. I have not had that either in two years.

I have the sleep apnea machine and am adjusting to it. The quality of sleep has improved, but now I have to adjust to sleeping on the board (just thankful it's not the pipes). I'm still waiting for the hernia surgery, and it keeps getting worse. I'm not exercising at all anymore and gaining weight because of it.

It's crazy around here, you should see it. There are lines for everything, and everyone always hurries to get in the front of the line. Sometimes I feel like we are a bunch of lab rats. When the truck came up with the new mattresses, they guys scrambled like they were handing out gold. Even at lunch, everyone runs to get to the head of the line. Even the 20 percent or so of us who think we are somewhat intelligent find ourselves running right along with them, even asking ourselves why we are. It's crazy what herd mentality does. We are like a bunch of chickens stuffed in a cage that's too small. Like I say when you don't have anything important to do, very small things become important.

We are now in final stages of sign up for classes. Actually the official sign up is finished, but this is still an important time. More guys are still coming.

After asking about it two times in two weeks, I finally asked the question if they, indeed, had sent my surgery request to the regional BOP. I just got an e-mail from them saying that they just sent it today. I assumed too much in thinking they would follow through. Well, now it will take about three more weeks. Then, if they follow through and call the surgeon, he assured me he would get me in within two weeks after that so it looks like five weeks.

I don't fancy going that long, it is growing pretty fast. I'm afraid I'm going to look like some of these other poor guys around here.

20

10/6/11

I have signed up for a Microsoft class and have class on Monday and Wednesday. This is the first week, and so far both of my classes were cancelled because the education guy forgot to put my number in. I can't get a pin number to get into the computer. Since he is on vacation the rest of the week, I don't have that class. That's pretty much par for the course.

We have some interesting comedy (if you can call it that). The lunch line continues to get deeper as the guys anticipate the dining hall experience. They kind of keep changing the rules as to where the head of the line forms. Today we got pushed way back, about a quarter mile. Don't know why, but it's the captain's desire that we do that.

Today is pay day, when we have to sign our pay statements. The captain had us all line up in alphabetical order, and he said he would give us ten minutes to do that. I wondered, "Why ten minutes?" Then I found out why. For guys that don't know the alphabet, this is a real challenge. What a scramble. I finally had to go down the line and just tell them where to stand. Even some of the guys that knew the alphabet in order had a hard time knowing that "G" was before "U." We never had to do this before so of course everyone was wondering why we are doing this. This one guy was saying, "Dude, I been in dis place long time before dude even worked here. He wasn't even pushing a pencil. Dis place used to be good place. Now it bad place. Dey don't need do me like dis. I ain't puttin' up with this [expletive]. What dey tink I am? I ain't no [expletive]." All the while we are in line, this big guy from Chicago that wants to play pool instead of standing in line, keeps moving back and forth saying, "Scurs me. Scurs me." This place is a zoo.

The CO said they are adjusting our pay, and so we had to go into his office to sign in case we wanted to discuss it. After half an hour it was my turn. He handed me my sheet to sign, and I noticed my pay was less. He hadn't said anything so I asked him why the reduction. He said, "We are paying for the hours actually worked. How many hours do you think you actually work?" I just grinned and said, "I'm okay." I went from $14.25 per month to $10.75 per month. So how's that for contract negotiations? Then he said, "I thought you were changing jobs to the visiting center." I said, "No, I turned that down; I like it here." He said, "Well, you're doing a good job." Now that's the first "atta-boy" I've had since I got here. Wow! I guess a good job means that I'm keeping the two toilets supplied well with toilet paper. That's mostly what I do.

Steve and I are trying to meet. He works in the dorm and can't be in there because of inspection. I work in the rec center and can't be there because of inspection. So, we try to find a place to talk. We meet on the street, and the announcement comes over the PA system, "No congregating on the street." We go in the library, and the guy comes through saying no loitering in the library. Ends up, they don't care where we are as long as they can't see us.

10/11/11

Classes started last week. We now hold two classes in one night. The best size class for us in doing it the way we do is twelve to fifteen people. We have twenty in our 6:00 p.m. class and twelve in our 7:20 p.m. class so we are more than pleased with that. This is without any publicity or promotion. It was impossible to promote it because they wouldn't let us know what time we could have it. So that's definitely a praise. God is working, and the word is getting around.

I finally got the nerve to ask my dorm roommates if they minded if I had the guys in our room two nights a week. They know I have Bible studies, and they have been watching me for a year now. None of them have ever said anything about it; I'm sure they were afraid I was going to bang them over the head with my Bible. Anyway, I asked the three guys individually and privately if they would mind me using the room. They all agreed it would be okay. They said they would disappear, and I said they didn't need to and they could stay and read if they liked.

The first nights they were gone, but the last two nights they stayed and read. I could tell they were curious. Our group has now grown from three to five. The Bible study guys were a little uncomfortable with my roommates in the room. In our dorm there is a room where the mop buckets and floor buffers are kept. There is a table and benches in that room where the guys play poker. I asked the guy who seems to be in charge of the poker if there was a time when it wasn't being used for that so we could have a Bible study. He said, "Just put a sign up in there and reserve it." So I did. The one night I did someone took the sign down. I don't know for sure what that means, but we canceled the meeting that night anyway. We will try again. I think our group will grow larger because we can handle more people.

My Mexican roommate, Francisco, asked me about my Bible. He asked me if he could look at my Bible. I gave it to him. He opened it, and then he went to his locker and took out a nicer leather Bible that looked new, at least unused. He compared the two and said they say the same thing. He said his sister sent him that Bible two years ago. His sister and two of his brothers became Christian and go to church. Francisco laughs at all that, but this time he seemed a little serious. I told him I would like to read some of it together sometime. He didn't say he would. It's just amazing to me how long they watch, and what they observe.

My roommate Jerry is asking questions. Jerry told me his people are all Lutheran and German. It seems that he didn't go to church much, and he never goes to church and has not been willing to come to a Bible study even when it's in our room. This morning Jerry asked me, "Bob, what makes you think all that is true in the Bible, like Noah and the ark, and the flood. Did it cover the whole earth, and what about the whale swallowing Jonah?" He talked so fast and didn't let me even answer. We would get into an argument. He kept repeating that he didn't want to get into an argument. He said, "You know science is fact. There is nothing about religion that is fact. It's just a story."

I questioned him on science and who figured out science. He said men did. I said yes, men—the creatures God created—figured out science. The Creator created the creatures who can figure out science. Isn't that amazing? Then he wanted to talk about man coming from apes. I said, "Jerry, you know that's not true. God made Adam in his own image. If anything, Adam was even more intelligent than we are because he did not carry the decay of sin in his body."

Then he said, "Well, all you hear is science, and everyone believes it."

Well, it's interesting what impacts different people. I knew he came from Amana and that is Lutheran; I said, "Jerry, when you were young you went to Sunday school, and they taught you the catechism, didn't they?"

He said, "Yes."

I said, "They did that, and then you were confirmed, weren't you?"

He said, "Yes."

I said, "And then it all stopped, didn't it?"

He said, "Yes, that's right."

I said "And since then all you've been getting is the science and evolution side of the story and nothing from the Bible isn't that right?"

He said, "Why I guess that's right."

Then he said, "Yes, I remember those stories when I was a kid, but I picked up your Bible one day when you were out. I tried to read John, but it was so complicated and confusing. I couldn't get anything out of it."

I said, "Well, let's read it together, and you can get it."

He said, "No, I don't want to do that."

I got a copy of *Good and Evil* out of my locker and gave it to him. I showed him how the cartoons were all from Scripture, and the verses were on the bottom of each page. That was yesterday morning. He read through the whole book by last night. I had told him before that if he really wanted the proof and solid arguments against evolution that I have a book from my cousin, Bob, that really goes into that. I said, "I don't really study that myself, but if you're interested, I'll get the book." He said he wants that book.

This morning, Jerry said, "You know, it's really true. We were taught all these things when we were kids, but after confirmation it all stopped." He repeated that several times as though that was the most important point of all that I said. I think that is really the shortcoming in most churches today; they do not consider that Bible learning should be lifelong and not just for children.

10/12/11

Saturday I was going to visiting, and the walkway leads right along side the chapel and heads out of the camp. There was a man there, about thirty years old. He was standing there just in his green pants and white T-shirt. He looked very bewildered. I asked him if I could help him. He just mumbled, "I don't know what I'm doing here; I don't belong here. I'm doing everything wrong, and everybody is mad at me. I'm really in trouble right now."

I said, "What are you in trouble for?"

He said, "I missed head count, and I don't know where I'm supposed to be." I asked him if he was in bed at 5:00 a.m. He said, "Yes."

I said, "Then you didn't miss your count; they count you in bed at 5:00 a.m." I asked him where he is from.

He said "Wisconsin."

Then he looked at me and said, "Why are you being so nice to me?"

I said, "I just want to help you out."

He said, "I'm so confused." (I knew he was on suicide watch and probably was medicated for it). He said, "Well what should I do now?"

I said, "I think you should go lie down in your bunk and sleep. Tell your roommates to be sure and wake you up for the ten o'clock count. It's a standing count."

He said, "Okay," and was gone.

Sunday, he was in church. I shook his hand and called him by name. He was surprised I remembered his name. Early in the service, he got up and walked out. Jim followed him and met him outside. Jim said, "Why are you leaving?"

He said, "I don't know. Why is everyone so nice to me?" Later, I met him coming out of the library. I greeted him, and he was pleasant. Then he said, "Maybe we should take a walk."

I said, "That would be good; let's do it." I wanted to make conversation with him so I asked him how long he is going to be here.

He said six months and then, "Why does everybody ask me that? I don't want to talk about that."

It was quiet so I asked, "Do you have a family?"

He said, "Why do you ask all these questions; I don't like that. I don't want to talk to you anymore."

So I said,"Okay." Well, that is my new friend. He is a very troubled man.

I had a book given to me by a Christian guy in my dorm. It's on end times. I have never been a student of Revelation, nor have I been fond of having discussions on end times. This book has really caught my attention, probably because of what I experience a lot of right here in the chapel and on the compound. The book is *God's War on Terror: Islam, Prophecy and the Bible*. It's written by Walid Shoebat who was born and raised in Bethlehem, Israel, by an Arab father and an American mother. He grew up a terrorist, but when he married a Christian woman he was challenged to examine the Bible in 1993 and compare it with the Quran. Shoebat says, "Only biblical truth has transferred my way of thinking from being a follower of Muhammad and idolizing Adolph Hitler to believing in Jesus Christ."[1] This book is about end times, but most everything in it is happening today. Being here where I am and living with the ones I live with makes the book very believable, and I believe it is important for every Christian to read it.

It's interesting how childish some of these guys can be. I was eating in the mess hall. An inmate sat down at the table and just looked at his plate and pouted. He was pouting over the small portion of meat he got. He just sat and sulked. I was quite entertained by that.

Regional has now approved my surgery, and they claim they are waiting for the doctor to have time for me. I don't believe that, because when I was downtown I asked the doctor how long it would take for him to get me in. He said, "Almost immediately, two weeks at the longest." When they sent me the e-mail that I was approved, I e-mailed back asking if they would verify for me that the doctor had actually been notified. He wouldn't answer that. It's part of their vague communication, which serves their purpose. It is true that we are waiting for the doctor's appointment, but it may not be true that they have asked the doctor for an appointment.

10/14/11

Well, it's Friday again. The weeks really do go fast, and that's a good thing. Now that the classes are going we have a lot going on. We have new guys in class who I now meet with individually too. They are rescheduling their days so they can meet with me. This is so great. Now, tonight and Sunday night we have two studies in the dorm. We will study Romans tonight. Guys are actually saying through tears that they thank God for sending them here. They never expected to find this teaching in prison.

Some of the dorm counselors now are recommending our class to some of the guys. I don't know how they choose the ones they recommend, but the guys they send are really good guys who I would pick to invite.

There was a threatening fight in the theater this week so they closed it down for two weeks. It makes a lot of guys hanging around at night with nothing to do. I hope it doesn't spoil our meeting room for the study tonight.

10/16/11

What a great week! Our classes are overflowing, and still more want to get in. The challenge now is space for our small group studies. Last night I thought I had it figured out. I found a place in the mop locker in our dorm. It has a table, and we brought in chairs. There were five of us. We no sooner got started when guys started coming in with their dorm cooking. The microwaves are in the mop locker. It was not only a steady stream of guys wanting to cook their food, but there was also a line up behind them. Some were cooking fried rice and mixed in all their strange seasonings; the smell alone almost drove us out. We had the window wide open, and it got cold but cold was better than stink. We kept going through the work for about a half hour, but after that we gave up. We were quite a spectacle for the guys, though. Some were glaring at us for being there, and one can only guess what was going through their mind. I realized that what was going through my mind was wrong, though, because one guy said, "What is this, a Bible study? Can I join you?" As we were leaving another guy said, "Was this a Bible study? I wish I would have known."

My daughters often ask me if I ever cry. I usually don't, and I haven't for quite a while. I did cry last night. I was thinking about the question "Can I join?," the comments "I wish I had known," and the looks on the faces. I know if we had the space in the dorm there would be more, maybe many who would like to be in a study. Most of the things in the chapel are either very loud with a lot of drama or repetition with a loud voice and drama. Not a lot of thinking because phrases are repeated, just rearranged in different ways. Or they are very loud with a lot of preaching, finger pointing, and scolding. I find that what these guys respond to is not preaching or screaming but sitting with a Bible in each hand, just pointing to the Scriptures, having them read and discover, and, when they have questions, just answering and clarifying. It isn't rocket science, but real thinking is something that is foreign to most of what goes on here. I think this is what most have experienced on the outside as well, either preaching and screaming or bland sermons about parables where someone else has done all the chewing and digesting and the audiences passively listens.

In my bed, the scene somewhat overwhelmed me, and I had such an impression of the lost nature of the souls that are in these bodies, many who, because of their outward appearance and actions, I pass by because I can't imagine them as Christians or interested in Christ in any way. We just don't know by the outside cover. I went to sleep thinking that I have two years left in this place and, if God wills, these might just be the most productive years of my life.

We have a new lead singer for the quartet now, and it sounds really good. It's just a traditional quartet sound, but it seems like it's a sound that never really gets old. The guys really respond to it. The chaplain does such a good job. It's so good to have a chaplain who loves God. The chapel is now full every Sunday.

Price grew up not knowing his father because his father was incarcerated as long as he could remember and still is. Price said his mother took him to church all the time until he was about twelve. He said after twelve you didn't need to go to church anymore. Price was a shy boy and never got very well-acquainted with others because they moved a lot and were always changing schools and churches. His mother told his older brother to take him with him so that he could be around boys and men. Well, his brother and all the men he knew sold drugs. Everyone sold drugs. His mother often asked him if he was going to turn out like his dad and brothers, and he always said, "No." Yet, when he got to be seventeen years old, he started using marijuana and started selling drugs. When he was nineteen, he was arrested and got a twenty-year sentence because he was selling cocaine and got charged for crack. (The penalty for crack is four to five times stronger than cocaine.

While Price was in jail on the front end of his sentence, a retired minister came through the jail three times a week. Price went to all his classes and accepted Christ. Then, in Milan Federal Prison he said he had Bible studies every day. He was there for ten years, then Kentucky for three years, and now he just came to Duluth where he will be for two more years. Then he will be released. Price is such a mild-mannered man. He has a true and reasonable plan laid out for his life, for both ministry and business. He works in recycling here and wants to make a business of recycling garbage when he gets out. He wants to teach that to people, and also gardening. He has taken a gardening class and believes he can have a business and ministry with those ideas, and have them centered around faith. He said he loves our classes because they require him to think and write. He said he never had to do that before, and he needs to develop his writing skills.

21

11/4/11

I had an interesting experience yesterday. Eagle Tail is the leader of the Native American rituals here. He seems to have taken a liking to me, but I also think that he wants me to go in the sweat lodge with them. I'd like the sauna part, but I don't think I will do it because I believe it involves communicating with spirits, and I don't want anything to do with that. Besides that, it would send the wrong message to the others who would notice that I did it. I am very watched around here.

Anyway, yesterday Eagle Tail said, "Goris, did you see the eagle?" I said, "No, where is it." He said, "Out there; come along." I was in the middle of a project and really didn't want to go, but I was afraid of offending him, and I went along. He led me out to the Indian ceremonial place, through the fence. I felt strange being in there because usually it is only for Native Americans and for ceremony. They really guard that place. There is a fence around it, and the gate is locked. We went through the gate. I followed Eagle Tail and did what he did. We shook hands with everyone there and moved on to a tent-like enclosure where a lot of men were standing around a table. I moved in and on the table was lying a dead eagle. I stood there with them, not knowing what to expect or what to do. One man was talking about the eagle. He had a feather in his hand, and he was talking about that.

It ends up that this eagle was found dead in Colorado. It had been shot. The people there put it on ice and shipped it here. It was a solemn atmosphere, very quiet. Eagle Tail went to the little shack where they keep their ceremonial things. He made a ball out of some sage and other material, handed it to one of the guys to hold, and then he lit it with a match. It gave off the smoke that they use in the ceremonies. I was wanting to leave but did not know if it would be appropriate; it was like a funeral. Suddenly, one of them said, "All right, get the [expletive] out of here we got things to do". I looked up, and he was talking to me and another guy. He escorted us to the gate and locked the gate behind us.

We have thirty-two guys between the two classes, and they take it so seriously. We start the class right on time, and nobody is late. They are so attentive and do their lessons so thoroughly. They really want to learn. The assignments always include their writing and then sharing in class what they wrote. The discussion is around their writing.

We have two older gentlemen (but not as old as me) in the class. They hadn't met before coming here, but they are both from the same denominational church. They have a very different church doctrine that is intolerant of any musical instruments in the church, insists on communion every Sunday, and that states you are not saved unless you are baptized. There is no problem with what they believe, but one in particular almost always wants to take over teaching the class. He was wearing hard on a lot of people, and I thought I would have to talk with him privately. He is a tutor in education, and on Tuesday afternoon the cops came in very mysteriously, took him away, and put him in the hole.

I don't think he did anything wrong. I think it has to do with isolating him as a witness to a trial coming up in upstate New York. It was all very strange. Anyway, a couple of the guys said, "God works in mysterious ways," as if to say this is the way God delivered us from his interruptions.

Well, it is very fulfilling to see these guys grow and think through these things. Tonight, I am meeting with Dario. He is very diligent with his study Bible. He has not yet shared his faith with his family. He never sees them. He prays for their salvation every day.

He has shared with his wife, but she has been confused by some Jehovah's Witnesses. His sixteen-year-old son told him he is taking a religion class in the public school. Dario is very excited about that, and tonight I am meeting with him to tell him how to write out the gospel to his son.

11/9/11

I have been thinking about pain and suffering. It started with my thoughts of my granddaughter, Larissa. Larissa is in her very early twenties and has been suffering from rheumatoid arthritis for some time. I found myself saddened for her as I thought about the limitations this might place on her life.

As I thought of Larissa, I thought of many others who have lived and are living lives of real restrictions, pain, sadness, and sometimes failure and who are almost always broken. My thoughts came back to myself and my prison, and I realized that all these cases are various forms of prison. They are obstacles and barriers that keep us from living the life we want to live. Some are speakable and easy for others to sympathize with. Others are unspeakable because they implicate others or carry shame and guilt that is not known to others. They may be addictions, failures that others don't know about, or possibly marriages that are dysfunctional or broken. It might be the broken heart of a divorce and the pain of living a single life again in a married world.

I have about a dozen books that I am always reading and never finishing because I underline, go back over, and read it again. I try to retain them all because they are so good. But my mind seems like a sieve. It's like I am carrying water home in a sieve, and when I get to where I want to be, it's gone. So these books by Piper, Sproul, and the men they often quote, the classic Christian writers like John Bunyan, William Couper, and David Brainerd, are books that really feed my thinking, and I want to use an idea but have forgotten where I got the idea.

I have come to think that I really don't have an original thought. Every thought I have came from somewhere else. Someone once said that if you find an idea and use it three times and experience it then it becomes yours. I don't know if that's right, but I'll use it for convenience. One of the dozen books I'm reading is *The Hidden Smile of God* by Piper. It's one I started several times in the last six months and just couldn't get into. Suddenly, I opened it, and it spoke volumes to me. It's interesting how our thinking and circumstances affect what we read and need. This time, it's like God is speaking to me. I believe God is allowing me to live out something of which these guys are speaking, and I am praying that God will lead my mind as I am writing this letter to all who suffer and all who live in their own kind of prison. Bunyan spent twelve years in prison, and he was in prison when he did most of his writing. It was his prison experience that gave us *Pilgrim's Progress*. William Couper had a mental illness. It was his illness that caused him to write songs for troubled souls. He wrote the song, "There is a Fountain Filled With Blood." It's a favorite of many.

Sometimes, the world seems so upside down. The things we once thought so important are later found to not really be important at all. Some things we dread the most become the most valued. God's way is to take all the things we would like to boast about and crush them. First Corinthians 1:26-29, 31 says, "Not many of you were wise according to worldly standards. Not many were powerful, not many were of noble birth, but God chose what is foolish in the world to shame the wise, God chose what is weak in the world to shame the strong. God chose what is low and despised in the world, even things that are not, to bring to nothing things that are, so that no human being may boast in the presence of God. . . . Let him who boasts, boast in the Lord."

Have you ever read James 1:2-4 at a time in your life when it made you angry? I have; it says, "Consider it all joy, my brethren when you encounter various kinds of trials . . . Knowing that the testing of your faith produces endurance." This can only be read with joy and only after God has already done a work in you. Yes, I think I understand that now, and it does bring me joy.

I think of those who suffer through difficult and failed marriages and live with the pain of the effects of that. I think of those who suffer with addictions, and their families who live with shame and sometimes the secrecy of that. And these loved ones of God who faithfully live out their lives in a ministry of suffering but may not know it is a ministry. You who suffer are important to God, and I think he wants you to know that. So it is to you who suffer that I want to write and hope that you find courage and peace in it. God has placed you in a place of ministry when he wants to show himself to the world through you. God has entrusted you with this. When we have prayed, "God, take this circumstance away from me" for so long and he hasn't done it, we must come to the conclusion that all this has passed through his hands. He could have changed it, but he didn't. We can then only conclude that this must be his plan, and he must have a purpose for it. If it's God's purpose, it is good. I would pray that God would give us each courage and faith so that our prayer would be, "God, have your way with me."

On the outside, I have had discussions with people who were skeptical of believing strongly in the sovereignty of God. They would make the claim that believing so strongly in God's sovereignty, and living with such submission to it, would produce a passive, fatalistic mind-set. I am experiencing for me, and observing the lives of others, that it produces the opposite. I see it as empowering, encouraging, and bringing abiding peace. I have seen, and I want my fellow inmates to see, prison as nothing more than what God has designed for us. Rightly or wrongly in man's eyes, it is all in God's hands. John Bunyan wrote, "So being again delivered up to the jailor's hands, I was had home to prison, and there have lain now complete for twelve years. Waiting to see what God would suffer these men to do with me."[2]

11/13/11

There are parts of this that are such a blessing, to be with men who are at such an important time of their life. A week ago, we had our conversation in class on baptism. Almost all want to be baptized. I would love to do it right now, but I know that some are unsettled on the amount of water that should be used. Last night I thanked the guys for the seriousness with which they have approached the class and this issue. I encouraged them to be sure to honor their commitment to God on baptism, and not let that fade away. When men come to faith in prison, other inmates (non-Christians) laugh and say, "Yeah, he found Jesus, until he hits the door." Many on the outside say the same, and when they go to church on the outside they will find the same reception. It is really difficult for a new Christian inmate to have confidence in his new found faith. They feel overwhelmed with the idea of the changed life. We talked about this last night.

I used Philippians 1:6, where Paul says to the Philippians, "I am praying of this, that he who began a good work in you will bring it to completion at the day of Jesus Christ. It is right for me to feel this way about you because I hold you in my heart, for you are all partakers with me in grace, both in my imprisonment and in the defense and confirmation of the gospel. How I yearn for you all with the affection of Christ Jesus and it is my prayer that your love may abound more and more with knowledge and all discernment, so that you may approve what is excellent, and so be pure and blameless for the day of Christ, filled with righteousness that comes from Jesus Christ to the glory of God."

It is so natural to look to ourselves, even after salvation, for righteousness. We must always remember the only righteousness we have is outside ourselves. It is from Christ. We talked about how to live the Christian life when we have such a tendency toward sin and temptation and what a struggle it is if we have to work so hard at keeping sin out of our lives. If we can extract one sin problem, it can leave a void where another comes in.

I used an analogy that a law in physics says that nature abhors a vacuum. When a vacuum is created, air moves in to fill the vacuum. A tractor cab company used this principle to create a tractor cab that had only clean air in it. In the field, the machinery kicks up so much dust that it's impossible to seal a cab tightly enough to keep the dust out. What they did was build an air system to filter and blow a constant stream of clean air into the cab creating a positive pressure in the cab. The dust cannot come in, because the pressure in the cab is greater than outside the cab. I like to say that the same is true in nature as it is in the spiritual world; our souls abhor a vacuum. With the Spirit of God in us, cleansing us and purifying us, if we fill our lives with the things that please God and are important to him, we will have much less trouble keeping the sin of our life out. It's a metaphor that seems to make sense to men. Some people have just enough Christianity to make them miserable. They have enough to know they sin but not enough to live the Christian life. The best thing we can do is to confess and acknowledge that we have wayward wandering hearts that cannot be trusted. It is because our desires are wrong that we do the wrong things.

Jesus said it so well with the metaphor of the vine and the branch. John 15:4-13 says, "Abide in me and I in you. As the branch cannot bear fruit by itself unless it abides in the vine, neither can you , unless you abide in me. I am the vine, you are the branches. Whoever abides in me and I in him, he it is that bears much fruit, for apart from me you can do nothing. If anyone does not abide in me he is thrown away like a branch and withers; and the branches are gathered, thrown into the fire and burned. If you abide in me and my words abide in you, ask whatever you wish and it will be done for you. By this my father is known."

The men were encouraged, humbled, and challenged. We are all humbled as we get even a glimpse of God's holiness and the complete adequacy of Christ, his work, and the power of the Holy Spirit to finish what God has begun. We can be sure that our salvation is rock solid because it depends on God's sovereignty and faithfulness. At the same time, from our perspective, it is fragile because Jesus says all we need to do is abide. His metaphor is that a branch that is grafted into the vine is a fragile picture. When the graft is new, it is important for the branch to not move until it takes. Even after that, the vine doesn't do anything to produce fruit but to abide in the vine. The vine produces all the fruit, and the nectar that comes out on the branch. The beautiful fruit looks like it was produced by the branch, but it is actually from the vine.

Assurance of salvation is an important thing here for the guys, and the tension of it is tremendous. I have had men who pray the prayer of salvation and then just walk away from everything. I don't know if they lose interest or think they are saved from hell and that's all they were interested in. Others have prayed, are saved, but are still worried that God might punish them in eternity because they aren't good enough. It's an interesting mix, and we get it all here. Sometimes I wish we could have class daily rather than weekly.

11/18/11

The surgery is done. I went in yesterday morning at 6:00 a.m. The surgery was at 10:00 a.m., and I was back to the room at 12:00 p.m. The surgery was a bigger deal than I thought it would be. Back at the room (in the hospital), they added pain medication until I had no more pain. I was concerned about how it would be when I got back because it's hard getting the medication the doctor prescribes. He assured me he was sending plenty to last me the duration.

I felt good in the room. It was nice having a private room with my own TV. I told them I wasn't in any hurry to get back and to keep me there as long as they could, and they did. I enjoyed the day. I got back to the camp at 7:00 p.m., and, just as I thought, the pharmacy was closed, and I couldn't get any medication. I was told to come back at 6:00 a.m., which I did. They didn't have it ready and told me to come back two more times. I do believe God took care of it all. I only have a little pain when I first stand up or sit down. Other than that, I have almost no pain. I took one pain pill when they finally got them to me, just to see what they were like. They made me sleepy so I'm not taking any more; I don't need them. I think that is pretty amazing. I know how many are praying. God truly hears and answers prayers. I must testify to that Sunday in the chapel. God is so good.

The guys did the class without me last night, and they were all so concerned for me. What a great group of guys we have in our classes. I don't think I have ever enjoyed the studies so much. They are so appreciative, in awe of God, and humble. We don't have any show-offs, even though several know the Word quite well. Tonight and Sunday we now have Bible study in my room. We are studying Romans. It is very uplifting.

We are having our first real snow. It is warm and all white outside, and the snow removal guys are at work. I think it's time for it with Thanksgiving next week. The Thanksgiving menu looks great again. Just like last year, we are having turkey, ham, sweet potatoes, apple pie, and more. It's the best meal of the year.

11/25/11

It is Thanksgiving. Here in Duluth that translates to a nice service in the chapel from 8:30 to 9:30 a.m. It was nice because there were different people participating. I think church here like everything else runs like a cartel. People push and shove to get into position, and then they and their friends do most of the "performing," whether it is praying, preaching, or whatever.

This morning it was different. I don't know how it got to be different. I think maybe the chaplain stepped in and said we are going to use different people. It was good to see that there are others. I think often it is like that in church on the outside as well. Leaders don't see it as their job to continue to scout for people who could take a position of leadership. Leaders usually have a tendency to protect their own turf and see others as threats. It was good to be in church. There were many expressions of thanks.

At 11:00 a.m. the dining line started. Our dorm was first so at 11:25 a.m. my Thanksgiving dinner was done. It was very good, very traditional, and topped off with a big piece of pumpkin pie. Everybody was happy about that. It is such a beautiful day that I will stroll a little bit between e-mails. I still have to take it a little easy.

I realized this week how much of my life is in the teaching. I feel gratified and purposeful when we have the space to teach and do Bible studies. This week education was closed so we didn't have class. I had three in my room at night but need to be careful of imposing on my roommates. Also, we have no sign of approval for any space for class the next quarter. We had four nights and now one night, but the education guy just doesn't make decisions. Like the rest of the government employees, they talk a positive talk but never take the step to make a decision and say this is it. Our new chaplain has talked a positive talk, but she keeps saying she is going to have a meeting that doesn't happen. I don't know what it will be like here if we can't have any class.

Nick is about 60. Twice every day, he sits in the group of men right next to me during count. This group is led by a man named "Bull Head" from Fargo. Bull Head just delights in mocking all religions and has a vulgar mouth, but he also has a tremendous gift for entertaining stories even though they are laced with "Anti-Christ" theology and centered around his humorous but dirty stories. The group grows and wanes, but Nick is always there. I also see Nick every Sunday just ahead of me in chapel. It makes me think Nick is searching, or maybe possibly God is doing something in him. I feel the need to talk to Nick. He seem sincere when he is in church, and he is profane when with Bull Head. They have a Thanksgiving concert in the theater at Thanksgiving and Christmas. Bull Head was asked if he is going to tell stories during the Thanksgiving concert. He said, "No, I'm saving it for Christmas, I'm going to tell my Jesus jokes." It is blasphemous. Until now I have felt it best to be quiet and say nothing. I'm not sure how long I should do that.

11/30/11

I kind of got buried in defeat over here. It's funny how negatives, despair, and discouragement build. I usually manage to stay above it, but things just are so crazy.

It started with them closing education for a week "to wax the floors." (The staff likes to take their time around the holidays). Then, with my surgery I missed the next week. We are now two weeks from the end of the quarter, and we still don't know if we will be able to have classes next quarter. We have been fighting for space ever since we started, and it's getting old. It seems e-mails go down, get lost, and communication breaks down. Life gets boring, and I get boring.

When things slow down, stuff starts playing with the mind. I start feeling sorry for my little grandkids who are all so excited when they come, and I start wondering if they can really stay that excited if we never do anything. Now, I know that is all stupid thinking, and last night I received a lot of help. In my praying I came across Proverbs 4:23, which talks about guarding your heart. This proverb says to me that God has placed his wellspring within me. All I need is what God has already placed within me. I need to be drawing on his wellspring and not be depending on others.

I have a new friend by the name of Matt. He is from Kansas City, Missouri. He is so much fun to have in my classes. He is in everything I do. Matt grew up in a Christian home, attended a legalistic Christian school, and then really pulled away from it. He moved to California and was involved in large fast money things, which got him here. While in California and after, he was involved with charismatic Christians, some health and wealth people. Matt is now growing so much and is so excited to see God as he is, a sovereign God who does allow pain and suffering to shape us and mold us into people he wants us to become. Matt is so bright and a quick learner. He is up at 4:00 a.m. most mornings with his Bible and devouring everything I give him to read.

We have some others who are struggling a bit with depression and sadness. It's always hard to know exactly how to read that because it causes them to respond in different ways. By and large, everyone is really on track; I just wish we could have the classroom space more consistently. It would add so much.

Today, we had a choir rehearsal with a whole different group. We have a goofy guy here who cleans in the chapel, and he thinks he is running the whole music program. He is a Minneapolis ex-cop who graduated from law school and is serving a ten-year sentence. He wears the big prison glasses that they issue for free, doesn't bathe enough, and has a pony tail with real stringy hair. Doug isn't sure if he believes in God or not. Some days he does, and other days he believes in the universe or the polarity of the earth. When the Catholic bishop comes, he is Catholic, and when he wants to play for the Protestant services, he is Protestant. Well, he has this song he learned in high school which is a Latin song, and he wants us all to sing it for the bishop when he comes. I can't remember the name of it; it is only about four Latin words that are repeated over and over. It is going to be sung in rounds with three groups. It's really strange, but I think might turn out good.

Tonight, we finally have class again after a long layoff. Next week, we have one more and then shut down already for the holidays. I don't think anybody here, other than the staff, likes the shutdowns and holidays. Oh, to be a government employee!

22

12/4/11

It's Sunday afternoon and a beautiful day. Harry Potter is on in the theater, and I tried it out but just can't get into it and just can't sit in a dark theater on a beautiful sunny day. I figure it's a good day to write and be walking the track between my fifteen-minutes e-mailing intervals.

Our study class this week was on legalism versus freedom. It seemed like a pretty easy discussion and that everyone in here is free from being judgmental. I think almost 100 percent feel they are not judgmental. One would think that would be the case, sitting here in prison, that any tendency of being judgmental would be gone. I used to think the only people tempted with being judgmental were Christians, and especially church people. I left the class thinking that it went a little too easy. Since the class, having pondered it more, I am haunted by the fact that it went way too easy. Inmates as a rule don't like the government, the justice system, or the law. Yet, oddly enough, I find inmates to be extremely legalistic. While I used to think that non-Christians are the least judgmental and legalistic, I find they have as great a problem with legalism as anyone.

Isn't it true that every thought in relationships either falls on the side of legalism or the side of grace? I find the hardest thing for non-believers to become Christian is the whole idea of grace. They don't object to gimmicky grace or cheap grace (getting something for nothing and thereby beating the system of hell), but, if they get by that one, it's the challenge of total and complete acceptance by God because of Jesus and accepting his redemption. Legalistic people don't like the idea that one can become totally reconciled by God by grace alone through faith. It is easier for them to accept it if there is something they can or have to do for it.

Is pride closely connected to legalism? I have a friend here who is totally out of money. He is a very proud man. On commissary day, I ask him if he's all right and if he needs anything or if I can get him something. He always says, "No, I don't want to owe anybody anything." Then there are a few things he needs, and I get them for him. Then he says, "I'll add it to my list that I owe you." I tell him I don't have a list, and I don't want it back. He says, "Yes, I will." I really don't think he will pay me back. I wish he would just accept it as a gift. It's no big deal; it's just something that I thought of as I was thinking about legalism. Read Romans 14. Is being judgmental or being legalistic kind of like being humble—the minute we think we have it mastered, it's gone?

What a great day outside. I don't know the temperature, but I walked three miles today and am feeling really good. I am so glad I have the freedom to be outside. I am really an outdoors person, and I can't stand to be inside. When I can't walk anymore, I will bundle up and find a place to sit in the sun and listen to Christian radio. What a blessing Christian radio is too. I have access to so much good music, sermons, even some talk shows that aren't too bad.

In helping my brothers here in prison understand the gospel, I have found it necessary first to help them understand God. As I said before, most gospel stories jump into the middle of the story and begin with how to receive forgiveness from sin when the unrepentant really don't understand why sin is so bad because they don't understand why God hates sin so much because they don't understand a holy God. The question always comes up, "Where did sin come from anyway? Did God create sin?" We have spent quite a lot of time studying what was going on in the heavenly places even before creation. We read in Job how God communicates with his principalities in the heavenly places and then in Isaiah and Revelation about Lucifer and how he was before and after the fall. I find it so interesting and also damaging to allow ourselves to be ignorant of Satan and how he works; we need to have an understanding of him without becoming infatuated with him and honoring him. Sometimes that difference is a fine line.

Our comfort is that Satan has lost the battle. In the timelessness of God and the Scriptures, we know that this is true. We know the end of the story. For now, Satan's tactic is to separate us from the love of our heart and sneak into the story of our lives through fears and wounds and thoughts of inadequacy. I believe this is what I was dealing with over the Thanksgiving holiday. Satan doesn't work just within the bad; he also works within the good. I had grown to love the communicating I had with so many through e-mails that I got used to e-mails bearing me up. Then, when they stopped, I dropped. That's where I learned from the "wellspring that we have within us" that my peace, comfort, and joy can come from within me, from the wellspring within me.

I see not only within myself but also within my brothers here that Satan is constantly wanting to reinterpret our own individual stories in order to make God our enemy. He is always working at condemning God to us, and condemning us to God. He says to us, "Do you really think you are important to God? Do you really think you can satisfy God's requirements to save your soul? If God really cares about you, why are you having to be treated the way you're treated?"

12/4/11

ARDAP is the drug treatment program here. It's a program where they move into a special dorm and live there for about six months. If they take this program, they are supposed to get from three months to a year off their sentence.

Evidently, there is a lot of experimentation going on with the program. I just visited with a guy who was in the program for two weeks and then signed out of it. He said he just couldn't take it anymore. They do things like make them do skits and tell children's stories. They have to color with crayons, moon walk on the stage, and then they ask them questions they have to answer.

They have to tell on one another if they steal an apple or an orange or cross any lines they're not supposed to. This guy was telling me about how the guys make up stories to impress the staff, and how they will go to every treatment meeting when they get out. They cry and say how much the program has already helped them. He said it's a big joke. There is a blind man in the program and a man in a wheelchair. They were in the TV room and got in a fight over the TV. The guy in the wheelchair said, "Well you can't see anyway; I'm going to change the channel." The blind man said, "I may be blind, but I'm not deaf, and I want this channel". He reached over and felt for the guy in the wheelchair with his hand, found his face, and sucker punched him in the jaw. I think they are both in the hole.

12/12/11

While biding my time, I have some great conversations with guys. We are in the last week of class in our book, and the last sessions are all about application of what we have learned. These are the best times; the guys share through tears as they find new meaning and purpose in the gospel and how it applies to life.

John Eldredge's book *The Sacred Romance* is one of my favorite books, and a keeper that I won't loan out for fear of losing it. I go back and review many parts of it. Of course *The Sacred Romance* is all about the relationship that God wants to have with us as he did with Israel. It's about how God has created a place in our hearts that he wants to fill. Even as Christians, as we love God, we still go out and find other things (lovers) to sometimes fill that spot. We fall in love with other lovers.

He talks about "resignation." When very young, we might say naively that there is complete absence of resignation. We think nothing is impossible, and the choices are all ours to make. I think of that every year as we go to high school graduation parties. I notice there are so many pre-med students. I listen to them knowing that by the middle of their freshman year in college more than half of them will have changed course. They are beginning to learn about resigning to the true facts of life. Resignation to reality brings change. Resignation is the acceptance of a loss as we move on to something less painful.

Eldredge states, "It also is a case when we live with or alongside of something of great beauty. Resignation is when we choose good as no longer startling in its beauty and boldness, but simply as 'nice.' Evil is no longer surprising. It is 'normal.'"[3] His whole book is on the romance God wants us to have with him. He calls us to love him as his "lovers." He has created a place in our hearts for him only. He wants to occupy that place, and he is jealous of that place.

One chapter in his book is titled "Less-wild Lovers." His point is that God's desire for our relationship with him is to go so deep in adventure that it scares us. We are not sure of it all so we settle for less wild lovers. We fill that space in our heart with achieving, accomplishing, recreating, building wealth, credentials, and fame. Sometimes it is sports, alcohol, drugs, or entertainment—whatever the lover of our choice may be. The beauty and awesomeness of Christ and our salvation becomes mundane to us, and we are drawn away to seemingly more exciting things but end up trading the relationship for something that is so much cheaper and will never measure up to the adventure there is in loving God.

Then he adds, "But this side of Eden, even relationship with God brings us to a place where a deeper work in our heart is called for if we are to be able to continue our spiritual journey. It is this desert experience of the heart where we are stripped of the protective clothing of the roles we have played in the smaller story of our life."[4]

Wow! I am so convicted of that. Thinking about my life leaves me with questions about so many things I have invested my time into. This experience

I am having right now is a real awakening for me. I don't think I will ever be the same. I hope I'm not the same.

12/15/11

It was a bittersweet weekend. My brother-in-law, Rog, has suffered with Lou Gehrig's disease for the last eighteen months. He went to be with the Lord a week ago Sunday. Almost my entire family was at the funeral; Amy sang, and I always love to hear that. There were two weddings in the family this summer, this funeral, and all the holidays—that's a lot to miss in one year.

I must confess, though, that events like this do bring emotions of some anxiety for both Jan and me; I am thinking of the day I walk back into Willmar again after my time is up. There will be a concern of stigma, discomfort, and being a spectacle—there is all of that for me; plus we are concerned for Jan. The discussion in our class Thursday night came around to guilt and regrets, and I shared with them my regret that Jan needs to go back and face the public without me. I was concerned for her. They all prayed for her and some even in the night because they asked me the next day how it was for her.

I think ahead to two years when I get out. You need to know that people like me in here give a lot of thought to that. I wonder what it will be like coming back to Willmar when I get out. There is a part of me inside that says I don't want to go. Yet when I hear from my supporters, I feel I owe so much to so many. I feel like someday it would be nice if we could just gather, maybe in church in Willmar or some place so that my family and I could be with everyone all at once. I would need to be careful that it is not something that looks like a celebration of me and not just my freedom. It would need to be a time of expression of the goodness of God, and how I know—and I really do know—that he provides, he is all we need, he is more than sufficient, he is sovereign, and he is faithful. That is all that needs to be said. If I can bless others, I would be so thankful. I am nothing, and he is everything. I don't need to talk about me ever again. His saints are good. Those who are redeemed know what it is to be redeemed, and they know what they have been redeemed from. In him, there is love, there is hope, and there is joy.

I've thought about Rog a lot. I watched him live life. I noticed the things that excited him and that he made much of. I've noticed in his family that there is an attraction toward beauty. They all love flowers. They all love making things pretty. Early in our family's life, we traveled somewhat together. He liked adventure and seeing new things. I'm thinking today about Rog's first days in heaven. I saw Rog's amazement with many things in life. I know that the amazement he saw and felt here can't begin to even shadow the amazement he is feeling right now: seeing the face of God.

12/23/11

If the day before Christmas is Christmas Eve, then today must be Christmas Eve Eve. At "Camp Walk-a-way" we are already celebrating Christmas. We had lockdown this afternoon so they could bring us our bag of Christmas goodies. It must be a ten to fifteen pound bag of cookies, crackers, candies, and a whole lot of other stuff we shouldn't be eating. It does create some excitement though because the guys get busy running around trading things and selling their bags for stamps.

One guy wanted only buffalo wing flavored pretzels. So we all gave him our pretzels for anything else in his bag he didn't want. He is going to make some kind of a dish out of his pretzels, and then I'm sure he will turn that into stamps and make his little fortune that way. The only thing I liked in the bag was shortbread cookies so I gave away my strawberry Newtons, and the guy gave me his shortbread cookies. Wow! Exciting!

After that they released us dorm-by-dorm and we went to the chow hall, we each got an eggnog, a bag of four cookies, and a little tub of ice cream. I am full now. I will skip the supper tonight, which is chicken alfredo. I know it sounds good, but it's made in one big tub ahead of time, allowed to set, and then warmed up. It is served with an ice cream scoop so what you get is a perfect round ball of alfredo. Yeah! It's not that it tastes bad, it's just that it's a let down the first time you have it because of the big expectation that it makes. I'm skipping the meal because I want to finish my e-mail.

12/26/11

Periodically throughout my Christian life, I have thought about the use of the word "blessing." When something really great happens in a believer's life, we say "God has really blessed you." When a new baby is born, when a significant job promotion comes, when a person comes through a very bad accident unharmed, etc., we say, "What a great blessing from God." It is indeed true that each of those things is a blessing from God, but what about the devout Christian whose new baby was stillborn or who was not promoted or who was permanently disabled in an accident? Are they not blessed by God? Do we see blessing from God as only evident in the things we really want to happen? Are those believers who are suffering in some difficult trial not blessed by God? One of the definitions of blessing is "something promoting or contributing to happiness."

12/28/11

These thoughts really occupied and lifted me up on Christmas Day as I pondered the truth of the Gospels and all the paths it led me down in thought. As usual, I woke up and wrote my thoughts. In the morning I didn't like what I wrote so I decided to e-mail my thoughts. I do have a lot of mental notes though.

In my younger years, I didn't think God would ever use me in this way. I know that in certain situations I may look extroverted, but in tests I'm 60 percent introverted. I identify with Moses when it comes to original confidence. I have felt like Moses many times. Almost all the time, I find myself in situations where I am in way over my head. God gave Moses Aaron as his mouth piece. Likewise, God has given me tools, and he has placed me here where I get to use them over and over again, perfecting their use. All my life, I recognized that I am not overly bright; I have to read slowly and review a lot. My strength is that I am a hard worker. If I have tools and know how to use them, I can be successful because I work the tools hard. I find a lot of people like myself, those who have a desire to serve God but don't have confidence in themselves. If they have a good tool, they will use it well. I think what I am doing here is very transferable, and most people can do it. I want to show them how.

23

1/1/12

I'm still absorbed in thoughts of the blessings I am receiving even now. Frankly, when I was going through the time prior to the trial, I really thought that getting hit by a semi or dying of cancer would be so much better. It would be so much easier for my family to explain and so much easier to understand. I thought there are things that are worse than death and this is one of them. In panic and terror, I tried so hard to fix my problem that I sought advice which actually made my problem worse. I couldn't imagine anything that could possibly be worse than this and didn't know of any possible good outcome.

Today, after experiencing God's faithfulness and seeing how he answers prayer and provides for my every need, I feel like I can go through anything now without ever feeling that kind of terror again. I want to be able to express that for a reason. I think days are coming when being a Christian is going to be much more difficult than it is today, and it may be in the lifetime of many who are alive right now. I don't know if people, or the church, are ready for that. I think it is quite easy to strike terror in the hearts and lives of people, even Christians. If there is anything in my life that my story can help people with, I would like to be available for that. I remember a few years ago when someone placed a bunch of stickers on car windows during church. I don't remember what they were about, but someone in the community protested that it was illegal for a nonprofit organization to do that, and we felt panic over the fact that we could lose our tax-exempt status. I hope when the day comes to stand tall for some principles that the tax-exempt status won't be an issue.

I must be honest that I am still working through it, and I'm not there yet. But I am seeing benefits in having less to take care of, less to be distracted with, and to have more time to grow, study, teach, and serve. I have known much fulfillment in all that. I feel blessed in it, amazingly blessed.

I have become very fascinated with what goes on in the heavens, even what was going on in heaven before creation. I enjoy reading about and thinking through what was going on in heaven when God was expressing his pleasure with Job. I have been reading in Hebrews, which has drawn my mind and imagination back to that.

Hebrews 10:19-25 speaks of drawing nearer to God with a true heart in full assurance of faith with our hearts. On Christmas Day, I woke up at 3:00 a.m., and I took my Bible and note pad to the broom closet and sat at the table and bench; there is good light so it is great for reading during the night. I was reading and visualizing a great cloud of witnesses, and my mind went to thinking about heaven. I was thinking about that Christmas morning along with the cloud of witnesses who are there. In my imagination I thought of Rog, my brother-in-law who had passed away several weeks before. It was so amazing.

As I saw Rog (in my imagination or whatever it was), he was a little at a distance, but I could see him well. He was not old, and he was very fascinated with what he was seeing. I could not see what he was looking at, but it was very bright and the brightness was shown all over him. The remarkable thing about Rog was the expression on his face. It was an expression of complete innocence. There was nothing that would indicate he was thinking about himself, and he was totally absorbed in what he was seeing. It was so very real, yet I was not asleep. I was totally aware of being where I was.

Then I thought that if I can see Rog I can see my dad and mom too, and I did. I saw them together, but they were not focusing on each other at all. They were completely absorbed and taken in by what they were seeing, like it would have been totally inappropriate to disturb them from their concentration. The most amazing thing was Mom. When Mom was with us, she was always self-conscious, timid, and a little unsure of herself. When I saw her, that was all gone. She had the look of innocence too, but she looked strong, confident, and very certain of herself. Dad and Mom both looked to be in the prime of their life. All of them looked, in the brightness of the light, to have a golden hew to them, like any color was washed by the bright glow they were facing.

I don't know what you think of that, and I just call it my imagination. But my imagination is a gift from God, and what I imagined came from reading in Hebrews, Isaiah, and Revelation. It was very real to me and lifted me up so much that I felt the exhilaration of it all Christmas Day and even now. Christmas Day was a great day and so unlike Thanksgiving Day. I was not lonely, even though there wasn't much going on. I took it as a gift from God and not anything of authority of how it is or will be other than that it is more wonderful than any words on the earth can express. I feel so very affirmed that God doesn't intend for us to see this place as our home, and he probably doesn't want us to get too comfortable here. This is just a tent, a vapor, a mist. The real thing is to come, and he is preparing a special place for each of us.

One of the guards committed suicide here last night. He shot himself in the head. They locked down the compound at 7:00 p.m. I guess that's when it happened. We were in the middle of a movie when they called us back to the dorm.

1/7/12

Wow! We kicked off our winter quarter classes this morning, and I'm eager to report to you how it's been. The classroom is reported to hold twenty people, but this morning we had thirty-one show up with another five wanting to get in. That is the first class.

We have two classes in the morning, and the second (advanced class) has thirteen with more coming. We are truly blessed, and it has an interesting mix of people. We have two that can't read, two attorneys, and everything in between. I was concerned about this and prayed a lot. I wanted a strong gospel presentation initially as introduction, even though the entire course is the gospel.

The gospel came through, and the men were very attentive. Normally, these men have been going to prison classes, and they expect to get nothing but a credit in their file that they came. They intend to sleep. I told them if they wanted to sleep and didn't like the class to let us know, and we would make it easy for them to get out without getting a bad report in their file. They were so attentive and were very excited when they left.

So far we have had 185 men take our classes. It's way more than I thought. Jim is keeping the record on this. It's surprising how many of them have gone home already. This is such a great blessing to me to be able to bring the Scriptures to these guys. I just couldn't have imagined that I would ever have this kind of a privilege, and even though I sense the privilege, I sense a great responsibility.

On the lighter side, we are now in a new year. I can now say that I am going home next year. It sounds a lot better. This is what I have left: 85 hamburger days, 85 fish days, 22 liver and onion days, 44 beef stroganoff days, 44 pancake breakfasts, 11 bags of espresso for the guy who cleans our room (my share), 15 books of stamps for the guy who does my laundry, and 9,900 laps around the track. Well, that's enough, but who's counting, right?

1/7/12

I had nothing going on tonight so decided just to walk the track. The last two miles on the track, I met Dale. Dale is a fifty-eight-year-old man who I observed on the compound. Just a week ago, I happened to invite him to our class. He did sign up, and I saw him there this morning. Tonight, we ended up on the track together. Dale has done very well in life, financially. He is a builder and has ended up with quite a bit of real estate. He is an unpretentious and humble man and seems sincere in all he says. When I ask him about his faith, he just gives straight forward answers and says he doesn't know much about faith. He never took the time for it before, but he thinks one reason he is here is to learn about faith. I said, "Have you been in any classes?" He said he has gone to the chapel and that he tries to read the Bible but just doesn't understand it.

He asked a lot of very elementary questions, but he asked them very unashamedly. He asked about faith and how to get it. I explained that it is a gift of God, and we can pray and ask God for it. He said, "How do I do that? I pray all the time, but the only thing I know is the rosary, the Apostles' Creed, and Hail Mary's." I said, "You can just talk to God just like you're talking to me." He said, "I don't understand." I said, "Can I pray for you?" He said, "Oh, yes." I said, "We can pray right here as we walk. We don't need our eyes closed; we only close our eyes so we don't get distracted." I prayed just a simple prayer thanking God for our walk, our conversation, and our time together. Then I asked God to give Dale the gift of faith and to give him insight and understanding of the Word.

When I finished, Dale said, "Well, that's how I would like to pray. Where did you learn that?"

I said, "When you come to Christ in faith, his spirit will enter into you, and he will teach you much more." We talked a lot more about how we know the Bible is true and other things. Then I said, "If you would like, we could meet tomorrow afternoon and sit with the Bible, and I will show you how easy it is for you to understand the Bible." He thanked me so much for being willing to do that.

He said, "Nobody has ever talked to me about things like this or showed me this stuff."

1/10/12

Sunday afternoon we met in the chapel. We went to the balcony and got chased out of there by the chaplain because the Catholics had the chapel reserved. We walked for an hour and talked then went back to the chapel. We read in John. Dale had many questions. I was surprised that he didn't really know even the most basic Bible stories. I laid it out the best I could, but I really didn't do a good job, because I was so taken back by what he didn't know. We read where Jesus told Nicodemas that to be saved he must be born again. We went over the fact that salvation is by faith. Dale said, "You mean if I don't have faith I'm not saved? Am I going to hell?"

I repeated what Jesus said.

He said, "Well, how long will it take me to get saved?"

I explained it could happen right now as soon as he decided he wanted to have faith and be saved. I told him about confession, repentance, and Christ abiding in him and that he would then live for him. I didn't really want to proceed with him in prayer because I wasn't comfortable with the little he knew. He rather insisted he wanted to be saved and born again just like Jesus said. I said, "Okay, I will pray, and then I will stop and pray a prayer you can repeat."

So we prayed, and he did pray. We finished, and he said, "But I don't feel any different." I told him that is normal. It will take a while for him to fully realized what happened.

I went to the dorm totally exhausted. I have not ever been so exhausted since I came, even from working out. I was encouraged, frustrated, and happy all at the same time. I didn't feel I did a good job. With so little knowledge he had of the Bible, I just didn't know where to start when I had so little time. It was like eating an elephant: where do you begin? Well, my comfort is that it is in the Lord's hands.

1/22/12

A number of changes have been made here, and it's funny how a lack of schedule can really mess up a person's mind. I can really appreciate the problem with people getting "institutionalized." Your mind begins running along a track, and when they change the track, you can't remember where you are supposed to be or what you are supposed to do. These guys here who have been in for ten to twenty years are really bad with changes. Moreover, they are very possessive about the smallest things and crabby about details. It will be a good thing to get out of here when the time comes. I wonder how much of that crazy stuff I'll have taken on.

Matt is growing so much. He is so rewarding to work with. His room is only two doors down from mine so we spend a lot of time together, on average more than two to three hours per day. He is so bright and so energetic. I give him my thoughts and all my books, and he gets the material so quickly and has so much passion for it.

It is worth so much to me to have such a young man who is at a point in his life when all this is so meaningful. Matt has a wife and three children, and he is taking his household responsibilities very seriously from here. Charity, his wife, is going through our class materials with him via e-mail.

1/28/12

There is a gentleman here who is in his sixties but looks eighty. He should be in a wheelchair, but they don't give wheelchairs out very easily. He has a heart problem and a lung problem. He walks with a walker that has a seat on it so he can sit down and rest.

It's a pity to see him three times a day, trying to get himself through the snow (sometimes in a snowstorm). He will have to stop and sit and rest three times between the dining hall and his dorm. Often, I come along at night, and he is sitting there in the dark trying to catch his breath. He shouldn't be here. The older population is growing because of all the new and unique ways of getting here.

1/31/21

This is a time when there is so much going on in me. I want to express it, but I'm not sure I can articulate it in a meaningful way. It comes from what I am experiencing, and it is fed by a book I am reading by John Piper, *Sovereign Joy*.

All my life, I've been one who likes to experience things, and I have become excitedly passionate about a number of things in life.

I am a pilot and flew for forty years, logging about 13,000 hours during that time. At first, it was a way to use up my GI Bill, which I was entitled to being a veteran. Flying then became a tool which helped me greatly in developing my business over a five state area. I loved flying so much, and it made my business so enjoyable. I always felt so blessed to be able to experience the joys of flying on an average of three days a week. I remember when I finally got my instrument rating and was no longer limited to flying on sunny days. I had so much greater use of the airplane by being able to fly in and through clouds. I remember the exhilaration of taking off from Willmar on a dark winter day, in a time where we hadn't seen the sun for many days, climbing to 10,000 feet, and breaking out of the clouds on top into bright sunlight. Sitting in the sunlight, while the world just two miles below me was in dark cloudy winter weather, I would land in Fargo to do a day's worth of business.

In late afternoon, boarding the plane again for the reverse home flight above the clouds, I would see the sun setting while making the descent into Willmar. I would make all the procedure turns to line the airplane up with the runway, which I could not see, and I would then descend to the decision height altitude of 500 feet and break out of the clouds with the runway lights right in front of me. What a thrill! I would go home and try to explain the thrill of the day. It wouldn't translate. One just had to be there to understand the experience.

I also love to sail. I started with a homemade sail board belonging to my brother-in-law. I was hooked. We bought a little Sunfish, then a boat a little bigger, and then one a little bigger. Finally, we had a small cruiser that our whole family could sail on together. We would spend a day on the boat with a nice breeze, the girls sitting up on the deck. Amy would straddle the bow squealing as the waves broke and sprayed her with cool spray. Tom was a boy and took the helm learning to sail. Then, as the breeze died, we would just drop the sail and drift. The kids would jump overboard, swimming, splashing, and diving. What a day with the family! What joy! Life couldn't get any better than that!

I have been intrigued with snow skiing since I was seven. I got skies for Christmas. We had no hills, just skis. I didn't really know how to use them, but I loved thinking about skiing as I saw it in pictures. Finally, shortly after we got married, we went to Grand Rapids, Minnesota, and I got to try out a hill. I was hooked. The experience progressed. We got older and had children and then grandchildren. My ultimate memory is when we went to Winter Park with our children and grandchildren. I got to teach my grandchildren how to ski down the endless runs at Winter Park. It was amazing! How could life be so filled with joy? I was so hooked. I wanted more.

I have been very passionate about these activities as well as others throughout my life. I liked business, making money, and recruiting people to a business. It has given me so much pleasure and joy pursuing them. I knew when my time became idle that this is what I would think about. I knew I loved these activities and events. I wondered about the passion and the energy I had for these things. I thought about loving God, passion for God, and how it compared with my love and passion for other things and activities.

In realizing how I was led by my passions and desires, I knew that if there was any part of what I was doing which was excessive, God would need to either take my passion away or direct my passions and desires. I preferred the latter because I want to have passion, and I like to be around people with passion. My prayer became for God to direct my desires and passions so I would love what he loved and be passionate about the things he is passionate about. I did see some transformation take place.

24

2/9/12

I no longer have Bible studies at night in the dorm because of a complaint from a roommate so there is just less activity. I am so eager to get our study material here from Antioch School. Again, the red tape of getting it in is just a killer. I started this in August. We think we have it worked out, but the guy who needs to sign off on it was on vacation last week and in training this week. It's hard for these guys to do two things at one time. It's just a signature, but you can't approach him the week he is in training. He doesn't want to think about it, and if you approach them when they don't want to think about it they will just put you off another month. Matt is going to do it with me. We won't bring any others into it because we can't find a space to meet. Two of us can meet unnoticed, just sneaking space.

When things slow down, of course, time goes slower and then even thinking goes wrong at times. Feelings are wasted and you can have little pity parties, etc. There is not too much of that, but it takes discipline to keep your mind right. There is a big guy named Bob in my dorm. He came in with a mohawk; it was cut with the top so long that it ran in a big braid down his back. Bob is from Omaha and has been a drug dealer for many years. Bob seemed to want attention from me, but I didn't give him much. Guys like that have very childish ways of drawing attention to themselves, and I read his act as that. I did invite Bob to our class the quarter before this, and he said no. This quarter he came on his own; he just showed up. The first lesson, he had nothing written; I wasn't sure if he could write or even read for that matter. The third week, I made a point to get with him. I told him I would like to hear his story. This is his story:

> I grew up without my dad. I knew who he was, but he was never around. I didn't care. The important man in my life was Grandpa. He died when I was seven. Then my friend's Grandpa became my friend, and he taught me a lot. He taught me to fight. I was a tri-state Golden

Gloves champion. He died when I was thirteen. I had nobody so I just began running with the boys on the street and that became my life. I began selling drugs when I was fourteen. I got married, and I had two children with my wife. I also have two with other women. I have been very angry with God. I don't know why he takes everyone from my life who ever means anything to me. Just before I came in here, my mother died. My girlfriend of four years just left me after I came in. Another girlfriend is writing to me. She is all I got right now, and I need her because she puts money on my account. She's the only one that writes me. My wife wants me back, too, but I left her five years ago. I know that won't ever work out. I really want God now. I've gone to him before, but I never followed through with it. I always go back to my old ways. I'm an addict; I'm an out-and-out addict. Addiction is spiritual, and I want to help other addicts get over their problems. I want God, but I know that Narcotics Anonymous is the way to help people.

Can you see how Satan so completely deceived people and what a hole he digs them into? Now, I work with Bob knowing that this hole he is in is deep and the mountain he needs to climb is high. I can't imagine how he can work his way out of this. I only know that God can do all things, even this. One of the first things that needs to be fixed is this selfish love triangle he has going on in his life.

I have helped Bob write his lesson on salvation. He says he wants to be a Christian. He doesn't know how he will do it. He is in prison for the second time. If he gets convicted, he will be a "professional criminal," which means he will receive a twenty-five year minimum sentence. It's a big hill to climb for Bob. In all my imagination, I don't know how Bob can make it. We know, though, that God can do whatever he wants to do. It's only through miraculous conversion that Bob can make it. But then is it that different from any of us?

It's difficult being in chapel. There is so much self-service in the serving. Men like to be up front, and they like to add so much drama. The power of the flesh is so evident. The chaplain's message is good. It's communion, and I feel a real need to confess my judgmental attitude toward these men. I spend my time doing that and asking God for cleansing.

I came out of the dining hall with no plan for the afternoon. I went to the theater because I heard a movie was playing. I didn't know what it was. I liked the movie; it had a great message. Not until the end did I realize I was watching *Courageous*, which was made by the same company that did *Fireproof*. Again, I felt very convicted about my judging. Almost all these men in here never knew a father. They are searching for their own identity, wanting to be a man and not knowing what a man is. They didn't now their father, and they are raising children who don't know their fathers and who will raise children who won't know their fathers. How can this end? Where can it go? Here and there, we can pluck a few out of the fire, but what a mess this world is in. They need a Savior. As much as my heart is broken over them, so much more our heavenly Father's heart is broken over our sin.

2/11/12

Tom is from Iowa City, Iowa, and comes from a family of pastors. His dad is a pastor, and both his uncles are pastors. They are from a pretty black-and-white, legalistic mind-set. Tom bolted from that when he was young. He began selling drugs at the age of seventeen and has an unbelievable background. Well, Tom is still here. We can't say his deliverance is complete, but he really has a good start. He, like Matt, has early childhood exposure to biblical truth and feels very convicted. He is extremely excited about the class and the Socratic discussion. This week Tom said, "I'm in prison almost seven days a week, but on Friday morning from 7:30 to 10:15 I'm not in prison. I am in a new world." That is so encouraging to hear. Tom is very animated in class, sometimes argues, and most of the time is overjoyed with the Scriptures he holds in his hand.

2/26/12

This morning was the last class that Dan will be in. He goes home on Tuesday. We have had people leave before, but Dan is the first one who has gone through all that we teach plus Bible studies, sometimes five times a week and then later twice a week. He has grown so much and is a great example of what we would like to see produced from these classes.

We are just finishing a quarter now with fifty men. That is by far the largest number that finished any class that is offered in Duluth. We look forward to the next group.

2/27/12

Sometimes when my daughters visited me they would ask me if it might be hard when it comes time to leave to say goodbye to these guys here. I always said I can't ever imagine that there would be anything hard about going home. Now I get an opportunity to watch guys going home. Dan shared his story in class, saying he is going home, and it was very difficult for him. There were long pauses. Last night the guys set up a pizza party for him. I was really wondering how that would go. I've not grown up with parties for men, as in real men don't do that. When the time came, Matt had some guys make five big pizzas. The crust was made out of tortilla shells. They put them together forming a large circle on a piece of cardboard, put them in the microwave to harden, and then put the sauce and stuff on and then put them back in the microwave. Well, Matt gave me the job of watching the microwaves while he ran out for a while. It turned to chaos. The Mexicans and Puerto Ricans all wanted to cook at that time. We had the room reserved, but somebody tore down our sign. I thought a big fight was going to break out, and I didn't want to be in the middle of it. Matt came back just in time and got everything calmed down. Matt's a real peacemaker; he has a good way about him.

We sat down around this big table with nine of us from our dorm. We prayed for the food, and it turned out to be a really nice time. Two of Dan's friends were there who I am not usually with. One has a wife in prison too, and she has come to faith so he was interested in what we do with our classes. I think both those guys are going to be coming to class. They became interested just by watching Dan live his life here with them.

25

3/2/12

Many of the guys here have nobody on the outside putting money in their accounts and have to live on the sixteen cents or so per hour that they make. It's not that they work that hard, but any extra opportunity to earn a little extra money is snatched up in a hurry. The snow crew gets an extra twenty cents per hour for doing that, and guys are willing to go out at 3:00 or 4:00 a.m. to do that.

It was the big snow this week so we were kept inside (I almost said locked, but we have no locks here) all day, in the morning at our work places and in the afternoon in the dorms. Matt and I got our material this week for the leadership courses so we made good use of the time. I didn't think I could ever do this, but I actually spent nine hours studying that day. It's so much fun with Matt because he is so sharp and really gets the impact of the significance of this material. He just can't wait until getting out and using this material to teach others and pass it on and disciple and plant churches with it. It's so helpful for me to have that kind of youthful energy, enthusiasm, and brightness of a quick mind to study with me. I'm supposed to be tutoring him (and he says I am), but I often think I'm getting the best end of the deal. Matt gets up around 3:00 a.m., goes to the broom closet, and studies, prays, and writes. Then around 5:00 a.m., I wake up and go in there, and he is usually so excited with what he is learning. He preaches (kind of) to me for about forty minutes. I finally have to tell him to shut up so I can get my work done.

Matt and I just marvel as we read the Bible at how perfect God's plan is and that we are in his plan. How we got here is certainly our responsibility and a consequence of our choices. But God is in control, and he uses this for his purpose. We are content to be here until his purposes are all met in our lives and in the lives of others and in the world, if he has that as part of his plan. I really want to teach that. I believe understanding that about God is the way to peace. This is an interesting place to observe both sides of that discussion. You can observe it in the conversations and the faces of the guys. Being in prison is being so out of control. Men have things going on at home and with their families that they just can't do anything about. How can one have peace if you don't think that God is sovereignly in control of all things and that he works everything for his purpose.

3/4/12

Jim has a blood clot in his lung; it was diagnosed downtown as a chronic pulmonary embolism. It was diagnosed January 24, but since that date nothing has been done. He is receiving medication daily. I don't talk about this stuff often, and there is so much more. I don't talk about all of it because it is easy for it to become life consuming. Seeing the justice system and the government from this side is very different than the general public sees it. Most of these guys really hate the government after they go through this experience. I really do think that it's also much worse for minorities.

3/16/12

There were two fights on the compound last week. One was in facilities, which is a working area; it is warehouse space where guys sit all day long waiting for some work to do. Guys get real possessive about their chairs, and there is a pecking order as to who gets the best chair to sit on. The CO told Darwin and some others he wanted to get rid of a bunch of chairs. Darwin, who is a really nice old guy who has had twenty-seven DWIs, hauled out the chairs as instructed. One chair "belonged" to a guy who came from a medium security place and was really a bully about his chair. After hauling out the chair, Darwin was in the bathroom, sitting on the toilet. There are doors on the front of the stall, and the door was shut and locked from the inside. The guy claiming the chair found out Darwin took his chair and kicked in the door to the toilet stall, put a big gash in Darwin's head, and then commenced to beat him over the head with a toilet plunger. The guards came in and put them both in the hole. Darwin might get out in a week, and I suspect the other guy will get shipped to a medium security place. All night long, they were calling guys to the lieutenant's office to question them as to what they saw.

Same day, Bob (the old guy with the walker) was in the pill line waiting for his medication. This particular lady that hands out the pills is really, really slow. A line forms and what should take twenty minutes ends up being one-and-a-half hours. There are two brothers who made some remark to Bob. Bob started pushing his walker into one of them in response to some of their remarks. Bob called one a "bitch." I didn't know it, but that word is a very bad word to call anyone around here. There are a lot of words that I thought were worse that get laughed off, but that word evidently means fight. Well, the two guys beat up on old Bob. Now Bob and the two brothers are in the hole. And there were more calls through the night for guys to go to the lieutenant's office to see if they could tell them anything about it.

I have a new neighbor right across the hall. It's a really noisy room; they are crude and loud, and there is a lot of chest pounding with a lot of curse words. And they never stop. Well, this new guy came in; he's from Arkansas, and we call him Arky. Arky has a heavy accent, and I can hardly understand him. I asked Arky if he has a family, and he told me about his children (an older set and a younger set) but no children with his current wife. Arky is about forty-four, and he tells me he has a twenty-one-year-old wife. Arky says, "Yeh, and she's a real good one too. She'll do anything for me. She cooks and clean the house; she's a real good one—and I know too cause she's my fourth one." It was really funny the way he said it. But I notice Arky doesn't hang out with the guys in the room, and I mentioned that to him. He said, "No, I stay out of that room as much as I can—I watch TV a lot." I saw him again in the dining room. I moved over by him and sat down. He prayed when he ate so I asked him if he's a Christian. He said, "Yeah, my mama took care of that before she died. She made me promise I'd go to church, and I'm gonna too cause I don't wanna put my family through any more of what they've been through with me. I've been using meth since I was sixteen years old, and I'm gonna quit now for sure. I told him about our studies, and he asked me to make sure he doesn't forget it when the sign up comes. Arky ran a large drying business for a rice farmer in Arkansas.

I thought I was done with this, when just an hour ago I was sitting on the porch, and Bill from Alexandria came up from medical. He said he was there with a man who just came back from the hospital. He had heart surgery and back surgery both at the same time. He's all bandaged up, and they were making him walk to the dorm alone without a wheel chair. He was having a lot of trouble so four guys were trying to help him. The doctor told them they had to quit helping him and leave him alone. They left the guy standing there by himself, with a lot of pain. We went over there after about fifteen minutes had passed. I guess the attention of the crowd around the guy made the doctor give in, and he gave him a wheelchair but told him he had to return it in two days.

Another guy who has had trouble getting taken care of evidently got the attention of Senator Grassley from Iowa. Grassley sent him a letter which the mail room did not open before they gave it to him. They open all other mail including legal mail from attorneys. It's against the law for them to do that, but that doesn't stop them. Things have improved a lot for him since that, and I think some others have gotten better attention too.

One of the guys has his wife do research on the outside. The BOP has a website showing all the prisoners in transit as well as the numbers who are indicted and waiting. She says that the number of inmates in transit are enough to fill two more prisons. There are as many indicted who are waiting to get placed as there are in prison camps right now. I hope that raises some questions in some minds about the philosophy of how crime is being dealt with. Just why do we have more people incarcerated by far than any country in the world. Is there so much more crime here? Is the way it's being treated working? Are there better ways that would cost the government less money? This certainly is not an inexpensive proposition for the tax payers.

25

4/8/12

I have been moved out of my room into a less desirable place. I am learning to fret less over things. Although the place I am has its faults, the whole end of the building smells—too many guys that don't shower enough and eat a lot of bad food. There is also unbelievable noise. I had no idea people could be so noisy. Some guys just do not have a conversational voice and just never stop talking. If they don't have somebody with them to talk to, they will holler out their conversation to someone at the other end of the building. If they have nobody there, they just talk anyway. I met this big guy coming down the hallway just talking really loud. I said to him, "Who are you talking to?" Then I asked him, "Who's listening?" He had some answer, but also you can't understand these guys. They have really lazy talk and don't finish their words, and even though they are third generation Americans they can't speak the English language.

We got on the computers for the first time this week for our Antioch University course. This is Matt and myself. It's really great. We feel like we are getting so much accomplished, and the time is flying. This week typing classes start so we won't have as much access to them, but it will still be good.

Now, in my new room, we will be having Bible study classes. The guys are wanting it. Isn't that amazing! Where I was, nothing was happening. God moved me against my will to where he had something for me to do.

4/13/12

It's Friday again. It's always good to come to the end of another week, and Friday is always good because that is when we have our classes. This week our new Bibles came, and they are so nice. They have a great gospel presentation—three pages just like the study Bible—and it is exactly what we need. The guys appreciate them so much. We are not able to give them out though because the CO won't allow us to distribute. I am hoping that when we distill it down to the real serious ones, we can work it out to have some less expensive (maybe soft cover) study Bibles sent in to the guys who prove themselves. We can have them sent in directly from the outside. The BOP cannot refuse that.

It's been an absolutely crazy week. Last week the regional inspectors were in and evidently they said the COs are not being tough enough. So this week we have a bunch of new rules, or just rules being enforced more strictly. They are after us more for walking between the lines when crossing the street even though there is no car traffic. The captain loves to holler and scream about that, and I do mean holler and scream. I've had it happen twice. They locked us out of the dorms yesterday and spent half a day in each dorm going through lockers looking for contraband like cheese, meat, eggs, sour cream, cottage cheese, etc., from the kitchen. Some guys got reprimanded for that.

They left with two big roller containers of stuff they took. They locked the gym and also the activity center where the TVs are and where I "work." Well, they did it without notice. I have a big heavy book bag that I need for the day. When I went to lunch I left it in the activity center because you can't have bags in the dining hall. They locked the activity center and my bag, books, notes, and everything I needed to teach my classes this morning were in there. The class went a little differently from how I had planned, but it was okay. Yesterday, we were all out on the street since everything was locked. We are not allowed to loiter on the street so we just mulled around. Whenever we would see a cop, we would move a little so we weren't congregating. I felt like we were a flock of sheep, huddled up and moving a little for the sheep dog.

This morning a man came up to me after class. Our lesson was on Peter getting the vision that the gospel was now for the Jews. This man wanted to know where the Jews came from. I said Abraham was the first Jew, and he asked who Abraham was. I asked him if he had ever been in a Bible class or church before. He said, "No, I just want to figure some of this out. I don't know anything." He seemed simply sincere about it too.

4/23/12

It's been quite different for me now that I am doing the Antioch studies. I'm kept really busy with that and haven't had the time to e-mail as much as I used to. With e-mailing, it isn't just the time it takes to do it but also the time to think about it, and now my thinking is kept busy between the two classes I'm teaching plus studying. The two classes are soon to become three. We are getting an additional time slot in the chapel for that. So we thank the Lord for that. The classes are getting good reviews with the staff and the warden.

It's not hard getting a full room anymore. Now I need to begin to turn some of the teaching over to Matt because Matt is in the Antioch program with me and needs to get the practicum experience as part of his course. Second, it's what needs to happen anyway because we need to develop new leaders to carry on.

This week we worked on repentance. Sometimes in the Scriptures it just talks about believing and having faith. In other places it talks about repentance. So this week we really dwelt on repentance. I drew an illustration on the white board of a chair representing the throne in our life with self on the throne and Christ off of it. Then, I drew it with Christ on the throne with us off of it. I'm sure you have seen the illustration. They really attached to it. It triggered conversation that was so good, and they were learning so much from one another.

Matt has two guys in his room who are really wild guys. I never dreamed they would ever come, but because of the way Matt lives and the respect they have for him, they became curious and finally interested to the point of being willing to come. They now meet with Matt between meetings with their questions. It's so amazing to talk to guys who know absolutely nothing about the Bible. It's hard to imagine anyone living in America, Christian or not, that can know absolutely nothing about the Scriptures. So it takes meeting between classes just to keep them from getting lost. The biggest motivator for them is their small children on the outside and wanting something good for them.

The guys in my room are progressing. We will have Bible studies with them too. I think it will be two Puerto Ricans and a Mexican. It will take a lot of refereeing on my part because they always communicate by shouting and arguing. In so doing they never get anything accomplished. Chas (my Puerto Rican friend who I first met when I came in) comes in all the time and fights and argues with them. Then when he wants to talk to me, the others holler and preach at him about how he needs to spend more time with me and what a sinner he is. So I have a chair beside my bed. I have him sit on the chair, and I sit on my bed; I made the rule that when Chas is sitting on that chair he is my guest and the others are not to speak to or about either one of us. It's really a circus. I have to shout and scream, too, just to be heard. When we do a study, I will have strict rules that nobody is allowed to talk about one another. If they talk, they can talk only to me and about themselves. They all talk about how Christians are judgmental, but they themselves judge constantly just to get the attention off themselves when they know they are wrong.

4/30/12

Matt did some teaching Friday, and he did so great. I know he could take the whole thing over right now and have no problem. Now, I'm hoping the chaplain will allow us to take over a little more space in the chapel and double our classes.

Still, not all things are easy. One of my friends has had a blood clot. It was never dealt with. The doctor downtown said he should be hospitalized. Ninety days later, he had large lumps forming under each arm pit. On four occasions, the nurse said he needed immediate attention. Nothing has been done. Inmates have rights and are allowed to register formal complaints. He has done that. There was no response the first time. Now, the second time he was called to medical, and they said they have approval for him to go downtown and want him to sign withdrawing the complaint. He said, "No, I'm not signing anything." He lives in fear of being shipped in retaliation.

Another inmate has been down a long time and has seven months left. His daughter is graduating from high school. He qualifies for a three-day furlough. He asked for a furlough, and he was told if he paid $500 more per month then he could have the furlough. His family got together and raised the money. He signed for the restitution, and the furlough was denied. Most people think that the government tries to do things the honest way. Not so, guys in here deal with this all the time.

I'm in this room now in "the ghetto." It's not a bad situation, but it's very noisy and smelly down there. The senior guy in the room is a short Puerto Rican and has a bad case of Napoleon complex. He also needs to control everything. One night I was flossing my teeth in the room. "Napoleon" has a store in his locker, meaning he buys stuff in commissary, marks it up 50 percent, and sells it to guys that don't plan ahead. This is common in here. They call it "their hustle." "What's your hustle" means "how do you make money?" So one night the room was full of guys buying from his store as usual. One Mexican guy said to me, "Hey, you supposed to floss your teeth in the bathroom." I didn't say anything, but this set Napoleon off. He said, "I never thought about that." First it started as a joke, but as it went on Napoleon got louder and louder. I didn't respond in any way. Everyone flosses in their own room. Then he said, "I think we should put some of these guys in a six-man room; maybe that's where they belong." He said it to someone else, but he was talking about me. After, he went on like this for about thirty minutes. I said to him, "You need to know when you've said enough." I mean, he got his point across, and needed to stop hollering about it. Then he got mad at me saying I was threatening him. It was really crazy. Now we have this room with this bad air in it. I guess this is normal prison life.

All of that—my good stories and my bad stories—is to say this. I have learned the importance, and the joy in living in the gospel. I live in the gospel first of all because I teach it every day. But in living in the gospel I find that it is a way of life that God wants me to live. Sometimes we live it in the light, but sometimes we live in the darkness. Diamonds are beautiful in the light, but even more beautiful with a dark backdrop. I find the gospel to be like that. It shines much brighter when the background is dark. My friend from India said to me one time, "The gospel doesn't usually progress as fast without persecution."

26

5/22/12

It was a different kind of class yesterday. The classes have been going so smoothly though. I had Matt lead the last two weeks, partially because of my laryngitis and partly because that is what we need to do. We need to let new leaders gain experience. This is the fifth week of the class, and it has gone so smoothly. I told Matt last week that it's a little scary. I don't know if it's supposed to be this way.

It's been hard getting things done. We have had recalls twice this week where we all have to go back to the dorm for the entire morning. It's hard to get one whole hour uninterrupted so I can get at least an hour's work done. Also, the disorganization of everything we see in here of the government is totally maddening. Now, instead of possibly getting space for two additional classes the next quarter we may lose one of the two that we have. Also, after the sign up, the applications for taking the class have to be sent to the COs for approval. Can you imagine how happy Duke will be about that? These guys absolutely hate every little piece of paper that has to cross their desk. So it's kind of a transitional time for me. I'm passing the baton to new leaders, but I will still keep my hand in it.

There are not a lot of new things in here to talk about. I recognize the problem though of just thinking about myself. That is really the poison that makes everything work. My salvation in this place is staying plugged into others. I guess that's true at all stages of life though.

27

6/3/12

It's Memorial Day weekend so tomorrow is treated like a holiday in here. It means we have the weekend routine and a special holiday lunch. I guess it's going to be larger than the normal hamburger patty and a polish sausage. It seems like the rest of the world is having a lot of summer heat, but there is some kind of a weather system between here and Minneapolis that is keeping it cool here. It's in the fifties with a strong easterly wind blowing fog in off the lake. It's really cold, and guys are wearing parkas, stocking caps, and some even mittens. Many are watching the Indy 500 where it must be right at 100 degrees.

I find I need to work harder at being positive and sensing the joy of the Lord. There are stages in life when it doesn't necessarily come easy, and I find I just need to purpose to do that. Psalm 16:11 is a good one for me. It says, "You make known to me the pathway of life, you fill me with joy in your presence, with eternal pleasures at your right hand." Sometimes I ask myself why it's so hard sometimes to feel the presence of the Lord when he is so available all the time. I know it's about me and not about him because he is always near and I am not always open. I can fret and fuss about things that are not going right, but I need to remind myself that it all belongs to him: the hearts that seem closed, the schedules that don't open, the assignments that don't get done, the competition from other activities, etc. It all belongs to him.

6/11/12

Summer is here! The weather is so great. There is nothing like summer in Duluth. I know most of you have never been up here and don't know anything about the wonders of Duluth: North Shore Drive, the South Shore, and the Apostle Islands. After four months of submitting and resubmitting my visitor list, I finally got my changes approved so I can get a handful of new visitors. Also, I have initial approval for a twelve-hour furlough this summer! The warden needs to approve it yet, but the COs have approved it. It's going to be so amazing. I think my whole family might come up to spend a day. Wow!

6/14/12

I was sent down town for a prostate exam. They did the deal with the camera up my urinary track. It looks like I'm going to have a procedure where they reduce the prostate. I'm not worried about it. It is a top medical facility here in Duluth. Just a little BOP medical comedy here. The doc here ordered a test a month ago because the doc downtown wanted it before this last procedure. I got downtown yesterday and of course it had not been done so they did it there, and we waited a while for the lab to complete the examination of the blood. Today, I got called to the medical lab here. I asked if this was for the test. She said it was. I said I had it yesterday downtown. She said, "Well this was ordered a month ago, and I have no record that they took it so I'm taking it again." I couldn't talk her out of it. Oh, for government medicine!

Arky has just finished a quarter now with our class and has been really doing good work; he seems to really be changing. About two weeks ago I asked Arky how is wife is doing. He said, "Not good. I think I'm going to divorce her. I told my sister to get the divorce papers ready."

I didn't say anything at the time, but in class he did his life application, and he seemed really sincere. This week, I was walking the track, and Arky just came along. I said, "Arky, I've been thinking about you a lot and wanted to talk to you. You want to go a couple lapse on the track?"

He said, "Sure."

So we walked, and I told him my appreciation for the work he's done in the class. He assured me he really wanted to change. He had also told me that next quarter he couldn't be in the class for the second book because of conflicts with other classes. I told him I appreciated his work in the class and especially his application, but then I said, "I'm concerned about what you told me a couple weeks ago, about divorcing your wife."

He said, "Yeah, I've been thinking about that a little bit. I think I'm going to call my sister and not send for the divorce papers yet."

Well, who knows? Maybe something as small as that might make a difference.

28

I have been heavily involved in studying and have started a new course on Paul's letters. This is a whole new level of studying for me. For our next assignment in Paul, we have to read all of Paul's letters, which is about eight books of the Bible. Then we have to work on three projects. Matt needed to step aside from teaching. Matt is a high-level person around here, and he gets asked and invited into many sporting/fitness activities and hasn't learned to say no. We addressed that, and Matt responded so tremendously well. He is stepping down from leading a lot of those things and knows he has to guard his time better. We now are on track to get our courses done by midsummer next year.

The guys are so excited and encouraged to see that new leadership can rise up through these courses. In prison everyone guards and protects their spot in leadership so much that it's always a struggle for leadership. I announced to the class this week that Matt has proven himself and is in a bachelor's program to get his degree in ministry and that the teaching he is doing is his practicum for his course. We now have three more guys who want to take the bachelor's courses. They expressed it before, but I wasn't sure about their seriousness. Now I see they have not relented on wanting to do it. Basically, they will have to go for certificates and not a degree because we don't have enough time for them to finish before I leave. They will have to live somewhere where they can finish it, or if they really do well, we will build a group (church) around them wherever they are.

Also the finances would be a challenge for the degrees; it's about $200 per month per student. For the certificate, it's seventy dollars per course. If they have resources on the outside to help them with that, we prefer they raise the money themselves to connect others with their progress.

A new guy, Rome, showed up in our class Friday morning. The first week in class, I always have the guys tell a little about themselves. I asked him if he is new to his faith. He said, "No, not really, but I don't really know. I always believed in God, and I would just pray to God like, 'Please help me not to shoot someone today.'" I asked him if he lived in a pretty tough part of town. He said, "There wasn't anybody that wanted my route." I'm quite sure he was referring to his drug route. I'm surprised he's in the class, but we are glad to have him. A number of these guys would say if they were here for crimes that they really did, they wouldn't be here in a camp but in maximum security. It's just the opposite of some who feel they received a lot more time than they deserve. We have all kinds.

7/8/12

Rob, a new guy, came in this week. I just spent two hours with him. He is not a Christian, but he wants to be. He feels so guilty about asking God to save him because he has pushed him off for so long. He said, "I feel like I'm just coming to him because I'm in a tight spot." He said, "I've been so controlling with my wife and family. I've been so jealous, and I thought I was protecting my family. Now I am afraid I'm going to lose my wife." They have been together and have seven children between them. He has lost his house and everything. His wife is afraid she and the kids will be living in a shelter. He said, "Sometimes she is nice on the phone, and sometimes she is going to leave me." He said he just can't imagine life without her. These are very typical experiences for families in this situation. I prayed with him, he comes to our class, and he wants to be a Christian. He said his parents divorced when he was seven. He always wanted to live with his dad, but his mom wanted the child support so she wouldn't let him. He said he loved his dad, but he died six years ago; he felt he lost so much. All this was said through many tears. He said he is sure she will never come to see him; she has no money. His sentence is two years.

The Fourth of July was good. I studied in the morning, and at noon we had barbecue ribs; they were really good. They fixed them outside so we could smell the barbecue all over the camp. We also had corn on the cob and watermelon. They treat us pretty good on the fourth. The rest of the day there were volley ball tournaments, soft ball tournaments, and chess tournaments. The tournaments went on through the rest of the week. I sat under a tree and talked with Steve for about two hours. It was a nice day. Actually, about three o'clock it was cool and I needed a sweatshirt. It's funny how cool it is here, and I hear how hot it is in Minneapolis. We had only one day when it was really hot. It is always cool at night, and I need a blanket on. We have no air conditioning.

I was told that I am eligible for three furloughs. At my last team meeting in May, I asked for my first one, and the two COs (one of which is Duke) agreed they would recommend me. I was to see Duke to get it through. I have chased Duke for two months since. He seldom comes to work, and when he is at work he is in his office and won't answer the door. The times I did see him, like catching him going to the office or with his door open, he just says, "Not now, I'm busy," or he says, "Just get the [expletive] out of here." This has been going on for two months. An inmate told me that he needs to just give me a form. Finding that out, I went to Mr. Baker who is his boss and told him my problem. He was really nice and said, "I think I can get you a form." In two minutes he logged onto his website and printed out the form and gave it to me. I said, "It's only three weeks away; is that enough time?" He said, "I don't know why not." I filled out the form and saw Duke in the dining hall. I said, "Mr. Duke, I need to see you." He said, "What for.?" I said, "About my furlough. I have the form all filled out." He said, "I'm not going to see you; you can report me to the administrator, the warden, or your senator. I don't care. I don't have to do anything." Well, we have been hearing that he retires this month, and he might not be back. I thought he was gone so I went back to Mr. Baker and asked him if he would help me. He didn't let me tell him the problem; he just said he would talk to Duke on Monday. The problem is that Duke is saying I did not request this in time, and it needs three months. I said, "I started this in May." He said, "No, this is dated July 3." I said, "That is when I got the form and signed it." He said, "No, Bob. I know what it says." He is making his case that I am requesting a July 20 furlough on July 3.

This is just the way everything I have done with the government works. I saw Mr. Baker in the dining hall and only got three words out. He said he will talk to Duke on Monday. First, I don't know if Duke will even be here, and he doesn't either. Second, Duke will tell him I didn't apply until July 3. This is the way it works.

Nevertheless, we have our plans made for my twelve-hour furlough. All my family will be here. We are going to Gooseberry Falls State Park to watch the children play in the pools. We will walk the beaches and have a barbecue outside. We will sing, and I will have some things to say for the family. It is my dream. I'm looking forward to it as the best day of my life. I know it's in the hands of these men. I know that God is in control. What God has for me does not depend on men.

7/16/12

Well, my furlough was denied. They said I didn't give them enough notice although even the COs said they would approve it. People have so much control and are so unaccountable and hidden; you can't uncover what they have. It is frustrating. When inmates come here, we go through their briefing to let us know how to conduct ourselves. They really make a big deal out of saying, "If you really behave yourself and take the courses they recommend and stay out of trouble, it will help you when you ever ask for something." It is so much bologna. I told Duke, "I've done everything they've asked. I have even taught two classes a week as long as I've been here." He said, "Oh, it's not about you; you're really doing a fine job. It's your file." Well, so much for that. I'm going to put in another application anyway.

What really keeps me going here is what is happening in the hearts and lives of the guys. Hardly a day goes by without some very meaningful conversation about real-life issues. I have watched Jim for over a year. He really has a sense of humor and creates a lot of laughs on the softball field and everywhere he goes. He said he has never been married and has no children, but he still would like to some day. He said, "I really would like to have some children. It would be so nice to have somebody. I'm so all alone." We talked about his trade, and he said he was a union carpenter on the outside and managed the construction of a number of tall buildings. I said to him, "Jim, if you keep coming to class, and if this all makes sense to you, wouldn't it be great if God would use your skills for his kingdom purpose somewhere where you could build a building just for God's purpose." Jim responded, "That would be so good. It would be so awesome to be needed."

I thought to myself, America is such a throw-away world. We throw away our cars after a few years and tear down buildings after twenty years, and in here we have throw-away people. Amongst the scrap heap of undesirables, there are God's elect waiting to hear someone's voice with encouragement and truth.

7/24/12

We are supposed to change our visitor list every week if we want to, but Duke has a rule of only every six months. I have been abiding with that rule, but even that made him mad. He usually shreds my requests for change, and I have to go to another CO. All this made him angry. Yesterday, Matt and

I walked into the dorm after our workout to get rid of our wet gym shirts. There were at least twenty other guys in the dorm, but he selected us out (me first). He said, "Bob what are you doing?" I said, "I'm putting my wet shirt in my room." He hollered, "Get out." I said, "Can I put my shirt away?" By then I was standing by my room. He said, "Get out." I walked out, and he hollered, "You can expect a room change too." I didn't say anything. He yelled, "Did you hear me?" He was disappointed he didn't get a big reaction from me. I said, "Yes," and kept walking. He has one day left at work before he retires. This was his last hurrah. At noon, Matt got moved to a six-man room. In the afternoon I was told I was moving to a six-man as well. I spent the rest of the day moving. When Matt was packing his stuff into his locker in his new room, one of the guys was so excited because he said now I have someone who can teach me faith. The other guy in the room hollered, "I don't want to get saved." I thought that was really funny.

Well, I moved to the six-man. It's really crowded, and the worst part is the lockers are smaller. I have to share a locker with another guy. I had too much stuff and had to throw some stuff away. I do have a bag of stuff stored in another guy's locker. Some of these guys are new and just don't have anything in their lockers. I really thought it would be worse than it is. Now, I have all English-speaking guys and that is nice. They are older and want the lights off early. I have a big light right by my bed and can read as late as I want. It is much quieter. I really slept well last night. I think maybe the noise in the other room was bothering me more than I thought. Duke has told me at least ten times that he hates white guys. I think the reason is because white guys get more visits.

Most of the Mexicans are from Texas and California, and they don't get many visitors. Most of the dorm orderlies are now Puerto Rican. Together, they get what they want from Duke, and all-in-all a move was eminent. Bummer! But again, God is in control. I think things will work out.

29

8/7/12

Tom is a young man in our class. He said I could write about his story. Tom's dad and all his uncles are ministers in small southern churches. Tom's dad left the family when he was seven. He remarried a woman with a four-year-old daughter. Tom had a sister who was four at the time. Tom and his sister were left with a very depressed mother. Tom's dad came around with his stepdaughter and showered her with good things while Tom and his sister got nothing. Tom was on the street a lot and at the age of twelve started selling drugs. By the time he was eighteen, he had already served three years in jail. Tom called himself a Christian all those years, but he lived a terrible life of sin. He went to church regularly but committed acts of sin with girls he met in church and that became his mode of operation. He made large amounts of money selling drugs and spent his summers at rock concerts selling drugs and living in orgies.

Tom got married when he was eighteen, to a minister's daughter. Both called themselves Christians, but both were going out on each other. They now have two children together, but she is living with another man who, Tom says, is worse even than he was. He is wondering what to do: now that he feels he is really saved for the very first time, he wants to know if it is right for him to try to go back to her (if she would have him) or to continue with a new relationship. I didn't give him any answers other than some references and told him to get everything in neutral and let God lead. Tom is really, really changed. His attitude and countenance are just totally different. Before he couldn't stand me because of his father, and I couldn't stand him because of his attitude. What a change!

8/19/12

The Lord is causing people to see me in favorable ways. I know Duke didn't, but in spite of the medical department here, I am getting good care. There are a number of guys here walking around with bags on their legs with catheters in them. They can't seem to get surgery. Some have gone six months this way. I was called in last Thursday for my pre-op physical. They are going to do my prostate surgery next week. I told the doctor downtown that I didn't want to come back with a bag, so he said he would keep me over night. The BOP has approved that so I will stay overnight. I feel very blessed and unworthy.

The courses are going well. We are making great progress now. Really the days just fly by. We are getting good time to study, and we put in long days on it. We are studying the Epistles now, and it's amazing for me to experience the transformation in my own thought. It is good to see Matt's progression of thought as well. Matt has started a class of six guys, teaching them the Acts course on a non-certified basis. I didn't think they would get it because the reading is hard and they are required to write projects, but they are really getting a lot out of it. They are amazed at the large picture God has for the progress of the gospel. Almost everything they have been exposed to is, "If you give your heart to Jesus you can go to heaven and not hell."

A friend sent me the book *True Spirituality* by Francis Schaeffer. I think it's going to become my new favorite. This is just one little piece I love so much. It helps me examine myself:

> Coveting is the reverse side of the law of love. Do I love God with heart and soul, mind and strength, or do I covet against God, that is, do I desire God's prerogatives for myself? Do I worship and serve myself, and pursue my own desires for comfort, pleasure and security, or do I worship and serve the Lord himself? Do I love my neighbor as myself, or do I covet against my neighbor? Do I desire what he has and envy him for his gifts, possessions, or leadership? Would I secretly rejoice if he lost his position of leadership, or be wretched inwardly if he gained recognition that I do not receive? When there is such a "coveting" there is no purity.[5]

8/29/12

It's Thursday evening. Yesterday morning the cop woke me up at 4:30 a.m. and told me to report to control by 4:55. I knew what that meant. I got surgery, and the doctor downtown kept me overnight so I just had a two-day retreat in the hospital. What a great hospital, great doctors and nurses, great food, my own personal TV, and even my own remote. My heart is so full of gratitude to God. I am so blessed.

I got in the hospital for surgery at 5:30 a.m. I didn't have my surgery until about 2:00 p.m. It gave me a lot of time to sit in the hospital room by myself. I began thinking that if I was on the outside I know Jan would be with me, and some of the kids would be with me. It's not that I would need it; it's just the way they are. Then I realized that they were all praying for me at that time, and I began praying for them. I didn't pray for a long a time, but I sat there half lying and half sitting up as you can do in a hospital bed, but what was so amazing was that I had a wonderful sensation of the presence of the Lord and how good and wonderful everything is and is going to be. I wasn't thinking in words and can't say the Lord was speaking to me, but I spent a long time sitting there being assured how good things are because he is in control. It made me brave, not just for the surgery, but for all the things I have asked the Lord for.

The surgery went so well, about two hours, but I stayed in the hospital all night and all the next day until 3:00 p.m. I have no pain. I didn't need any pain medication. I feel the doctor just did me a big favor by letting me be in the hospital that long. I know God answers prayer; he is good, and all good things come from him.

30

Matt and I talk often of how we sense the Lord's presence. We really miss being with our families, but the sense of purpose we have here is something we are so grateful for. We would rather be here with this purpose than to be out without it. God is so good and showing us his works every day. I'm so glad Steve talked me into working on my degree in ministry. Matt and I are gaining great vision from the study of Acts, and now we just finished the Epistles. We are just beginning the course on "Sound Doctrine." So far it has really challenged us, sensing God calling us to ministry beyond what we had dreamed or thought before.

We are seeing how important the home is in the progress of the gospel. It brings to bear such a bigger picture in husbands loving their wives and wives submitting to their husbands than we can ever grasp without seeing it as actually part of the gospel. When we see how our marriages and homes are meant to actually adorn the gospel, it calls us to commitment beyond even our marriage. It has an eternal purpose, and it is transformational for the guys to understand that.

It was two months before Bob could get into a class, and I was concerned about that much time passing. But when class started, he was there. We have ten weeks of class, and for the first seven weeks, Bob had a lot of intellectual resistance to how we know the Bible is true and how a holy God could send anyone to hell who hasn't, for example, heard the gospel. It always seemed he was being skeptical about everything. The last three weeks his tone has changed. This week he said for the first time he is feeling peace in his soul. Then he said, "What worries me is if I die and go to heaven and my wife and daughters don't; I'm going to feel bad about being there." Tonight he called me out of my room and told me he has about two hours per day he would like to put to good use. He wants to start reading the Bible and outlining what he reads, and he was wondering where to start. I told him to read John and then James. It's so good to know that we are not on our own when it comes to ministry. The Holy Spirit works long after we have said our last words.

9/23/12

I picked up a staph infection. When I got back from the hospital, I got boil-like sores under my left arm. It took me four weeks to get an appointment with the nurse. He put me on "bacterium" for two weeks. The next day (yesterday), I got taken downtown for my post-op visit. The doctor there confirmed it was staph and also confirmed they have me on the right medication. I was thankful for that. As an aside to that (rather humorous), yesterday, when they took me downtown for my post-op appointment, they woke me up at 4:30 in the morning. I woke up with a flashlight in my face. They only told me I was to report to the central office by 4:50. They never tell you what it's for, but I figured I was going downtown. I only thought it was strange so early in the morning.

When I got to the office they said I was going downtown and wouldn't be back until 4:00 p.m. This sounded really strange, but I went. The town driver dropped me off in front of the surgery center. I roamed the empty halls of the hospital until I met a lady who said she would look my name up on the computer. She said, "Your appointment is not until 11:30." Then she opened the sealed envelope I was carrying for the medical staff. The order in my envelope was that I was to have surgery at 9:00 a.m. Well, of course, I explained that I already had the surgery, and the hospital knew it because of their records. I was to wait until 11:30 for my doctor appointment at a different building. So at 5:30 a.m. I was wandering around downtown Duluth (in the skyway) and really enjoying the scenery. I saw the sun rise over Lake Superior, I could see Canal Park, and I saw the lift bridge and all of downtown. It was a beautiful scene. After about an hour of that, I found a really nice waiting room where people sit while their child is having surgery. No one was there, but there was a fresh pot of coffee and a basket of fresh cookies and a big screen TV. I had the channel changer all to myself and watched whatever I wanted. I sat there for three hours. Then I went to another waiting room and read all their magazines. Finally, at 10 a.m., I went to the waiting room where I was supposed to report and turn myself in. All that is to say that God's blessings come disguised in various forms, and they need interpretation. It made me a little upset that the medical people here in the prison can't seem to keep their records straight at all, but being on my own in downtown Duluth for five hours was rather nice.

The after-surgery report was good. Everything is working fine for me. I had forgotten that it is normal to not have to go to the bathroom all the time.

I can't believe how great this is! I had a great doctor, and the hospital here is first class. I was glad I could have the doctor downtown look at my staff infection, and he confirmed that they were giving me the right thing. All-in-all, the trip downtown was great. It was a nice reprieve from the mundane.

9/30/12

Right about now is the beginning of my last year here. This will be my last winter. I have been counting the seasons more than the days or weeks. I'm thinking it goes faster if I don't count. I hope time doesn't slow down. There are always rumors that there are going to be big cuts and that home confinement time might be doubled. That would be nice because it would give me another five months off. I don't really dare think about that (although I just did, didn't I?).

Jim finally got downtown to have the lump under his arm taken care of; he had a biopsy and had surgery. Part of it was cancerous, but they felt that they got it all. After three weeks, he got another call that he had to go downtown to see the doctor. He didn't know why. When he picked up the form that morning it said it was for surgery. Well, Jim knew my story about the surgery so he thought it was just another mistake. When he got downtown they took more biopsies. He waited in the waiting room, and the doctor called him in and said, "Well, we are going to save your arm." Jim kind of laughed and wondered if this was a joke. The doctor said, "Didn't they tell you? We called you ten days ago to tell you that we think you might have cancer, and if you did we might have to take off your arm to save your life. The tests came out negative." Jim didn't take that very lightly; he said he would never have let them take his arm off. When he got back he addressed the doctor on the compound. He said, "You were supposed to tell me." The doctor said, "Well, I just thought I wouldn't upset you, and you would find out in due time."

31

10/14/12

It's Monday, a federal holiday. The difference here in a holiday is that it's just like a weekend. We can sleep in late if we want, and there is no work call. For most of the guys, it's not a welcomed change. The routine of going to a work site and the moving around that it involves makes the day go by much faster. They do give us a holiday meal which today was turkey and mashed potatoes. I think in reality they just moved the Thursday meal to Monday and called it a special meal.

I have a new roommate named Will. He is forty years old and has been incarcerated for seventeen years; he has five years to go. He claims to be a Christian. He is a nice guy but a hard one at the same time. Guys that have been in prison a long time really become interesting and difficult people in many ways. He explained what life is like in a medium security prison. It's much more harsh than it is here. He said they are totally separated by race, gang, or other. He said you better be part of a group, or you're in trouble. He said you can go to the laundry room and wait in line and just keep on waiting because guys will come in and let others in line in front of them because they are of their group. You just won't get a washer (laundry). When you go out in the yard and want to sit on a bench, you can't sit on that bench because it belongs to a different group or gang. He said if you don't want to join a group or gang, you go it alone and you'd better be ready 24-7 to take care of your-self. You just don't dare turn your back on anyone, even sleep half awake all the time. You will either get beaten or raped or extorted. If they see that you shop and buy things in the commissary, they will say, "We see you have a lot of money coming in. We will have 40 percent of everything you buy in com-missary." He said if they catch you urinating in the toilet rather than the uri-nals, they won't talk to you about it. They will go to the head of your gang. No gang wants another gang to "take care" of their people. Their own gang will take him into the bathroom and beat him while the other gang stands at the door to be sure it's done well enough. Fortunately, there is none of that here, but when the guys come from those systems they think a lot of this should be operated like that.

10/18/12

For the most part, they try to keep prison life to somewhat of the rhythm of civilian life, that is, the weekend is (kind of) something to look forward to. For those who get visits, it really is. For the many others, it's a struggle, but Saturday night usually means movies in the chapel, movies in the theater, an open gym for workouts, the activity center for watching TV, playing pool, or playing cards. That's how it's supposed to be. Today is different. I had a visit so I didn't get in on the excitement, but someone stole a DVD monitor so they did a recall, and everything is shut down and everyone must stay in the dorm. We just had dinner (spaghetti and meat sauce), and now we will be back in the dorms again for the night. I don't know how long this will last, but they want us to believe it will be until someone confesses to the action. I doubt that will happen. I hope this doesn't continue all day tomorrow.

There is word going around again now that due to the cuts coming there is a bill going before Congress again that would double our good time. As it stands, I get six months good time (time off the sentence). If this bill would go through that would be changed to a year. It means instead of going home in October I would go home in April or May.

It's hard to know how to pray for this. He knows the purpose of this much better than I do. At the same time it would be so awesome to go home in April. I really don't dare think about that too much. Matt would get a year off his sentence if it went through. I think it would be a really good thing. I have a hard time seeing how extended time here does anything at all for these guys. It is expensive. They say for young guys it costs the government $45,000 per year to have them here. For men over 60, it runs $60,000 per year because of medical costs. It would be a good way to save some money. The report is that they are 35 percent over capacity in the whole system anyway. Men are being held in county jails waiting to get in.

32

11/11/12

Rob is now in the marriage class. I emphasized in the first class that he wouldn't be able to fix his marriage until he fixed himself first. Of course that means establishing himself in the ways of Christ, which Rob says he has done (but he has so far to go). His talks on the phone are never pleasant because he gets frustrated because he always ends up telling his family how to live. This morning we told him again that he just needs to focus on himself. When the guys say they just can't do anything about their marriage and family until they get home, I tell them they must begin to do things now. First, they need to pray for their own heart—that it will change. Next, they need to write to their families about things they can't say: how they know they need to change, how they are praying for change, and how sorry they are for not being the husband/father that they should have been. This is terribly hard to do, but the guys who have done it have strong testimonies as to how it helps their family and relationship. Rob has been very depressed, always has red eyes, but now says he is starting to get a measure of peace. He still refers to this process as "getting religion." We are working on that.

11/22/12

Two weeks ago I had Antonio with me. Antonio is Portuguese and trains leaders throughout the entire Portuguese-speaking world. I did not know that Portuguese is the fifth most used language in the world. We are praying and working to keep that ministry supported. Also Javier, who does this training throughout the Latino world, was here, but I did not get to see him. Today, Thinigarin was with me. Thinigarin is from India. He works with the same material we use here in Duluth FPC and is training leaders through a network of leaders.

I want to tell you about him because so often we think of internationals as uneducated and needy people. This is really not true. Both Antonio and Thinigarin have their doctorates in theology and train at a very high level, and they do so on very little financial support. Thinigarin trains leaders of leaders in fifteen different church expansion projects. He is training them in the course material I am taking. Most of these men have been in ministry for ten years or more. They, in turn, are each training fifteen pastors who train pastors. Each of them oversees a church planting movement and trains fifteen pastors leading churches. This means 1,500 men are being trained and have 75,000 men in the same courses we are teaching here. The strategy in India is exactly the same as the strategy we want to implement in Kansas City and beyond.

11/25/12

I'm still in a six-man room, and the protocol there isn't the most pleasing. An inmate at education got jealous of the time we are on the computers and got the head of education to put us on a timer so we can't be on the computers whenever they are available. We have to wait until the time expires and that greatly reduces our time. I got a "shot" (can be serious and mean losing visiting privileges, commissary privileges, and even loss of good time) for walking on the street with my radio on and ear buds in my ears. I'm losing my inspiration. I have been told that the last year gets like that where things get on your nerves a little bit more. Three days ago a second CO committed suicide. The other one was about eighteen months ago. One of the guys rode to town with him awhile back. He said he hated his work but had twenty-one years in and couldn't quit now. His funeral is here in the chapel today as I am writing this, which means he has no church and has hardly any family. The COs never go to church here so this is a little unusual that his funeral is here. It's really sad for people who live and die without the Lord.

A few days ago I just came to the realization that I'm not thinking about or asking God for vision like I used to. I used to ask him daily to show me his glory. I realize I have stopped doing that. I stopped asking, and I stopped looking for it. During that time I also began to think and be concerned about getting out and going home. What will it be like? Will I face challenges I don't face here? Will the reality of my life changes hit me harder than I expect?

I realized that the things I used to be thankful for I already take for granted. I came to the understanding that it all depends on my pursuit of God. If my pursuit of God continues as it did when I came in, I don't think I will have a problem. I will need ministry. If I pursue God for it, he will give me a great appetite for ministry, and I will find it. If my eyes become attached to people and circumstances, my heart will wander, and my soul will become unsatisfied. It seems that pursuing God is not a passive thing; it is active. It takes time and attention. God is so good.

It's been about four days now since I began thinking through all this. I am back to asking God to show me his glory and his purpose like I used to do. I ask God for that throughout the day and am conscious of him on my walks.

Several days ago Peter asked me a biblical question. I told him I had my Bible in education so we should go there. Peter is a Christian, but he has chosen to take a hard, legalistic view of God and how we should expect others to live life. He has a beautiful family. His wife is Korean and a very bright, talented individual. They have five boys and one girl and a remarkable family; they are well-behaved and very loving. She is in Chicago with the family and has had to move from a very large house (they had been doing very well) to a three-bedroom apartment. I have been hearing through Jan, via his wife, that Peter is leaving her when he gets out, and she was asking for help. I have to be very careful in prison about "getting into someone else's business." A lot of trouble can come from that. Peter would never open up to me. This day Peter opened up to me about what he perceived his problem to be with his family. Peter is very smart and knows the Bible extremely well, but he is very legalistic and always goes back to the "original Greek" to prove his point. One can't win an argument or discussion with Peter. This day I was able to have my first real conversation with Peter, one where we set the Bible aside and Peter let me in on what really is bothering him. We talked for two hours. Although Peter has resigned himself to a divorce and not going home when he gets out, I feel there is a crack in his hardened heart.

Two days ago, I had to meet with the committee to determine what should become of my shot demerit that I got for listening to my radio on the sidewalk. I met with the three guys. They asked me if I had anything to say about it. I explained that the report was right and that I had been walking the track (where the radio was legal), I got called to education, and forgot to take my radio off. I noted that the CO from the kitchen felt his question was answered. I was told to leave for a few minutes. Then I was called back. He asked me if I would be willing to do ten hours of extra duty in place of the shot. I said I would and was told to report to the CO in the kitchen for the extra duty. I went to him the next day. He told me to give him my paperwork. I did. He marked it with the date, and he credited me ten hours of work. He said, "See that piece of paper there on the floor? Throw it in the garbage; you're done."

Yesterday, another friend whom I meet with a lot came to me. He said, "I've been wanting to talk to you, but you look busy every day." I said I wasn't, and he just wanted to tell me how great his visit was last weekend with his family. He has been troubled by not being able to share and open up with them about what is going on in his life. He said he is now doing a Bible study and corresponding through the mail with them. When he said we need to pray together, his youngest (who he was afraid was drifting from him) jumped up on his lap and offered her prayer, which he said was so good.

There is an application to be made in writing after each lesson. One man has been married and divorced three times. He said, "Now I know I married for the wrong reason every time. If I ever marry again it will be a lot different." The next man has been divorced four times. He said, "I don't think I will ever marry again, but I need to spend time with my adult children. I need to get this information to them."

One man is married with six children. He never talks in class other than to tell us how broken his marriage is, how much guilt he has, and how depressed he is. He doesn't know if he can save his marriage. He says, "It is my fault. I have been so controlling. My wife has not had a good life

One man has a wife and four small children. He tells how when he came to prison he had been unfaithful to his wife, thinking she couldn't give him what he needed. When he started the classes he began writing to her. He said now his marriage is so good, and he never thought they could have a relationship like this. He has sent her a copy of *First Principles*, and they are going through it together through the mail and talking on the phone. One man said that he is saddened in that he was not a spiritual leader to his family. He thought if he provided for them and made sure they got to church on Sunday, he was doing a good job. He said how bad he feels about not being a leader to them. He said, "I thought it was other people's responsibility to teach my family."

After a lot of straining and sweating, he finally got a letter to each one of his children and his wife. He said they appreciated it so much. He said it took a while, but now when they come he prays with them and talks about the Lord. He said the first time he did it he was just a basket case emotionally. He said, "I cried like a little girl, but it was an amazing time." He is now doing a study on the book of John with them through the mail. Guys are learning what it means to be the spiritual leader in their homes. They usually say, "I will do that when I get home; I can't do it now because I'm here." I tell them that this is the best place for you to learn it. As a man, I have found, it's easier to open your heart in a letter than in person. You have time to collect your thoughts and say what you mean. And if you don't begin now, you will never do it when you get out. It is true. The pressure of being incarcerated, or any crisis in life, puts the pressure on a person. It squeezes us like an orange. It is up to us to yield ourselves (give up the juice) to Christ so that by his grace good things can come out.

33

12/4/12

Well, Thanksgiving's gone, and Christmas is coming. I think we are making headway. I had two interesting requests this week. A Mexican inmate named Flaco, who is a Latin King and just kind of a joker and is hardly ever serious about anything, asked me about the class. I told him the next one starts in January. He said he wanted to be in it and to be sure to let him know. This week he said, "Goris, take my information so you can sign me up for that class." As I was taking his information, X, who is also a Latin King and started the class once and dropped out because he always had Jehovah's Witness objections, said, "I want to take it now too. I got rid of all my Jehovah's Witness stuff, and I'm not Jehovah's Witness anymore."

Now the challenge comes that we have a third man who is also a Latin King. He is a friend of Matt, and Matt says they might not open up in class if there is another gang member from the same gang because of the commitments they have had to make to the gang. I don't know what to think about this, but the Spirit blows where he wishes. If God is in it, it will work. But only then.

The more I comprehend of the depth of my fallen self, the more amazing the grace of God becomes. Oh, that I could comprehend and communicate this more clearly. Can it be done? Has it taken seventy-four years for me just to understand this myself?

This is the message I would love to be able to communicate more than anything else while I'm here and when I get out. The travesty of sin is such a big idea. The holiness of God is such a big idea. The grace of God is such a big idea. Nothing is so deep, so vast, so important, or more exciting. Romans 11:32-36 says, "Oh the depth of the riches and wisdom of the knowledge of God! How unsearchable are his judgments and how inscrutable his ways! For who has known the mind of the Lord, or who has been his counselor? Or who has given a gift to him that he might be repaid?"

12/8/12

Rob said his relationship with his wife, Peggy, has gotten better, but it's so hard being on the phone with her because she just cries all the time. They have seven children, and three of them still at home. The ones at home are sixteen, fourteen, and ten. He was a carpet installer and had a very good business because he is the best in the area and takes really good care of his customers. He has always provided for his family, and his wife did not work outside the home. When the economy slowed down, he started selling things on eBay. His neighbor brought him some things to sell, and it was a good business. Later, he found out that the stuff he was selling was stolen, but by then the money was so good and they needed it so bad. He kept doing it. Finally he quit it because he became convinced in his mind it was wrong.

Two years later the FBI contacted him, and he was arrested. He said he had a nice house they were renting, a new truck for the business, and a thirty-two-foot camper that they used a lot in Door County. He had it all financed, and he had only a few days to get things ready to go to jail. He sold his truck and car and got an older car so his wife has that. He moved his family into a small duplex unit to lower the rent to $450 per month. His wife dropped him off and that's when she was not wearing her ring.

Peggy got a job and is one of the top people there, but business got slow. She is one-and-a-half months behind on rent and some other bills. She bought a ham so they could have a Christmas dinner, but it was delivered to the house and stolen from the front door. Someone broke into the house and got her computer information. The credit card company stopped her credit card because someone was trying a lot of pin numbers trying to make it work. She said she has no money for Christmas and can't even get to the boys' wrestling events.

He says he can't focus because of thinking about his family. Today he said he never thought of himself as a criminal and still doesn't so he doesn't talk to anybody in here because he doesn't want to have anything from these guys rub off on him. I asked him what he does all day. He said he just sits in his room and looks at the wall. Rob says he goes to the chapel about five times a day to pray, but he doesn't know what to say anymore. He thinks God is mad at him and is punishing him. I tell these guys that this is not punishment. Punishment will come in eternity for those who do not repent, and it is hell. This is discipline, and for those who repent, this is to condition and prepare us for greater things. Rob says he is encouraged now. Peggy now talks a lot about him coming home and that she never did stop wearing her wedding ring. She just told him that. Rob says that's been hard, but it's been good for him because it caused him to look over the edge and see that he really could lose his marriage. It does make him more committed to changing his attitude and demeanor at home. One last thing Rob said was that when Peggy was fifteen years old her stepfather sexually assaulted her. She attempted suicide at that time. He said he doesn't like to think this way, but he is concerned for his wife now. She is so desperate.

12/12/12

Jan visited me on Saturday and gave me this verse to have as our Christmas verse: "Rejoice in hope, be patient in tribulation, be constant in prayer (Romans 12:2)." It's appropriate for us because we can only do that because of the Christ of Christmas.

12/19/12

Thursday night I walked out of the library, and Rob was waiting for me. Every night when Rob gets off the phone, it is a very difficult time for him, hearing of the stress his family is going through. Thursday night it was different. It was like Rob was a whole new person. He said his wife got five Christmas cards and five hundred dollars in them (from our prayer partners). He was laughing and crying at the same time. He said Sue was so happy. She went right to the landlord and paid some rent. She said some of them even had pictures, and the family was going to read the cards together and then watch the movie *It's a Wonderful Life*. Rob said he just didn't know what to say, because they have never experienced anything like this. It was a wonderful experience for me as well. It was like a wonderful Christmas present for me, and I am so happy for them: to think that a family can be so happy to get money for Christmas so they can pay the rent, let alone have any presents.

It is now Sunday. Now, they have received $1,200. They are so thankful and in disbelief. Rob's wife is now going out to buy some underwear and school supplies the kids need, and that will be for Christmas. They have never seen anything like this.

I spend hours every day talking to guys who have come to Christ but deal with very much depression and regret. Sometimes, the more they learn about how the family should have operated, the more regret they have. That's the way it is with Rob. But I know that as we give of ourselves to these people, we need to give them as to the Lord. When we do it for the Lord, their response or lack of, will not slow us down or disappoint us. We never waste our energy or resources when we do this for the Lord. After all, he is the one who does all the important work in it.

12/20/12

Since our room is somewhat of a transient room, two of the beds change constantly. Of the four of us who stay, one is Mac. Mac was a stock trader and managed a portfolio. When 9/11 happened, the portfolio went down, but he lied to his investors thinking he could build it back real fast. He didn't and was convicted and got a ten-year sentence. His children at the time were ages six, twelve, and sixteen. Two days after he was indicted, the FBI told his family they had to move out of their house. The church helped them with a small apartment for a few years, and now they have a very small rental house in a not-so-good part of Chicago. The church has had to help her get her heat turned back on several times and has been very good throughout the years, but the last years they said they have so many to help they can't do much anymore. His wife Laura has on-going depression to the point that it makes it hard for her to function and make good decisions. Mac gets out in May.

It is now Monday. As I was writing, the family surprised Mac and showed up Sunday and stayed until Monday. I asked Mac how they did it, and he said she just spent money she didn't have. When he asked her she said, "I just won't be able to pay the bills this month." He said that is what she does. I met the family. They are very nice, polite, and personable, especially the sixteen-year-old. He loves to talk.

12/24/12

It's 8:00 a.m. on Wednesday. An hour ago I was watching the news on TV. Bob, the attorney from Oregon, came to me and said, "Can I talk to you?" I said yes, and he led me off to another room far in a corner where nobody was sitting. He said, "Bob, I've had the most wonderful experiences these last few days and especially this morning. I've been going to the chapel to pray. I get down on my knees and this morning I had a wonderful and real overwhelming experience with God." He said, "I am so sure that God is real and what he says about creation and how the world was formed is all true. Bob has a twelve-year sentence, and although he is from Oregon he was incarcerated first in Brooklyn and then Minnesota. Finally in his seventh year, he is going to be in Oregon at a camp twenty minutes from home.

Then he said, "When I was in Brooklyn, the government wanted me to do something for them." They said they had an additional case they would put on him if he didn't and would get another twenty years if he didn't do it. He said, "I remember saying, 'I wish I could die.' That night, I got a terrible pain in my stomach. It was severely painful, and I didn't want to die. I started saying the Lord's Prayer, and my pain went away." He said he wasn't a believer, and when he met me he was saying that intelligent design and other things couldn't happen. He was too intellectual to believe that. About a year ago, Bob prayed to receive Christ but couldn't get into our class. I didn't have much contact with him, and I doubted whether his salvation was real. He has come to class now for twenty weeks, and I have had personal time with him. He has been growing.

I told him this morning that these sensations that he is experiencing are signs from God especially for him. I cautioned him to realize, though, that God doesn't live in the chapel, and that his spirit lives within him and he can call on him at any time. The signs and wonders and miracles are wonderful, but the Lord doesn't want us to live for them. He wants us to allow him to open our hearts and minds to his word and to pray before opening the Word so that the Holy Spirit will reveal himself. I always sense that Bob, though having a brilliant mind, isn't into the Word like I would like to see. He asked me again what he should read, and I suggested him reading James five times. He said he would.

He was very excited this morning and said he believes so strongly now, and he almost feels like he should become an ambassador for this. It's interesting when people are fresh and don't know the normal lingo Christians use. It's refreshing. I told him God wants him to be a normal Christian man enjoying life and being very open and honest about his faith in Christ. That is exactly what he said he would never do before when he wanted to become a Christian. He said he would never talk about it. It is wonderful to see God's hand moving.

34

1/1/13

Rob just has a smile on his face all the time. His family has changed so much, and his phone conversations with his wife are all pleasant. She sounds like a really great person. The newest thing that has happened is really miraculous. Rob had two children before marriage, and Peggy had two from a previous marriage; they have three together. They have raised all seven together, except for Rob's oldest son. They were raising him in their home, but he had an incident in the home when he was twelve and another when he was fifteen, and Peggy couldn't have him in the house anymore. He was sent to a foster home and then to a halfway house where he lives now. He is now twenty.

Rob said he had to choose between his oldest son and his family, and it has been very difficult for him. Peggy said she never heard the right kind of apology from him and couldn't have him in the house until he did. Now, while Rob is here in prison, his son is on Facebook. Peggy "poked" him, and now they are friends on Facebook. Yesterday, because of the Christmas money, they were driving to the place where they shop (about fifty miles away), which is right near where the son lives. Peggy arranged to pick up the older son and take him with them for the day. She reported back that they had such a great time together. The children all hugged each other and were so happy to be together. Rob has not seen his son for three-and-a-half years. He said it's just a miracle that probably wouldn't have happened if he was home, because his wife had to have the freedom to do this on her own. Rob just said, "This is a miracle."

A friend said his church would like two inmates' names who live in the area and that they would like to do something for them through their church. One of the names I gave him was Tim. Tim is a good friend and has taken some of our classes. Tim has two sons but isn't married. Since Tim became a Christian, I encouraged him to explore the possibility of marrying his sons' mother. After some time he said he just didn't think it would work out. At Christmas they all came up for a day to see Tim. After the visit Tim came to my room to tell me that the visit went really well, and it looks like a good possibility they might get together. Tim assures me they won't live together, though, unless they marry. I believe him. Sometimes, just a little bit of help, resources, and human interest can go a long way in healing lives. I enjoy this so much, but I am careful. I get thanked by the people who receive the gifts, and I get thanked by those who give the gifts; still, I know that none of the thanks goes to me. I'm just the messenger. All the glory goes to God, and he is jealous for his glory. I don't want to rob God of his glory.

I talked to the guys this week about anxiety, and I find myself talking a lot about how God wants us to learn to live and depend on him day by day. This is a big lesson for me to learn myself. I talk about the children of Israel in the wilderness for forty years. Jan and I took a biblical studies trip to Israel with a man who has his doctorate in Old Testament history. He took us out into the wilderness where Israel spent forty years. I always pictured the wilderness as desolate, but I never saw desolation like that wilderness. It reminded me of millions of acres of a gravel pit. It's just rock and boulders—hills of it, with nothing growing and no water. I tell the guys how God wanted Israel to live one day at a time. He gave them manna for food, but they couldn't gather more than one day's supply. He wanted them to trust God for each and every day. I'm trying to teach them something that I'm not sure I have learned myself, but I want to learn this. I believe it brings more glory to God.

1/6/13

I'm going home this year. I've been waiting a long time to say that. Time is going fast, and I am thankful for that. Yesterday, I moved out of the six-man room and into a four-man. It is so nice. I had become accustomed to the six-man and had forgotten how nice it was to be in a four-man. There is still one other empty bed, but my roommates are Mexicans and very clean and respectful. I was really concerned at first because other guys on the floor call the room "The Casino." They told me they do play cards, and I thought I might have to leave again soon. Some of the guys are very noisy when they play cards; they slam the cards down and use constant vile language. My friend Peter, however, always looks after me, and he got me this room. He took the guys out in the hallway and told them they needed to take care of me and respect me. He said I am a "holy man." How about that?

Asians and Mexicans really respect age, and I do benefit by that. They played cards last night but were very quiet. I have ear plugs. I used them and put a sweatshirt over my head to block out the light and went right to sleep. I never slept with ear plugs in before and thought I had grown accustomed to the noise, but I really slept last night like I haven't slept in a long time. I think this will be a good room.

Today we had prime rib and shrimp for dinner, at least prison's version of it. The meat was way overcooked and the shrimp mostly bread, but it was good anyway. The Rose Bowl game and movies in the chapel will be the program for most of the guys. Also, they have an inmate concert in the theater. It is mostly hollering and screaming into way over-amplified sound systems. It's a good place to stay away from.

I have been reading *The Zion Covenant*. It's a historical novel of the lives of the Jews during Hitler's regime and includes events leading up to World War II. It has deeper meaning to me after going through my experiences of the last two years, especially the experience of being under investigation and prosecution.

One of the hardest things for me was that the government lied three times before I even got to trial about why I was a flight risk. The flight risk accusation got me seven weeks in county jail, including the horrible ride and being shackled in the van to, from, and between prisons. Then there was the great bus ride to Duluth with prisoners who committed any kind of crime, with a shotgun escort. The flight risk is still on my record and came up the last time I asked for a furlough. The other thing that stays on my record is "felon." There was a man in the news last week from upstate New York who killed his wife with a baseball bat twenty years ago. He and I have the same classification because there is only one. We both have the same restrictions: no guns (I don't really care about that), can't ever vote again, and many problems if I was young enough to want to be employed in a lot of places. It's really not bad for me but think of the thousands of young men who have many years to live with that, some for as little as making too many deposits in your bank account just under $10,000. (Did you know that is a felony?) It is a classification that is the same as a murderer, and it is for the rest of your life.

Of course, my experience was only a shadow of what the Jewish people went through, but it did add drama to my reading about the Jews. So this is what I've been reading, thinking through, and imagining. I try to imagine what it was like for them to be separated from their families and be shamed and disgraced with all the humiliating things they did to them. There must have been some of those who were trusting God for their salvation from this right to the very end; some who lost faith in God for allowing this to happen; and some who didn't lose faith but trusted God for all time and eternity. I imagine this, and I wonder if anything I have felt is anything like what they might have felt.

My faith is so strengthened because of going through the last five years. I know the glory of the Lord is all around us, and he is working in the hearts and lives of people around us. If we pay attention, we can see and hear signals of God at work. I see crises as necessary to get our attention and draw us to him. How is it for you? Has God called you to a ministry of pain, loneliness, disappointment, and heartache? Has he called you to a ministry in crisis? Ask him to show you his glory and his purpose, and let him show you and strengthen your faith so that you can encourage others who are walking the same path. God is real, his mercies are sure, and he is faithful. A verse that has come to mean a lot to me is in Psalm 28:13-14: "I believe that I shall look upon the goodness of the Lord in the land of the living! Wait upon the Lord, be strong, and let your heart take courage; wait for the Lord!"

Katelyn is one of Bob's daughters. Bob is serving a seven-year sentence in a very public case that was in the paper for weeks. He is a great guy, and it's so unfortunate he got caught up in this thing that turned into a crime. He has five years left to go. Bob and his wife have three darling children. We have become very close to them and are almost like Grandpa and Grandma to them. They have no church background to speak of. Anyway, their middle daughter is Katelyn.

Katelyn was four when we first met, and now she is six. She is the little girl that Jan wrote about. She would go over Jan's gospel message bracelet with her, nearly every week for almost two years now. Well, someone else saw how much Katelyn loved it and found one on the internet and gave it to her. She was so excited and had to come right over and show us and go through it with Jan. I often wondered how much Katelyn was really getting from this. I think at first it was an interesting gadget, but then it became a story she understood. This time when she finished, she said to Jan, "That's Jesus. Will I ever get to see his face?" Her words have just stuck with me ever since. I see now that Jesus has become a real person to her. I think she really does know and love Jesus and wants to know him more. I find this so amazing, that God allows us to see these things happening right before our eyes. Even little Katelyn wants to see his face!

1/15/12

Today we had what they call a town hall meeting. We were called to the dorms, and they called us into the hallways to tell us that we are under a flu restriction. We are all to wash our hands ten times a day and sing "Happy Birthday" through twice while we rub our hands with soap. I said to myself that when I get home Jan is going to have to get used to things. Not only will I be hollering "Clear?" every time I go in the bathroom, but I'll also be singing "happy birthday" when I wash my hands. They are putting hand disinfectant around the compound, and they want us to use it every time we pass it.

Pedro is not in our group, but he is in my dorm. He is always friendly to me, and I've known him ever since I came. He seems to like talking to me, and he knows I'm a Christian; he is definitely not. He goes home in four months and is finishing a fifteen-year sentence. He's a Gulf War vet and has seen a lot of bad stuff; he has a hard outlook on life. This is how he talks. Regarding marriage, "No, I spent $3,500 dollars getting a divorce, and it's the best money I ever spent." (He said this two years ago.) He also said, "I was a sharp shooter in the Army. When I get out I want to join Blackhawk and go over there and get myself shot. That will set my two daughters up. I don't have anything else to live for." (All that is laced with about fifteen expletives.)

I saw Pedro this week, and I asked him if he is still going to be a mercenary. He said, "No, I've changed." I asked, "If you've changed, did you find God?" He said, "No." I said, "Are you open?" He said, "Frankly, no. I've changed because we are pulling out of Afghanistan now, and there won't be enough troops over there to support us. I tried to kill myself twice. Once, I had a 45 in my mouth. I just started crying like a baby. Another time I overdosed on a whole bunch of drugs and passed out and didn't die." Pedro is not at all interested in considering God, Jesus, or anything religious. God is just not at work in him. He just might be one that God calls "a child of wrath," and he will face the wrath of God. Well, that's one kind of guy we have here.

On Monday of this week, spiritual warfare began for Rob. Rob's wife is a counselor for Girl Scouts. She started with fifteen girls and built up all the way up to 100. She takes it very seriously and is very committed to it; it is an important part of her life. I mentioned earlier that her neighbor (they share a garage) has been giving her a lot of trouble, including stealing her things, giving her a bad time about things, and this week went to the Girl Scouts' office and said that parents were complaining about the way she was treating the children and that she thinks Rob's wife is taking money from the cookie account.

She was called into the head office because they said they needed to talk to her. She went in, and they told her that because her husband is in prison and it's been in the paper and because of the complaint, she needed to quit the Girl Scouts and can't come on the property again. She was devastated, and Rob fell all apart Monday. He was totally upset. I was disappointed in Rob's response and told him, "Hasn't God taken care of you before? Hasn't he been answering prayers before? Why are you responding like this? We need to pray." We prayed, and Jan sent Peggy an e-mail suggesting a psalm. Rob said he hated to call home the next day because it was gong to be so terrible. When Rob called home, he found out that the next day the head counselor had called Peggy and said she wanted her to come back. She had received so many phone calls from parents. Six of them were going to take their girls out and there were fifteen calls she couldn't even get to because some of them talked so long. Also, she said she really liked the e-mail from Jan, and she read the psalm and then had her kids read it. Her fifteen-year-old son said, "Man, mom, I think I could really get into this."

Flaco is now my neighbor, and he is a friend of my roommates and around a lot. On Wednesday he came into my room and said, "Bob, can I talk"? I said, "Sure." He got two chairs and arranged them facing one another so we could talk. He was really on a mission. He said, "Bob, do you believe in miracles?" I said, "Yes." He said, "Then let me tell you something. My dad is in prison and serving an eighteen-year sentence. One time, when I was in another prison, I was laying in my bed. A man all in white came to me. There was a real bright light all around him. He didn't say much, but he said he wanted me to follow Jesus. His face was my Dad's. I told my Dad about it, and he said he was praying for me that night. He has become a Christian, and he wants me to read the Bible." Flaco teared up when he told me this. He said, "I grew up Catholic, but my Dad is now a Christian. I want to be one too. I think you can help me, and I want to come to your class." I told him that would be good, and since he is right next to my room, we should spend some one-on-one time together so the class will be more meaningful.

Mac came to me this week and asked that I pray for his wife. She works at the university hospital in Chicago, and her supervisor asked her to come into her office the next morning because she had an issue to discuss. She was afraid she was going to be fired because she sensed tension with her supervisor. We prayed that night for her. The next morning when she went in for the appointment, someone from HR just happened to be there and decided to sit in on the conversation. The supervisor had several issues that she raised. The HR person came to her defense and said it seemed the issues were more with the supervisor than they were with her. The interview turned out really well and it was because the HR person "just happened" to be there. Mac says his wife is such a conscientious, hard worker and that sometimes other workers don't like it because she may makes them look bad. Anyway, it's just one more thing to highlight this week.

1/22/13

I am so blessed to have a ringside seat, right where the action is happening. I hear this so much from the guys, and I heard it again yesterday: "When I'm with you, I feel so much peace." Now we all know I cannot bring peace. I am just thankful to the Lord that he allows me to reflect something of him so that people relate me with him. But God and the gospel really do bring peace. I am thankful for the continual practice I get in handling the Word, and because of the frequent opportunity to use it, I think it sharpens my skills. At the same time, I know that unless the Lord does it, skill doesn't matter.

Flaco has been meeting with me at least two times a week plus class time, and he also runs into my rooms several times a night with questions. Today he came and got me and said, "Mr. Goris, come here." I followed him to his room. He said, "Mr. Goris, I'm going to the dentist to get a wisdom tooth pulled. One time, I had a cut or something wrong on my arm. It wouldn't stop bleeding, and I almost died. I'm worried about this tooth." He wanted me to pray for him. So I prayed for him. He thanked me. After I ate lunch today and watched the news, he was waiting for me. He said, "I got my tooth pulled. The dentist said it hardly bled." I said, "Well, praise God." Yesterday he came and said, "Goris, is there some special prayer that I can pray like when I eat and in the morning and at night?" I said he didn't have to pray a certain prayer but that I could help with some ideas. So I've written some bullet points he can use when he prays. Flaco is the best friend of my roommate Pepi. Pepi is fifty-six and very short. He is from Peru and is a really nice guy and father figure for Flaco. They are like father and son. Pepi furnishes all the food, and Flaco all the cooking. Pepi eats way too much. He is really big around the middle. There is really a lot of comedy here. Pepi is a great roommate though. Pepi says he has never been to church and has never read the Bible but has so much faith. Flaco wants Pepi to come to our classes, but Pepi won't get up that early. I'll probably do it in the room with him, but he says he can't read and needs eye surgery first. That will be in about two months.

This week the lady that called the Girl Scouts and gave the false report on Rob's wife got booted out of their rental and fired from the job that Sue got her. She left very angry and made some threats against. Rob was worrying about that. I said, "Rob, hasn't the Lord shown you so much these last days? Isn't he going to care for you? Trust him." He also worries about the bills for his family until he gets out. We all have to learn to live by the day. Thinking way down the road gives us trouble. We all have to learn that, though, and I guess I can't fault Rob too much. Their bills are all paid, and their rent is now paid a month ahead. God is good!

1/23/13

Wow! These dorms aren't built for twenty-below weather and a fifty-below wind chill. I went to bed with long underwear (top and bottom) and sweats on over that plus socks on my feet. During the night I got up and put big wool socks over the other socks and put my winter coat over everything else. I also put double stocking caps on my head. Finally, I warmed up. I haven't been out today other than for lunch. I made chicken noodle soup for supper with a package of mackerel in it. That's home cooking in Duluth FPC.

35

2/9/13

I realize my time is short because they want me to take pills that will dull my pain. I have felt that I don't need them, but now at 6:00 a.m., Sunday morning, I realize I will need to take a sleeping pill tonight because I have only slept a total of six hours the last two nights and that can't continue. The problem with the pills is that they won't give me the pills to take to my room. We have to go to "pill line" at 6:00 p.m., swallow the pill, and then open our mouths and give them proof we have actually swallowed the pills. Some guys "cheek" the pill and then spit it out and sell it. The problem with taking this strong pill at 6:00 p.m. is that I will be drugged and a zombie the rest of the night.

Three months ago I began to feel something was wrong in my stomach. I knew the doctor here would say, "Let's wait and see what happens." Thirteen weeks ago I went to "sick call." There was a nurse that day so I filled out a form to get called, waited three weeks, and got no call. I went to sick call again, and the nurse was not there. So I filled out a form again. This continued for ten weeks. The tenth week, the nurse was there and entered my complaint into a computer and said I would get a call. This continued, and now it is three months since I first felt pain. Last Monday, February 2, I was taken downtown for a CT scan. On Friday, I was called in to the prison doctor's office. I got there, and the psych doctor was there with the MD. The MD handed me the report from the downtown scan and told me to read it.

It didn't tell me much so I said, "What does it say?" He said, "It's not good." I said, "Is it cancer?" He said, "Yes." At this point he is just answering questions and not offering me much help. I said, "So what's next?" He said, "Not much we can do." I said, "Can I go home?" He said, "We can apply for a compassionate release, but it takes two or three months to get it. The last four guys we had all died before it came through. I said, "Will I see another doctor?" He said, "We will send you downtown next week."

That was Friday. The psych doctor said, "Do you think you might do something crazy? I mean like hurt yourself?" I said, "Not a chance." (They fear corpses here.) She said, "How do you feel about this?" I said, "I'm all right; I just hate making the call to Jan." But, of course, I did.

Word spread on the compound, and I was amazed at the way the guys responded. There was a steady stream of guys coming to my room with compassion and concern. Guys who I have had on my radar and had talked to a little, now really wanted to talk. Pepi sat with me and felt so bad. Then he said, "Bob, I want to hear that story you said you have for me." (I told him I want to tell him about Cornelius because he reminded me of Cornelius, the centurion). So I read to him in Acts about the centurion who was a good man and who prayed to God. But he was missing something. He needed the gospel and needed to receive Jesus. Pepi said, "I am so honored that I remind you of a man like that."

Then I read how God came to him in a vision and told him about Peter. Then God gave Peter a vision and told him to send Cornelius with a message. I told Pepi, "God didn't give you and me visions, but he put us here in prison so that I can tell you what Peter told Cornelius." Then we read the gospel that Peter told Cornelius and how Cornelius's whole family believed and was baptized. Pepi said, "I want that. I want that for my children and my grandchildren." Then we went to John, where Jesus told Nicodemus he must be born again. Pepi said, "I want that. I want to be born again." Then we prayed.

Pepi went right across the hall to his friend, Lopez. He told Lopez, "Bob said I remind him of this man, Cornelius, and I am just like him." Lopez is a Christian and so Lopez came over and wanted to know where that was in the Bible so he could read it on his own. Pepi is telling everybody that he is born again, and yesterday Tony, who bunks right above me, was hearing all this. But Tony has always been very cold to the faith. Tony has warmed up to me, and I have told Tony many times he should think about Christ. Tony would never respond but would often joke and talk to me about money, work, and all those things.

Yesterday, I told Tony five times in five different ways that he needed Jesus. He grinned a little but never responded. Last night Tony said, "When I get out I'm going to have lots of fun." (Tony likes fun, laughing, and good times.) He said, "I know I will make lots of money because I believe in God." I said, "Yes, you believe in God for temporal things but not for eternal things." He said, "What's temporal?" I said, "Temporal things are all the things that are going to burn up some day and they will be gone." Tony laughed and said, "Yes, I know what that's all about. Just like when I came to prison." Tony had told me before that he owned a rental house, auto body shop, and other property. The government took it all when he came to prison.

Later that night when the other guys left the room, Tony said, "I like talking to you. Older men have wisdom. I am going to listen to you and take your advice, and you can tell me about the Bible. I will listen carefully."

There has been a steady flow of stories. Friday night I went to bed. I didn't think I needed a sleeping pill, but I went to bed and my mind was just running so fast I could not stop it. I thought about Jan and how the Lord has shown me how to love her so much more. I thought about all the plans I have for us when I get out. I thought about our grandchildren. I am a dreamer and a planner, and I have so many things to do with them and to say to them. I had plans of doing ministry with them like my dad did with some of his grandchildren. I wanted to invest my life in them.

I thought about how much I have learned here about ministry. I have taught these courses now to hundreds of men, some so rough and crude that they don't lean back but over the table as we talk about becoming a disciple. I thought that God would certainly give me many more years to use what I have learned.

I thought about all of that but mostly about my family. I know my time is being shortened, but at least I would have a few months with them now. I would get home, and we would sing around the piano. I have even been dreaming about getting together with all my prayer partners in some place, at one time, and just worshipping the Lord and marveling about him and his goodness. Oh, how I would love that! Maybe we can do it? It was 4:00 a.m. when I fell asleep, but I was not sad. God is good.

On February 8, I heard from Jan that the entire family is coming for the weekend, from Texas, Kansas City, and Minnesota. Jan told me how hard they are working at home to get me an early release. Matt helps me in the law library as we find out what we need for the release. I talked to a CO. He told me the staff here all know about it, feel bad for me, and will do all they can— but that it usually takes too long.

I went to the doctor to get my medical information for the release. He said, "Why do you need it?" I said, "I am applying for a compassionate release." He said, "Oh, you can't do that from here. Just wait until you get to the next place." I said, "What next place?" He said, "You will probably be shipped. You will probably be moved." I said, "To Rochester?" He said, "No, I think it will be to Butner, North Carolina. In fact, I already have the approval, and you will be going." I asked, "What about seeing a doctor downtown? You said I could talk to him." He said, "Oh, we have to set that up yet." I said, "Well, can't you do it right away? It's just a phone call. I thought you did it right after our last visit." He said, "We just haven't had time yet. You know we have other things to do, and there are other people besides you." I left the office very upset.

2/11/13

There is a medical doctor across the hall from me in my dorm, an internal medicine specialist. I gave him my scan report. After a little while of study, he seemed to know a lot about it. He drew a picture of my organs. He drew the tumor and its exact size. He estimates I am in the third of four stages. He said, "You have to see an oncologist really soon. They will tell you what type of treatment they can do, the percent for potential improvement, the side effects, and then you will be able to decide what to do. The treatment will be very severe, and they might not recommend it."

I went to bed Friday night with my mind just running, and I couldn't sleep now for my second night. I slept two hours and got up. These were my thoughts that I couldn't shake: there is so much about this that nobody knows; everything is so complicated; what I did to get here is so complicated and even my criminal defense attorney didn't understand it; I couldn't bear the thought of Jan having to visit me in Butner, a prison with barbed wire and all that sitting at night by herself; the cost of traveling to North Carolina to see me; and I also thought about me and being a failure and how I could put my wife and family in a situation like this.

2/12/13

When my family checked in at the visiting center, the staff told them, "We are going to let all of you in for the whole time." That is something that has never happened before. We were so amazed! Chris went to the motel and told everyone, and we had such a great day. We talked, cried, laughed, prayed, and sang a lot. Right there in prison, with the other inmates all watching and listening; nobody minded one bit. I felt and still feel so good. I have no pain, and I am carefully eating more. Last night, I ate a lot. I feel so completely normal. I don't know what is happening in me, but right now I thank God for every day of health without drugs to fog my brain.

God was glorified, and we were all so lifted up and strengthened. There is so much power in praise. I say this often to guys I am trying to help: "Praise and thank God for all the good things he has done. Don't let a temporary crisis cause you to lose sight of what God has already done." I believe that. There is so much power in praise.

I was enjoying the singing and praising so much that I thought, "This is what I want my funeral to look like." Now this may sound morbid to you, but it has been a joke in our family for years because when I flew the plane Jan was always so worried. She wanted to know how the funeral should go. We all laughed at the way I brought it up, and the family said, "No, this is how we will celebrate when you get home." I said, "Yes, either way this is what we will do." The family was all here for three days this weekend, and it was a glorious time.

2/13/13

I took "the pill" last night at six o'clock and went to the TV room to watch news. I got up to go to the dorm and was totally drunk. The guys had to hang onto my sleeves as if I was drunk. I got there, and they said I asked Peter to make me a bowl of rice. He did, and I ate it. Matt said he was there, but I don't remember him. He said he and I both prayed, and I prayed for the work in Kansas City. I fell asleep and slept through count this morning. I staggered over to Rec for count and just told them the pill was too strong. They weren't asking for an explanation, just concerned, and said I don't have to come for count anymore. I am only going to take half a pill from now on. I don't need any more of that drunkenness. I want to be sober. If I can't be sober, I won't take even half.

2/14/13

After visiting was over, I walked right past the chapel and a couple friends who had asked me if they could meet me to pray for me were waiting outside to catch me in case I forgot. I agreed to meet at the chapel at 3:00 p.m., and we walked into the chapel. It was half filled with people. I said, "We can't meet here; there is something going on in here. We need to go to the balcony." We went up into the balcony, and they had a chair there for me to sit on. I sat down facing away from the guys. Later, when I turned around, the balcony was full of people. All the people in the church had come to pray for me, and I thought it was some other meeting. It was really amazing.

I went to the dorm, and all the guys wanted to meet me, touch me, and wish me well. I got to my room, and it was a steady flow of guys who have been in my class, coming with tears and telling me they were praying. Then it became even more amazing. Non-Christians began coming because they heard that Flaco and Pepi had become Christians and were now curious. I asked them quite openly if they would become Christians too, and many said, "Yes, but I don't know if I'm ready," "I'm not sure if I know how," or "I need to change first."

I went to the library to get my e-mails. There I met Paul and Benito, who said they wanted to talk. We talked about how happy I was that they are reaching out to their families because their families have become Christians, too. They were crying, and more people stopped. I knew they wanted to say something. Not knowing what to say can become awkward. I just started giving hugs; I was hugging guys who I have never talked with before, but they knew me and had heard. They all told me they were praying for me, even people who aren't Christian say that but I appreciate it. Many tell me they are calling home and asking family to pray for me. And a number of them said their families are having their whole church pray, one church of 2,500 and one of 1,500. Some told me that their family's churches are having mass for me. I think if I add the numbers they told me, it might be about 10,000 people.

There were about twelve to fifteen guys around me. We were blocking the traffic in the library. I told the guys that I appreciate their prayers so much, and I really want to be healed to be with my grandchildren and my wife. I feel I have learned and prayed to love them more, and I've learned to minister more. I am really looking forward to getting out and doing all this on the outside so I would like to be healed. Then I said, "We should also pray that the 10,000 people who are praying, plus the tens of thousands in India in the villages and in Portugal and Cambodia and all over America, would be given a real spiritual experience and that God's love would flow back to them so that they sense in their praying that Jesus is alive and real and personal to them. I said, "That would be so awesome for me, even more important than life. My desire is to live, but I am ready to die. I just want Christ to be glorified in my life and in my death, and I want many more to come to him in faith to not only believe and be saved but become real disciples of Christ. By then there were many tears and people were shutting off the lights so we had to leave.

I thought I would need a sleeping pill that night, but with all the talking I forgot to go to the pill line. When I went to bed that night, the Lord gave me rest, with no pill. I am so thankful. I woke up Sunday morning feeling good.

Pepi tells me all the Mexicans swear so badly, even Flaco. I said, "Still? He still swears?" Pepi said, "All the time." Flaco was standing right there. These guys don't pull any punches with one another. I said, "Flaco, is this true?" He said, "Well, when I hang out with these guys to shoot pool with them, these guys are my friends. I don't want to tell them they can't swear." Pepi said, "Well, that's the other problem. It's the crowd you hang with." This went on for some time. Then I took my Bible and looked up scriptures on the mouth. I gave him Psalm 71:8, Proverbs 13:3, Proverbs 18:7, Matthew 12:34, Romans 10:9, and James 3:10. I read him the first one and he said, "Just a minute. I want to get my own Bible." He has a paperback we gave him in class. He reads it every day. As he read he got real serious. He said, "I will quit swearing. Well, I will try, but when I play pool, everybody swears." I told him, "Maybe you will have to quit playing pool." Then I said, "If your eye offends you . . ."

Pepi went after him some more about the guys he hangs out with and also about "that crap music you listen to." Flaco was thinking. I told him he needs to delete that gangster rap music on his mp3 player. He was thinking. Then he said, "Okay, I am going to stop swearing. By the time I get home in April, I won't be swearing anymore, but I will be honest with you. I will not delete my music because that would be wasting it. When I get home in April I will give it (he means sell it) to guys on the street. Then I won't listen to it anymore."

So now when Flaco sees me he says, "Goris (it sounds like "Gorees") I only swore two times today." Flaco loves his Bible. I really need to get him an ESV study Bible.

2/15/13

I was supposed to go downtown yesterday morning and fasted the night before. They gave me such a strong sleeping pill. I woke up, forgot what day it was, and ate two oranges and half of a piece of cake. When I got downtown they couldn't do the test. When I got back, I got a good chewing out. The cop asked me who I thought was going to pay for the trip and the cost of the medical cancellation. I said, "It's up to you." That was the right answer. He wanted to know what happened from my perspective, and I told him. He said he believed me. I could have been put in the hole for that.

I thought I would go today. I was ready, but they never called. I guess it is rescheduled for next week. I feel so good, and I feel like the cancer is gone. I have no stomach problems at all. I weighed myself and gained another pound. Everyone tells me they are praying for me, even those who curse a blue streak.

2/17/13

Pepi and the guys made pizza so we could have a time when they could meet all my new Christian brothers. They were afraid of running out, but everyone ate. There was even some left, and someone mentioned the miracle of the loaves and fishes. We met in the orderly room where they keep the mops and the microwaves. We ate, and toward the end of the meal, I told the guys we were going to have a special time. We shared the Lord's Supper: we saved a piece of pizza crust and a sip of Pepsi. I don't know if you have read it this way, but that's the way Jesus did it. It wasn't a service like we have in church. It was a meal, and at the end of the meal, they had Lord's Supper. We were all blessed. Those who have been in church said this was the best Lord's Supper they have ever had. For others, it was their first.

Four of the guys who were there are Christians of four weeks or less. We had them share their experiences, and the others shared a word of encouragement. It was an awesome time—a bit messy because others kept coming in to use the microwaves, but I'm sure Jesus's times were sometimes messy.

2/20/13

I just got back from the downtown doctor, and the report for me was better than expected, although it is not final until the pathology report comes tomorrow. They did the procedure through my mouth under anesthesia. The doctor said the good news is that the tumor is on the tail of the pancreas and is operable. The pathologist will not say that it is cancer, but the oncologist is sure that it is. If it isn't, he said it's some other kind of a mass. I said would that be good news? He said not necessarily and that it depends.

2/22/13

Pepi said last night, with his arms raised in the air and flailing around, "It really is something in this room. At least every hour, I hear the name of Jesus mentioned. I never thought it could be this way in prison. I don't feel like I'm in prison at all."

Pepi just cannot do enough for me. He is very giving. It's really amazing. Last night Flaco's first disciple prayed to receive Christ. He brought him over to my room for a little help. Now, I am helping him write a letter to his wife telling her about his first two changes. First, he is going to stop swearing (he said she won't believe it), and, second, he is going to love her the way Jesus wants him to love her, according to Ephesians 5. He said, "So she is the only woman in my life. That is important, and it will be hard."

2/24/13

I have changed my diet and now eat a little every few hours. I keep my pants unbelted and shirt out, and I feel pretty good. I look a mess, but I feel good. As I walked outside today, I was thinking about what a sorry sight I am here, but, of course, everyone is. I wear two stocking caps pulled almost over my eyes and look really stupid, but I am comfortable.

Yesterday, Matt brought me some chicken, and I put it in two cans of V8 and cooked it with a little seasoning. I ate a little at a time, and it lasted me all day. Lopez wants to do things for me and likes to bring me a burrito quite frequently. I like his burritos, but I decided tonight that I can't do that anymore. The spice and the beef don't agree with me. Today, I started off with two boiled eggs (contraband), and two eggs is now too much for breakfast. The guys bring me lots of fruit—more than I can even eat, and the apples right now are really large and tasty. Tonight, I had a pack of salmon with mayonnaise poured right into the pack. (Mackerel is better). Then I had a banana with a can of pudding with an expiration date of 2005. It was awesome: banana pudding!

According to the guidelines, I don't qualify for release. Yesterday, however, I was talking to the chaplain, and she was talking about getting me out. I told her about the qualification, and she didn't believe that. She asked me if I knew the warden, and I said I didn't. She said, "Well, he knows all about you. I will talk to him."

2/24/13

I have often thought and asked God to help me not waste my life in this prison. A friend sent me this tiny little paperback book by John Piper, *Don't Waste Your Cancer*. It is so good for me, and it confirms much of what I believe but don't dare to express. Everyone has more of an awareness of God than before. Everyone is reminded of the fragility of life like never before. Most did not know that death really has no sting or dread for a Christian. They are very amazed by the fact that it is giving me opportunities to speak to some of the other Bible study group, and address some important theological issues that need to be addressed.

2/27/13

Monday morning I was called for my visit to the doctor. I got downtown, and I was an hour early so I got to sit and look out over the city and Lake Superior. The receptionist said she would see if they could get me in early. I said, "No, please let the doctor be. I have plenty of time."

While I was waiting, I was wondering what my surgeon will be like. I saw this tall thin guy from a distance and from behind. The receptionist said, "That's your doctor." He had a long white coat on and a ponytail. I thought to myself, "Oh great. All I need is a hippy doctor who I can just visualize sitting in his canoe at the end of the Gunflint Trail smoking pot."

The nurse called me into the consulting room and took my blood pressure and weight. My blood pressure was good, and I was 196 pounds (I lost six), which is a perfect weight for me. For the rest of the morning, I could only respond, "Oh my God." And I wasn't swearing. It was so awesome. First of all, when the doctor came into the room and faced me, he looked at me with the most compassionate concern, understanding, and intelligent form I could ever ask for in a man. I thought to myself, where do these men come from? He probably does hundreds of surgeries per month, yet he talks to me like this is the only thing he has to be concerned about today.

After a short introduction, he said, "Let's see what we have here" (like he is looking at it for the first time, which I'm sure he is not). On this big double-screen computer, he pulled up this image of the CT scan, first from the top down and then from the bottom up. It's just like if you take a hog carcass, freeze it, and then cut it through the middle with a meat saw. All the organs stay in place because they are frozen. It was so amazing to see that and to know that the organs we were looking at were actually mine. He showed me the pancreas, stomach, liver, spleen, and a lot of other stuff.

He showed me the cancer, not on the tail of the pancreas as was told me but almost in the middle. He said, "This is what we can do. We can take about 60 percent of your pancreas, your spleen, and a mass of fat with it. We can cut far enough away from the cancer so the cancer doesn't leak out, and we can lift the whole mass out so that the cancer is contained in the mass of stuff they take out. It will be about a three-hour surgery, but it looks like it has not spread yet. I think we will get all of it. You'll be in the hospital four days and then back to the camp where you will get strong for a month. After that, we will do some light chemo, not to kill cancer but to prevent any small cells we couldn't see from growing. I said, "Is it that easy?" He said, "I hope so. We won't know for sure until after the surgery, but if this works, you might see eighty-five."

Then, he got a puzzled look on his face and said, "How did you know? How did they find this so early?" I said I had this lower stomach pain when I ate and it kept getting worse. He said, "That's strange. Usually there isn't pain with pancreatic cancer. That's why it is so dangerous. It's usually too far along by the time it's recognized." He questioned whether the pain is even related to the cancer. He examined me a little more and just said, "Well, we will take care of the cancer and see what happens."

I was thinking about being in the hospital for four days and wondering how I could even get information to the family about how the surgery went. I went to the chaplain to see whether she might help. She was busy. Last night, walking down the street here I ran into Mr. Baker. I think he is the one who can really make things happen here. He is the one who got my family in at visiting, all at the same time. I asked Baker if he would be in tomorrow. He said, "I'm in tonight. See me in about an hour."

I saw him and told him the good news on my surgery and asked if my family could visit me while in the hospital for four days. He said, "Usually not, but we take it case-by-case." He said, "When you went downtown today were you alone, without a guard?" I said, "Yes." He said, "We might do that. They could visit during regular hospital visiting hours." He said, "Fill out a cop out (request) and give it to medical in the noon cafeteria line. I'll be there and explain it to him." I did that, and am now praying that they will grant that. This would be so awesome.

35

3/8/13

I'm out of the hospital early because the news wasn't quite as good as we had hoped. The doctor made a smaller cut about three inches long right in the middle just below my chest to do an inspection before he took out the parts. He found the cancer had spread to the liver. He took out some samples to verify it also is cancer. He closed me up again. He said it is stage 4 because it has spread. Without treatment, he thought I would have a year or less. With treatment, it all depends on how the cancer responds to treatment. Evidently, there are many different kinds of cancer and also many different kinds of treatment. It will be trial and error. The tumor is large enough to measure so they will measure it, treat it, and check back later to see if it's smaller. If it's not, they will try something else next time.

The first night after the surgery was normal for me. I was supposed to be able to have Jan come and see me, but there was a snowstorm; also, the guard never came to see me so I could tell her to come anyway. I was going to use his phone because we are not allowed to make phone calls. I knew Jan, our family, and friends were anxiously waiting, and it was bothering me a lot that they didn't know. By night the guard still hadn't come. There was a phone in the room so I asked the nurse if I could use the phone. She said, "Yes, I don't care." I called Jan. I told her the news (very sad time). I knew I shouldn't have done it, but with all that was on her mind I couldn't pass it up.

While I was on the phone, the guard walked into the room and told me to give him the phone immediately. I did, and I left Jan hanging without an explanation.

The second night in the hospital was just an empty void. Nobody to talk to and not even much traffic passed the door. I was trying to adjust to the new information. I was disappointed with myself. I thought it would be a great time of thinking and taking notes, but I just lay there and had no thoughts.

I got back yesterday afternoon. Everyone was eager to see me. Last night I called about ten guys into my room. They were brand new Christians who had been praying for me. They were eager to come and be singled out for me to talk to. I told them how life needs interpretation, especially our prayer life. I knew they were all praying for my healing, and now it sounds like worse news. I didn't want them to be confused about that. I talked about the "cup." In Psalm 16 it says, "Lord, you have assigned me my portion and my cup. You have made my lot secure. The boundary has fallen for me in pleasant places, surely I have a delightful inheritance." The Lord gave me my portion and my cup. Knowing it is by God's design is a great comfort for me because then I know he has purpose even when I can't see it.

The guys in my dorm are so amazing. While I was gone, they washed my laundry, washed my bedding, and put all my stuff away. They said, "Mr. Goris, you won't do anything anymore. We will do it all for you." Wow, it is amazing. I get to see God's love around me, and they get to serve God by serving me. It's good for all of them. It was good for them to get together. They were honored that they were the first ones that I talked to. I do love these guys, and I respect them. Most of them are former drug dealers. They are scarred by society and by life, but they are all sinners saved by grace. And God's grace is great.

We had class this morning. The new Christians gave their testimonies along with everyone else. They are becoming bolder every time they go through it. It is such a privilege to be here and to serve God with them.

3/15/13

An hour ago I went to sick call because I wasn't hearing anything about going to the oncologist. The lady checked, and the appointment had not been made. She was disgusted and said she would take care of it right away. I asked her to let me know when it was done. An hour later, I was called to sign papers to go downtown. Then she called me into her office and said, "Mr. Goris, you need to be on the inside of what's going on. She said, "You are being transferred to another facility."

I said, "That would probably be Rochester or Butner then, right?" She said Rochester does not do cancer. So that leaves only Butner. She said I will go downtown, and they will do whatever they recommend. But as soon as a bed opens at Butner, I will be transferred.

I went downtown and saw the oncologist. He was not very reassuring. I think he was careful not to build any false hope. According to him, the cancer is in the bag that holds my intestines and is very hard to treat. Without treatment, he said I have four to five months. He said there is not much new technology for this kind of situation, and the old technology doesn't seem to work very well. He said we can try to treat it, and if it works it could give me an additional six to eight months. He said some have side effects, and some have very little. There is no way to know until it is done, however. I need to decide if I want to do it. I said we should set it up as long as we can cancel if we change our mind. It is set up to begin next Tuesday.

The nurse then gave me a three-ring binder with a lot of instructions about what to do with the various reactions. It started with taking my temperature as soon as I feel a chill. The first problem, however, is that they won't let me have a thermometer in here. Then she said that they are on call twenty-four hours a day and that if I have any strange feelings I should call in. The second problem is that I don't have access to a phone at night. She continued, and I continued to think that this isn't going to work very well. That is the way we left it.

When I got back, Mr. White, the medical director, called me into his office. He asked me how I'm doing, and I said fine. He said, "How are your spirits?" I said, "Are you talking about my faith?" He said, "That's exactly what I mean." I told him about my faith and that I am not discouraged because there are so many family and friends praying. He said, "That is what I needed to know." He said, "I am a Christian, and this is a very hard place to work for a Christian because I am so limited in what I can say. But I needed to know about that."

He then said, "I know you want to start treatment, but you're going to be transferred, and I don't want to start your treatment if we are transferring you soon. I don't want to put you on an airplane during treatment. I said, "Well, I don't want to postpone the treatment." He said, "We already have you approved for transfer, and it's just a matter of when a bed opens up in Butner, North Carolina. I will call now and try to expedite it." Well, I think that's the best. I really was wondering how it would be possible in any way to do it from here.

Then he talked about compassionate release and said all their staff is behind me and for getting me out. He told me to talk to the warden. Craig House, Lisa's husband, had all the paperwork for me to sign. He e-mailed it to me, and I gave it to the warden today at noon. He said they were talking about me in a meeting this morning, and they are going to try to expedite it. Usually this is a very slow process.

Wow! Things are moving fast. The atmosphere here has really changed.

Everyone is behind me and doing all they can to get me home early. The warden took the papers, and an hour later the case manager called me and was working on it. She told me to stay around because she wanted to get this done right away. Later, she called me in again, and she said she was finished. I said, "Now is this going to be submitted and slowly proceed like all others?" She said, "Oh no. We have this on a fast track. I called the probation officer (PO) and told them we want this expedited." I just talked to Jan, and the PO had called the house and wants to do the inspection. That doesn't mean it's near the end, though. It still has to go to the regional officials, Washington, the attorney general, and then the judge. Usually, this would be four months, and I'm thinking this might be one month. At the same time, they are expediting my trip to Butner. I think I will be going there very soon, and that is good. I want to get the treatment started.

I have so many thoughts. I'm rejoicing and just praising God. This whole place has changed. Everyone from the inmates to the staff. God is so good, and he has done all that we have asked him to do, and more. It is inexpressible. My time is really occupied. I wish I had more time to develop my thoughts on this. I have very little time for myself right now. That's a good thing, yet, at the same time, I'm looking forward to getting to Butner and quieting down. I will have more time for thinking, reading, writing, and praying. I feel I have some catching up to do.

Tomorrow will be our class, and it will be my last one. There are a lot of mixed feelings about my leaving. I have them too. I never expected to feel this way about this place, but God has certainly shown me his glory—many other people see it too. This has been a field of dreams for me. I have guys waiting to see me in my room as I write.

3/17/13

Well, it is official. Yesterday, they called me to R & D, which I think stands for Receiving and Departing. They gave me two boxes and told me to pack up. I did that last night. Today, they called me back and told me to bring my property in. So everything I own on this earth is sitting in two boxes and on its way to the next place that they won't tell me. By process of elimination, I know it is Butner. They don't send out on weekends so it will be either Monday or Tuesday. At whatever time it is, I will be called, and I will be out of the gate in a car. I will not know where I am going, but I know it will be to the airport. I think I will have an escort with me. They will give me some civilian clothes to wear.

Right now I'm sure the warden is over at Nordstrom's doing some shopping for me, and I will really look pretty good as I travel to Butner.

It is so amazing the way God has definitely led through this whole process. Even the guys in R & D were really helpful this morning. I didn't get chewed out once for anything. The items I couldn't take, for whatever reason, they nicely gave back and told me to use up over the weekend. I can only have five pairs of socks, underwear, etc. Of course, those are only what I bought in commissary, and the prison issued stuff stays here anyway. They went through it all and counted each piece and nicely packed them tightly in a couple of boxes for me. I had to send most of my books home, but they let me keep a generous amount over the five allowed. They were really nice. They asked me in their own friendly but gruff way when they were going to send me home and that they didn't think I should be here.

The guys in the dorm are so helpful but sad to see me go. This is really funny. Lopez, who loves to cook for me said, "You are such a holy man. I wish you could be my Pope." The guys who have been given Bibles are bringing them to me to write in them. Others are seeing that, and now they are all bringing Bibles to me so that I can write in their Bibles. I have a lot to do.

I said good-bye in each class, and it was a solemn but powerful time. During the first part, we read the parable of the sower, which I call "The Parable of the Soils." I said we are all soil. We used to farm on a farm by Prinsburg that was a rocky farm. We didn't farm the rocky farm. We farmed it, and every year we picked up the rock. And every year the rocks came back. I said that most of us are like that and that it's important to know that our rocks never stay picked. All through life, we need to pull the weeds and pick the rocks. I told them I have enjoyed serving them, and now they need to learn to feed themselves and stay strong with themselves and the Lord and to become friends with their Bible.

In the second class, I used the same chapter but different verses and talked about the farmer who sowed his fields. During the night, someone came in and seeded in a lot of weeds. The farmer said to leave them in because if you pull them out now it will pull out the wheat with it. I said, "I'm concerned that with all the Bible studies going on here, there are some that are sowing bad seeds. They need to be aware of that and use discernment." I feel the guys are prepared now, and Matt will do a good job in leading the classes. He really feels challenged by it and knows that he needs to grow and mature a lot. Matt is dealing with his own issues and is honest about it.

Most people here have said when they leave here they will never want to come back to Duluth again. I feel very different. I will love Duluth, and when I see this place, I will see it as the place where God was with us. Many feel the same way.

This is a good place and so amazingly blessed by God. It is also crazy and funny. Tony, my bunky that sleeps above me, reminds me of my grandson, Ethan. He has almond-shaped eyes and sometimes is very quiet. Then he comes out in broken English with words that let me know he comprehends a lot. I have been waiting for him to get through the book *Chicken Soup for the Soul* because he wanted to finish that before he starts on the Bible. He said, "What I read I have to go out and practice twice before I get it." Now, he's reading the Bible. He started in the Gospels and had so many questions. Today he said, "This stuff is really good. I didn't realize the Bible is one long story."

Today, he came in the room and just rolled on his bed saying, "How true it is, and it works." He said, "It says, 'Don't worry about the splinter in your brother's eye when you have a boulder in your own.'" He thought that was so funny. He said, "There were two black guys arguing, hollering at each other, and I told the guy don't talk about the splinter in his eye when you got a boulder in your own." He said they stopped arguing. He said, "Now, I got all I need. With *Chicken Soup* and the Bible, I got all the words I need in life." It is so much fun being with him. I will miss not being here when he goes through the Bible because he comes up with such good and crazy questions and comments. He said, "I can see where I'm going to have to start at the beginning of this book so I get the whole story." He read seventy-five pages that day so he did pretty well.

Tonight, I will meet with the guys to give my farewell talk to them. Whoever wants to hear it will come to my room. This will be just for the guys in my dorm. I will be using Philippians 1 as the focus for my talk. It's interesting how it is written to fit into my farewell so perfectly.

I think this is my last day here. I am so blessed. I am full of joy. I have no pain. I have a small sensation in my stomach that cannot be called pain. God has answered every prayer. My blessings are more than I can take. My cup truly is running over. I think my early release is going through, and I could easily be home in three weeks. Isn't God amazing? It is a miracle to have it go through so fast; this is absolutely unheard of. God has given me so much favor.

From Jan

We were faced with yet another challenge. Bob was diagnosed with pancreatic cancer in February. We were counting the months until his release in October, and now we're uncertain if he will live until then. I drove to Duluth on a blustery, bitter cold weekend. I stayed one extra night at a friend's home and hoped the weather would improve. I headed home in the morning, and while I was en route, I received a call from a dear friend, the wife of an inmate in Duluth. The passing of messages is illegal so they have codes. Her husband had e-mailed and said, "Bo Peep left this morning at 4:00 a.m. He came in my room and said good-bye." I knew that Bob was on his way to North Carolina for treatment. Once again, there were lots of unknowns.

A friend of Lisa had just moved to Charlotte and was willing to let me stay with them. I packed clothes for several weeks and headed east. Tom drove me there and helped me get acquainted with the area and rules of another prison. Once again, I was driving over two hundred miles every weekend to visit Bob, this time from Charlotte to Butner.

I was blessed with the beautiful scenery, early spring flowers, and the family and friends who were flying in every weekend to visit us. It was a wonderful young family who took me in. I was "Gramma Jan" to their little ones.

3/22/13

I am sitting in Butner. On Tuesday morning, the guard woke me up at 3:30 a.m. to report to control by 4:00. They had me change into their travel clothes, which are not civilian clothes. It wasn't a pretty sight. A CO escorted me—it's called an escort if they don't have a gun. We had a three-hour layover in Chicago. I had no breakfast and was really hungry, but they didn't provide any food. There is nothing like an empty stomach to add to my dilemma, and I had a real pity party for myself on that trip. We left Duluth at about zero degrees and snow, but it is fifty-eight degrees with the cherry blossoms in bloom here.

My first impression of Butner was that it is new; it's only ten years old. There are five prisons on the compound, ranging from a camp to medium security to a medical facility to something higher than that. Medical is a level three so it is more like a prison than Duluth in that there is razor wire around everything and has locked doors. The treatment center is four pods that join in the middle with the cancer patients all on the fifth floor. There are around 200 cancer patients on our floor.

The fifth floor is for the dying, where a lot are dying from AIDS and HIV. I think hospice is up there too. It was a big adjustment coming in; there always is in a new place. I told myself to withhold judgment for three days. I remember my first thoughts of Duluth were pretty ugly the first night. It's hard to believe how that place came so much to be home and how the men who I first thought were really strange and far out became good friends. I don't know if the same will happen here, but coming in it's hard to imagine. Many of these guys have been down a long time and are very institutionalized. In this place you don't just break into conversations with everyone and ask them questions about themselves. You kind of wait until spoken to and see how it goes. So I have spent most of the time trying to figure this place out. I walk and am lost most of the time.

I had my first visit with the physician's assistant (PA). The guy is in the National Health Service and wears a uniform like a Navy officer. He is a Captain, which in the Navy is just below Admiral. I am very impressed with the professionalism of the medical people. They are all very compassionate, just like the doctors on the outside. So the first to examine me was the PA, who is actually a student. Next Tuesday, there will be a committee of five oncologists here from several hospitals. The PAs present to the committee and provide information on each patient for that week. My oncologist is Dr. Carston. He is a Harvard graduate, and they say we are very privileged to have him here. I am getting a good feeling about the capability of this place.

It's tough to see all the guys going through treatment. Most of them seem to be prostate and colon cancer. Some brain cancer and others. They always ask me what kind of cancer I have, and when I say pancreatic cancer, they say, "Oh, [expletive]. That's a bad one." Also, I talked to a guy tonight who just had his second chemo treatment, and it wasn't good news. He said he's going to try one more, and if it's this bad he is going to quit.

It's hard to believe that my health is such a serious issue. I have almost no pain. I feel strong. I miss the guys in Duluth a lot. I don't have any of my property, meaning my personal stuff. They say it can take three to four weeks to get your stuff. They have toiletries here to hold me over, but I'm quite lost without my Bible, radio, books, etc.

I found the chapel, but it was locked. There is very little sign of any Christian activity other than a Sunday service. The schedule is full of times for Muslims, Wiccans, and every belief imaginable. It will be interesting to see.

We are two men to a room, and the beds are sheet steel with a thin mattress on them. The toilet is right in the room with no wall, curtain, or anything around it. One leaves the room while the other uses it, except in the night when the door is locked. When you flush the toilet, it sounds like a jet airplane taking off. It scares me awake when my celly goes, and he and I both go pretty often. I suppose it's all in getting used to it.

Some of the guys introduce themselves to me because the first day a new person doesn't have a uniform yet and wears "entry clothes," which are green like a fishing lure. You stand out pretty well. One guy who is really helpful introduced himself as "Jimmy the Fish." He seemed quite proud of his heritage; he was part of a mob. His father in-law was "Little Joseph," who he said was the mob boss who, supposedly, had to do with the Joseph Kennedy deal. I don't know. He's been down seventeen years, has brain cancer, and still has ten years to go. His wife is still with him, and they have two daughters. He seems like a pretty regular guy otherwise. He's helping me get some things.

My roommate is named Ghetto, but the way he pronounces it, it sounds like "Gwetto." He is a Mexican from San Diego and Tijuana before that. He is terminal, has been here seven months, and has had no treatment. He is here illegally and is in prison for wrongful re-entry into the U.S. He is trying to get a compassionate release, but his wife is afraid to assume his care because she has no money. She doesn't realize that there is help out there for that. Sad story. He seems really nice, but he also is not a guy I would stop and talk to on the street. I think I will tell him Pepi's story of Cornelius. I really do think that God is making appointments for me here, just like he did with Peter in Acts 10. I must admit that I felt a little undone since getting here. It just shows me that all that God has done in Duluth is not because of me because I am weak. I'm so glad that he makes strength out of our weakness because right now I don't feel strong. Not even spiritually. Goliath is looking pretty big. I'm not just referring to the surgery but to spending months here, trying to see God's purpose and plan. I do have faith, though, that he does have a plan, and that he will do it.

3/26/13

The R & D experience here is totally different than in Duluth. The COs here are much better, actually friendly, and don't seem to hate their work like they do in Duluth. They really treat us decently, not warm fuzzies or anything, but they are very decent. That's a big improvement. The food is the same menu, but, believe it or not, it doesn't meet Duluth's standards. I must say that the hamburger is not spoiled, however, and you don't get that awful smell when you walk into the kitchen. Visiting hours are much more liberal.

I walked outside for an hour today. When the sun shines, it is comfortable. It's still coat-and-cap weather, but it's comfortable. They have a real nice chapel library that is well supplied with really good books. I found a three volume set, *Exploring the Psalms* by Joseph Phillips. I believe God may have directed me here partly for this book. I love it. I thought I knew a few psalms pretty well, but now with this study book, they really come alive much more.

I found another small book that I would recommend—everyone should have five or ten of them in their car at all times. It is a very small and an easy read; you can read it in one hour. It would be a great little book to open a discussion with someone about how one becomes a Christian. The name of the book is *How Good is Good Enough?* by Andy Stanley. It would be good for the guys in Duluth to have for their use.

Upon leaving Duluth, I was at an all time high. The last weeks and months were so good, with the Spirit of God moving among the guys and the whole compound. Things did start getting better the second day here, and I really felt picked up and nourished by writing a few e-mails.

3/28/13

Weekends here are the longest. It was so nice in Duluth when Jan visited. Besides the obvious fact that it was nice to see her, it made the weekends go by faster. On weekends, all the activities stop, and it seems the clock does as well. When things slow down for me, I go to the psalms.

Up until a month ago, I thought my time on the earth was almost unlimited. I planned to live to 120 years of age. My only fear as I went to prison was that my life would be wasted. I asked the Lord not to waste my life. With that request/plea to the Lord, I knew that the purposes of God to me are more precious than life. Being in the center of God's plan is better than life itself. Then I was told I had four to six months of life left, six to eight months more with treatment.

3/29/13

I'm on my second week here. They did another CT scan. I was hoping to visit with the oncologist this week, but I haven't heard anything yet. I really would like to get this treatment started. It's over a month now since I was diagnosed, and I would really like to get things going. The social worker met with me, and it sounds like the compassionate release is continuing to be processed. The week after next it goes to the legal department and from there to the attorney general and the judge. I'm thinking I could be out by the first of May. We'll see, though; I must remember it's the government and that would be like a lightning strike for them.

There is a big mental health unit here, and it houses about 300 men. Some are out-and-about, and some are locked up all day long depending on their condition. I don't run into them other than out in the yard when I walk the track.

The first guy I met when I was walking was Cota. Cota looks like a cartoon character. He shaves his head and face except for a long black mustache that grows straight down and completely covers his mouth. He is very personable and speaks with a heavy accent that I wouldn't have detected was Spanish. He looks more Jewish. He loves to talk. In a minute's time, he is into his whole background. Cota is a tribal name because he is half Native American and half Spanish. He talks like this (and calls me "General": "So you see, General, I'm here on a study. I have no convictions; they are here to study my brain because you see, General, I worked undercover at the border because you see, General, I worked for the FBI, and they were bringing all these guns across the border. And they took these guys, General, out and Boom! (He pulled an imaginary gun up to his eye.) And they just left them for the coyotes, General. You see, General, they put this computer chip in my brain, General, and they downloaded it now. And they sent it to the Pentagon, General. They are going to reprogram me now, General. General, if you come to the library, General, you can read all about me." I had a nice conversation with Cota, and in all other ways he seemed pretty normal.

Then I met Stanley. I was just walking by myself. Stanley pulled up alongside, and I just greeted him. We had hardly talked, and he said, "It's nice to meet someone who is down to earth." I said, "Stanley, what is it that made you think I was down to earth?" He said, "I thought you would talk to me. Most people don't want to talk." Stanley talked quite a while. He is here because he made a terrorist threat. He said he got fired from his trucking job, and he was upset with his employer. He called him on the phone and said some bad things. He said, "I shouldn't have done it, but I didn't have no gun or anything, I was just talking." I said, "Stanley, have you ever been married?" He said, "Yes, once for a very short period of time. It didn't work for me; I shouldn't have gotten married." I said, "Do you know Jesus?" He said, "Yes, I've committed my life to him, and I've committed my life to be celibate too. I graduated from the Salvation Army Bible study, and I'm a Christian."

Then I met "Rooster." They call him Rooster because he has a red beard that sweeps down and forward and has spiked hair that is spiked up around the edges. Rooster seems normal in everything he says. I asked some leading questions about his faith, but he didn't pick up on anything. I moved on and plan to talk to him more later. He is in my wing.

The last guy I met was Gonzales. I knew Gonzales is having chemo. He is in my wing also. Everyone on my floor is in cancer treatment. Gonzales is a small Mexican and very nice, but you can tell he can be tough if he wants to be. Earlier that morning there was an incident with two guys who have had throat cancer and had their voice boxes removed. One was in a wheelchair, and they were having a serious argument and were trying to holler at each other. All you could hear was a lot of air coming out of the holes in their throats. Gonzales tried to step in and break it up so the guy in the wheelchair wanted to fight him. I heard Gonzales say, "Come on, don't be that way. I know you're bad. I'm bad too. If you like, we can go in my room, and I can show you how bad I am. But we don't need to do that. Let's not be that way. We all need to get along." So when I saw Gonzales on the track I asked him about his chemo; I wanted to know how sick he got. Gonzales said, "Oh no, I don't get sick at all. I give it all up to Jesus. It's covered by his blood." I asked him when he became a Christian. He said, "It happened when I came to prison four years ago, and it's so amazing the way the Lord is leading me." He lifted his finger up like he was following a line on the horizon and said, "I can just see how far he has brought me." He was genuine. It was so good to hear him talk about how good God is. It's interesting how God works when people just open themselves up to him.

I must talk to my roommate soon. Now he is writing to an old girlfriend in Mexico to see if she will take him. He is a nice guy. He has some Catholic things around his bunk, but I don't think he knows much. I thought I should let things season a little before beginning the conversation. It's a little more tense when it is your roommate, and you can't get away from each other. We need to respect each other's space.

3/31/13

Well, tomorrow is Easter, and I just got my property from Duluth. The main things were my Bible, my radio, and my MP3 player.

36

4/2/13

Well, I just had my first treatment this morning. It went well. I sat in a big La-Z-boy chair and took two long naps while they dripped the stuff into my veins. I don't think this is going to be too bad. I'm getting two cycles of treatment and then have to wait until the twenty-ninth to visit with the doctor so he can see how I'm doing. He will ask me how I'm feeling, try to see if it's doing any good, and then ask me if I want to continue. I feel like I want to do all I can short of burning up my insides. I don't think the doctor wants to do that either.

One part of the treatment is that I take a pill. If the pill works, I will break out in a rash and have pimples almost like acne. If that happens, it's a good thing and a sign that it is working. This cancer is a strange thing.

4/7/13

I've been here two weeks and two days now. I have started two of my three treatments. The pills I take have still not all come from the pharmacy. I hope they come today. Jan and Tom are coming today. Tom is driving her up in her car, and then he will fly home on Monday. It's going to be so good to see them. I miss Jan so much. At least when she is home she e-mails me a lot. On the road, of course, she can't do that. It's interesting how I don't realize the value of something until its gone. I guess that's our nature.

I've heard that there are some struggles in Duluth with the classes. It seems there might be a type of power struggle going on, not with the guys so much, but this is always what happens in prison when people move on. The mind-set is not about who is the most capable; rather, it's about who has been here the longest, and it creates turf wars. It's disappointing, but it's true. I think the classes have stopped for the moment.

I just had a conversation out on the track with an inmate. When he told me his story, I realized why I like my church. Joseph pulled up alongside me on the track, and this is how the conversation started. I had never met Joseph.

I saw him in a Bible study one night but never met him. Joseph just blurted out to me, "You know that a little Mexican dog can kill a Doberman?" I said, "No." He said, "When the Doberman swallows them, they get stuck in their throat." I don't know if that was a planned opener or not, but that's Joseph.

Joseph's story was that he was working for Ford Motor Company as a robotics engineer. He was gone almost all the time, and his family was under stress so he quit and went to UPS as a hazardous materials inspector. He has a wife and three children with the oldest being sixteen and the youngest eight. He said what he did was a really stupid and foolish thing. In opening material, he found stamp machines that validate passports. He stole one and sold it for $5,000. Over a period of time, he stole five more. The state turned it over to the federal government. They caught him with a hidden camera on the inside of a truck and saw him opening boxes. He was in jail eighteen months before his trial. He pled guilty and got a fifteen-year sentence.

Joseph said he has not seen his wife or children since he went to jail. His pastor went by the jail every day as he went to and from church, but in the year-and-a-half there, he only saw his pastor three times. His wife is very angry at him and has left him. He hasn't seen his children since that day. His pastor said he would appear for him and be a character witness. He didn't show. He said, "I went to that church for nine years. I tithed there. I always had my kids at all the church events. I sent the pastor a letter and apologized for what I had done. I asked him for help to try to get my family together or to help me to see my kids. I haven't even got a picture of my kids. My whole family has rejected me except two uncles." He said, "I have nobody."

Joseph does not have cancer. He is here as an orderly up on the fifth floor where men go to die. He said the nurses barely do their job. They are only interested in doing their job with the least amount of work. He said the inmates there don't get visits, hardly any of them. He said, "I tell them I'm going to try to be to you what I wished I had for me. This is the way I'm going to try to find peace."

I tell you this because Joseph's is not an isolated story. I have heard this from guys about their church way too much, particularly with churches that tend to have a legalistic view toward life. I think about how different my experience is. I have received so much grace, love, and acceptance from my church.

Let me tell you why visits and e-mails are so important. For me, I have more people who want to visit than I have room on my visitors' list, but I can receive unlimited e-mails. The reason they are so important to a prisoner is that in prison, and through the justice system, you are scorned. You reach the point that you expect people to respond negatively toward you. It means that if you don't hear from people you assume they think badly about you. Prison really has a stigma, not only for the inmate but for the families as well. I know so many spouses that have lost their jobs, even volunteer Sunday school jobs, because their husband is in prison. It is very hard on families even when they are accepted well. I'm sure this is why the Lord made such a point about "visiting him in prison." By the time men get out of prison, they are filled with fear of meeting the world again. They are broke, in most cases their families are gone too, and they have a history such that they can only get a minimal job, if any. Their lives are really ruined.

It makes me appreciate so much how my family has responded to me, and the acceptance I feel from all the e-mails. To me, a few lines on an e-mail is like a visit. It tells me people don't think of me in the way most people think of a prisoner.

When I walk into a new place, like the first time I walked into Duluth, I felt like I was walking in on a bunch of bad, undesirable people. After three years, I realize that they are not as bad as I thought, and I really am no better than they. I look the same, eat the same, and have the same rules they do. I'm inmate number 14451-041.

In my first days at Butner, I had the same shocking feeling. Everyone looked terrible to me. They looked different from the guys in Duluth; they looked older, sicker, and kind of like the walking dead. I've adjusted. I feel very much like one of them.

Joseph's eyes were welled up with tears as we talked. Fifteen years is a long time for him to sit with these thoughts. It's so sad.

4/9/13

Jan and Tom came on Friday. By the time they came, I could hardly walk to the visiting center. I tried to be strong for them, but I was so weak. I couldn't last until the visit was over. I had to excuse myself and go to the room. I walked the track, or tried to, for a while because I thought I needed the fresh air. I hurt so bad I went to the room. During the visit when we saw how I was, we started talking about Lisa and Craig's plan to put a hospital bed in their bedroom right off the living room. It would be such a nice place for me. It became evident to the three of us that the end for me was probably very near. I really felt like I was dying. We doubted I would ever go home by car. It was grim.

After they left I thought through my feelings and emotions. I realized it started a little bit on Tuesday when I visited the doctor. The first doctor in Duluth gave me three to six months. The second doctor in Duluth gave me six to eight with possibly another six months with treatment. When I went to the doctor here I was really hoping for another upward movement in the life expectancy. He seemed unwilling to give me any hope of life expectancy at all. He said three months, maybe six if treatment works. I didn't think I was affected much by that, but as I thought about it on Friday, I felt I was.

I enjoy writing. I started writing a book, and I got to the IRS invasion when my real sickness started. Thinking back, I tried to identify what it was. I never had a feeing of being mad at God in any way. I think I did feel disappointed that he wouldn't give me just a few more months. I'm disappointed in myself that I would become disappointed with something that I know is entirely in his hands. He has a plan. Talking about going home straight to a hospital bed made me feel badly. I have been visualizing Jan in our nice apartment and have been looking forward to just being able to go to sleep, holding Jan's hand at least one night. Now it doesn't look like that will ever happen. As I thought through the night, I became overwhelmed with feeling of failure, stupidity, and foolishness for the pain I have brought on my family. Usually I am excited about the grace I have received from God and everyone else, but I felt so totally unworthy and loathed myself.

I hadn't put this all together when I went to visiting. I only knew I was dying at a much faster rate than I was before. The night after the visit I was just thinking about this, and I asked God about it. Finally, at ten o'clock, I laid down for the night. As I lay there, a very evident change came over me. I noticed that I was so aware of its contact with the mattress on all parts of my body. Then all my pain just went away. Even pain that I did not know I had. I don't know if it makes sense, but when you get used to pain you ignore a lot of it. I felt such great peace and relief. I began to pray, just talking to God, and my praying went in and out of praying, meditating, and thinking. I felt myself loving and appreciating God again the way I was having a problem with before. It was sometime after 1:00 a.m. that I fell asleep. The three hours waiting for sleep were not bad hours; they were good, with perfect comfort. All my pains were gone.

The next morning I got up and ate a good breakfast of tuna on bread. I went down and met Tom and Jan at visiting, and it was like they saw me in Duluth. I don't know at what point it was, but I became aware somewhere in there that I had been through some serious spiritual warfare. I don't talk about that much in life, because I don't like giving Satan much credit for anything. I've heard a lot of that and tend to want to avoid it. But throughout the process of writing about it and the years of living through it, I think I understand more of what it is. I really think I know now that Satan still wants to have me. During those two days, I second guessed bold statements I've made about God and the strength he has given me. It was thrown in my face that day. I was caused to wonder if I had been foolish and if I had spoken too soon.

Tom and Jan came at a critical time for me. I know, them being here was a big part of me pulling out of it. I believe I really was that sick. I believe I really was dying. I believe the Lord really has restored me. Satan wanted to have me, but I know the Lord is going to use it to remind me of my dependence on him.

Today I was reminded that the guys in Duluth are also under attack. The classes have been stopped because of an incident Matt had. I think it will be six months before they can start again. That's not good, because they will lose momentum. But it is also discouraging for the guys. Matt has lost visiting privileges with his family and phone privileges for either three or six months. I'm sure there is a lot of discouragement there.

I realize so much what a privilege it was to present the glory of the Lord almost every day in Duluth. I really miss that, more than I realized I would. I just need to be sharing. There are plenty of people here to share with. It just takes time to get acquainted, find a place, and know the territory. I also hope to leave soon. There are five right now willing to talk. Also, the writing of the book right now needs to be a priority.

4/15/13

I'm so looking forward to driving home with Jan. I always said, "I can't wait just to get into a car and drive and drive." I had no idea I could do it so soon and so far. We will take three days driving home. I want to just poke along, enjoying the countryside and the beauty of creation. It will be spring and a great time to do it.

Visiting here is very different. I am patted down when I come in like at Duluth. When I leave, every time is a complete strip search, completely stripped, bend over and cough, and then dress again. If I need to use the bathroom during visiting, I must go with the guard, completely undress and use the stool while being watched. Then I have to dress again and continue to visit. It would be nice if we had clothes with just a big Velcro strip down the back that we could step in and out of. It's pretty amazing to me how soon these things become normal, and I don't think much of it.

What became more evident as we talked is that I'm not even mindful of the hardness of this place. I'm living on a floor with 200 very sick and dying men. I know this is not a place where children like to see their aging dad. But the amazing thing is that, for me, I don't really live here. I don't live in the reality of it. My reality is that I am the Lord's, and he is caring for me and meeting all my needs. I don't see that there is anything I need that I don't have. I have a hard time sleeping, and many nights I don't fall asleep until 5:00 a.m. For my family, that is terrible to think about. For me, I have found that it is not terrible to lie there all night. I lie there and am so mindful that my body has no pain.

The chemo hasn't been bad, and I am not sick. I have a rash, little pimples in my mouth and on my tongue, everything tastes bitter, and I itch, but that's nothing. The pills are working. I have a rash all over my body like chicken pox. The doctor said if that happens, that's good news, and we want that to happen. Well, it's happening, so praise God. I also feel so good. Even the pain that I had that got me to the doctor originally is completely gone. I don't know if the pain had anything to do with the cancer at all, but it seems that God just put it there to get me to the doctor. Isn't that amazing? Also, we have been approved for full medical coverage at the VA hospital. So when I get home that will all be taken care of at the VA.

4/21/13

Writing keeps me from engaging with inmates. Also, knowing I'm going to be leaving soon also makes it hard to set up a game plan for engaging. One thing that strikes me as different from Duluth is that there are a lot more typical felons here, in the way we think of felons.

One guy I've met is a really nice looking friendly guy who I always greet. We smile or have comments as we pass. He is really nice and from Georgia. One day I asked him what he did on the outside, expecting to hear a profession. Instead he said, "Oh, I smuggled lots of things. I started when I was a kid. It was so much fun. I was doing things around the city. But I must say I've had a good life, and I can't complain. I got a lot of time up front in those 747s. I've been all over the world. I just acted like a spoiled rich kid, which I was, because my parents had so much money. That's why they never knew where I was because they were always traveling themselves. They had homes in six different countries. I could have lived in any one of them." I said, "With all that money why did you do what you did?" He said, "It was the rush. Oh it was fun. The last gig I did I was smuggling hash out of Africa. I'd pack the stuff into suitcases with false sides. I would hire really good looking women with little children. I'd buy them a really nice dress and a first class ticket for them and the little kid. I just told them to get on that plane and smile like you don't have a care in the world. The cops would see her and say we don't need to check her; she's got plenty of money." "It was so exciting. I made $100,000 every three weeks. It was a rush." And his face lit up like he was talking about sky diving. Then he said, "I've got another fifteen years here, but I can't complain. I've had a good ride".

It does cause concern when I see a man here with the same pancreatic cancer I have, diagnosed the same month. His chemo offended his body so bad they had to stop treatment. They put him up on the fifth floor this week to die. There isn't anything they can do for him. He is trying to get compassionate release. His has been on the warden's desk for a month, and he hasn't heard anything. I did find out that he has violence in his past, and he still has twelve years left on his sentence. I do think that would make some difference.

4/24/13

One step has been made on the release. The social worker told me the committee has met and approved the release. Now he waits for some items from my case worker and others in order to complete the file to put it on the warden's desk. I found out who the warden is. He is new here, and according to the COs, he is a nice man who will listen to anybody. He stands in the lunch line almost every day and talks to inmates. Now that I know who he is, I will introduce myself so he can put a face with it. The social worker has no idea how long Washington takes.

I had a visitor last week who overnighted his request form to the CO. I talked to the CO and asked him if he had received it. He said he did and was about to key it into the system. He said he would do it right away. I didn't feel the need to check back with him again, but I should have. This CO is like Mr. Duke. He doesn't like doing his job. He didn't key it in.

My friend Steve came more than a thousand miles. I was visiting with another visitor at the time. He never came.

Yesterday, I was in my room, and the cop came and opened the door to my room and said, "Are you Mr. Goris?"

I said, "I am."

He said, "Come with me. I'm supposed to take you to the lieutenant's office."

Going to the lieutenant's office is not a good thing. It's the next thing to being arrested. We got to the lieutenant's office, and he must have forgotten we were coming. I sat and waited for thirty minutes thinking through my last days and wondering what I could possibly have done.

The lieutenant finally came. He sat me down on a chair, and he sat down and looked right in my face. He said, "Mr. Goris, do you know why I called you here?"

I said, "I have no idea."

He said, "You had a visitor this last week who was not on the visitors' list. Now I know the problem with the CO, and I can handle that. But your visitor called the COs home and left a message. That is a federal offense. Someone could go to jail over this. That could be considered a terrorist threat. The nation is a little nervous right now and we aren't putting up with that stuff. Now you call your friend and tell him he better drop this thing right here and never try it again. In fact, he better not try to come here again."

4/25/13

Jimmy the Fish (Jim) is on the Internet a lot, and I am on it a lot. He tried to tease me that I am writing a book, and I said I am writing a book. I could tell he didn't like it. My thought was that he was afraid I might be a snitch or something like that. I made a point to get with him.

He said "You got to realize you can't be on the keyboards there all the time. There are a lot of guys here that need those computers, and you being on there for hours is a problem."

He went on and on, and after a while, I just interrupted him and said, "Jim, that's all right. It's not a problem. I'm at a good place to stop right now, and I will. I don't want to be a problem for you or for anyone else." Then I said, "But I'd like to meet with you and tell you about my book."

An hour later he came over and said, "Okay, let's talk." I told him my story like I always do. It was my life story but shortened and modified to fit our situation.

It came to the ministry stuff, and he said, "Are you a minister?" He was smiling.

I said "No,"

And he said, "Let me tell you something. I thought there was something different about you. You are soft spoken, you don't seem to make an issue out of your own interests, and you just don't seem to fit here." Then he told me how he grew up in Dallas as an only child; he went to a Baptist church as a child, attended Dallas Christian Academy, and named his first daughter after the name of the church. He even showed me a big tattoo on his arm with the name of the church and daughter on his arm. Then he told me the story of how he became involved with the Mafia, married the boss's daughter, and grew deeper and deeper into crime on a global basis. That's a whole story in itself.

Anyway, after all that, he said, "Hey, your time on the computer really isn't a problem. Nobody has said anything to me about you doing that; I just wanted to get on you."

I said, "Well, it's not a problem for me to give it up. I don't want to offend anyone, and I just don't need to do that."

He said, "No, please, please don't change anything. Please, keep doing it. I'll be offended if you don't."

I've been here a month now, and I notice something happening here that began happening in Duluth. It just took longer in Duluth. People are starting to acknowledge me more. They are greeting me, and inviting me to sit at their table (some inmates set glasses by all the empty seats around them saving the seats for their phantom friends because they are fussy who they sit with). A lot of those things are happening.

I have come to believe that people are seeing something in me that has an attraction. It seems that as God has revealed more of himself to me, I gain more of an understanding of what it means to follow him. As he transforms me by the renewing of my mind and as I grow in humility and grace, it is easier for me to admit my shortcomings and failures. I am growing in a way that reflects Christ more, and instead of seeing the self-centered man of flesh that I am attempting to die to, Christ's spirit is transforming me. The Apostle Paul calls that an aroma. Instead of the old aroma of "death to death," it is the aroma of "life to life." It's interesting that he says we are the aroma of Christ to God. He is saying this is a pleasing aroma to God. It also seems that Paul understands how I feel with this because he asks whether anyone is sufficient for these things. I know I am not. In fact, only God is. It is only Jesus. I get to carry the aroma of Jesus because I am serving with him and something is rubbing off.

And there are those who carry the aroma of death. There is a lot of that here, but God's people smell different.

4/29/13

I just came from my appointment with the oncologist. He was very surprised that the chemo did not go against me. Also the chemo pill is doing its job and that he can give me salve for the rash and acne, He said now we will do another round of the same. We will do this every month. After four cycles he will do another CT scan and see if it's helping. He is surprised I am feeling so good, I have a good appetite. He is careful not to be optimistic, but I could tell he was pleased.

37

5/6/13

I have always heard people talk about fighting cancer and that really seemed strange to me. I thought, well, if you have cancer, you just have it, and there isn't anything to do. Now I find out it is fighting. I fight to eat, for example. Chemo on an empty stomach is a killer. The guys here have said it, and I find it to be true. At first I didn't eat so much because I was trying to eat healthy. There is no healthy food here so that meant I ate very little, but that's the wrong thing to do with chemo. Now I fight cancer by eating all I can get myself to eat. During treatment, everything tastes bitter. Even water tastes bitter. I don't get the metal taste because they give me medication before the chemo for that, but I taste bitter.

I also fight cancer by keeping my attitude up. I used to not have to work very hard at that. My time is getting shorter now, and I really want, and expect, a compassionate release. I have to work at staying positive. I have to work at practicing what I preach about waiting on the Lord and being satisfied in him. I think the wheels are turning too slowly here on that. This week I am going to approach the warden in the lunch line, and I'm going to ask for some account-ability from people who are supposed to be doing things. This week there was an article in the paper that stated that last year there were 125 compassion-ate releases granted and twenty-five of them had died before the release was approved. We have the Speaker of the House for the state of Massachusetts here as an inmate, and he says it's time to pull out all the stops on getting out.

I wanted to talk about Mother's Day since we are just one week away. The longer I'm married and the longer I realize the blessings of being married to a well-grounded biblically established wife, I know that for every man who is married, and appreciates his wife, we really have two mothers we should honor. The first is our own mother, and the second is our mother-in-law. As I marvel at Jan and what she means to me and how she serves and loves, I just see her mother in her so much. Although her mother, Francis, is with the Lord now, I thank God for her. She is the one who taught her daughters how to love their husbands and submit to them as their husbands submit to Christ. In all appreciation to my wife, Jan, I want to honor her mother Francis and all the godly mothers who knowingly and unknowingly have served God in their homes, always giving of themselves so unselfishly and never seeking honor or recognition for themselves. They have followed God's plan, and we are so blessed. Guys, remember the woman who gave you your wife.

5/8/13

God gave me a great boost today. I have been missing the ministry a lot thinking that my calling for this time is for my writing, and my writing hasn't been going that well, in my opinion. Jan was here for four days this week. We did a lot of praying together and reading, which may have lead to this guy approaching me today.

I was waiting in the commissary line, and a man started talking to me. He did not introduce himself to me; he just said, "You must be from North Carolina." I said, "No, I'm from Minnesota." He said, "Well, you sure get a lot of visits." I explained that my wife has moved up here to Charlotte so she can be with me on weekends, and we have a lot of friends who want to visit me because we just found out about my cancer. He asked how long we've been married. I told him fifty-two years. He said, "That's amazing. Were you always faithful to your wife?" I said, "Yes, I've always been faithful." I said, "We are Christians and being faithful is important to people who are Christians." He seemed quite sensitive so I asked him, "Are you a Christian?" He said, "No, but I'm going to be when I go home. I want my whole family to be Christian." I said, "I'd like to talk to you about that. The Bible tells us how to be Christians and exactly how we should be in our home if we are Christian. It will teach you how to be a husband to your wife, and how your wife should be to you."

He said, "I've been married twenty-four years, but I never knew what a good wife I had until five years ago when I lost my case." He said, "I wasn't always faithful to my wife. I mean, I never had sex with another woman, but I wasn't faithful to her. I thought I had to be faithful to my friends, and I thought my loyalty to them was more important. She always went along with it. But as my money went, my job went. Then my friends all went, but my wife stayed with me. I've apologized to her, but she just said, 'Oh, you've been a good husband.' But I want to be a whole lot better one, and I want to be a Christian and want to do that when I get home." I said, "Well, now is the time to start, and this is the place to do it. We need to find a place we can talk." He said he has a Bible, and he wants to meet in the library tomorrow at 9:30. He looked me up three times since then to be sure I remembered.

5/13/13

I just spent three days with Jan. I'm so pleased that we can spend three days together and the time never gets long. Most of the time is spent reflecting on God, what he is doing, reading his Word, praying, and marveling at who he is and his mighty character. I feel like it's a big part of keeping me as a tree planted by the river of living waters, and that from this I can bring forth fruit in due season. That's what I need. I need to bear fruit.

I met another guy; his name is Elijah. I noticed he always picks the chairs right next to us in visiting. He has a really nice wife. They are very hard working and have a very good potato chip business and an ice cream business; she is also an MET and a beautician. Elijah told me that when he gets out he wants to be a Christian, he and his whole family. Today, I walked with him and got a little more of his story. Elijah and Mary have been together as friends since they were fourteen years old. Elijah's dad beat up his mother so much that his mother left when he was about twelve. He took care of his brothers and lived with his dad and his dad's girlfriend until he was fifteen. He got kicked out at age fifteen and lived in his car, but he ate meals with Mary.

When he was eighteen years old, he worked on a chicken farm and had other jobs. When he was seventeen he actually made enough money that he was able to get an apartment. Mary moved in with him and got pregnant. They built several successful businesses, but he served five years prior for selling drugs. Then a year ago he had a friend who claimed to have a bad need for a drug, and he told him where he could get some. It turned out his friend was an agent, and he got another eighteen months, and that's why he's here now.

Elijah says that they are not Christians, but he said, "My wife Mary has the heart of a Christian. We both are always helping people." He said, "When I was twenty-four years old and had enough money, I hired a detective to find my mother. She was in a nursing home. I took her in, and my wife is taking care of her right now even as I am in prison." He said, "I know doing good works doesn't make a person a Christian. I know we aren't Christians, but we want to be." I said, "So, I'm here to show you how to be a Christian. Are you ready to start now?" He said, "Yes, that's what I want." Isn't this such a clear example of God doing the work and that there are fields ready for harvest? I told him today of my condition and that I don't have much time to live according to the doctors, even though I think they are wrong. I said, "I don't think I will be here long so we need to really be on a fast track here so you can learn what you need to learn." He said he will be available every day.

I did have an encouraging word this week on a movement of my file from the case manager to the warden's desk. It would be so wonderful if I could be home for Lydia's graduation on the twenty-seventh. But how do I dare to ask for so much when men are dying all around me? Last month they had a memorial service for eighteen men who died. This past week it was for twenty-six men. When we live in the middle of sickness and death, it seems selfish to ask for so much as a release for a graduation event or a release to be able to take a cross-country, springtime drive with Jan. God is good, and I'm glad he doesn't meet our blessings according to what we deserve. He is so gracious. I know he has been more gracious all my life than I have noticed or given him credit for.

I sat with Jan these last three days in this visiting center. It's not a desirable place. The circumstances were not anyone's choice, but I am so pleasantly amazed at how thrilled I am to be with her. We read Scripture together, not only because I wanted to but because I know how Jan loves to and how it feeds her soul when we do that. How it thrilled both our hearts to pray together, not out of obligation or duty but because the God of the universe made it possible through our Savior! We can have direct contact and communication with him. Together, Jan and I can share our hearts in a three-way relationship that we do not tire of. It's not a feeling of duty but a feeling of desire and pleasure.

After three days of doing just that and nothing more, I still got back to my room last night and couldn't wait to call her on the phone again, just to hear her voice. I had nothing more to say, but I wanted to hear her voice. I don't think I ever had this kind of love before, and I think God is doing something in us and changing us to a place we never want to return from.

I am really sleeping now. I take my medication early, I thought too early, but I actually slept last night from 8:00 p.m. until 6:00 a.m. That is so amazing. Also, my release made it past one more check point last week. I will talk to the warden tomorrow to see how he's doing with it. He has been very approachable for me.

God has answered every prayer, and I feel no pain. I do believe God is doing something in my body. I have no evidence of any cancer in me. I feel wonderful. I walk three miles a day, and I did thirty-five push-ups yesterday. I decided it is time to start building my muscles back. I am not going to live like I'm going to die. I'm going to live like I'm going to live. And every day the Lord gives me I will use to proclaim him at every opportunity I get. I will ask him to guide me so that nobody gets tired of hearing it and so that he will keep my testimony fresh and interesting.

One of my favorite jobs on the farm as a boy was swathing grain. Dad let me run the swather when I was ten years old. It was fun when the oats were standing straight and tall. When the cutter bar came to cut the oats, the reel would push the oat plant over at just the right time so that the oats would fall on the swathe canvas. Then the canvas belt would run them all to the end where they were dropped off. The grain would dry there for another ten days, and then the combine would come. The straw would go into the combine (all heads first and all the same way), and the beaters in the combine would beat the oat grain out of the straw. There was a fan in there with little doors so that you could regulate the amount of wind that came over the grain. Just the right amount of wind would blow the chaff away and leave the grain. Then the grain would fall through the sieves and into an auger that would auger the oat kernels into a bin to be hauled away and saved. The oat kernels were the prize of the plant. It was used for feed for cattle and people. The chaff would be blown away in the wind. It had no value. The straw would go out the back for lesser service. It would be used for bedding for the cattle until we cleaned the barn and it would then be hauled out as manure.

In the same way, the Lord of the harvest comes to harvest his church. How great it is when the church is all in agreement about the way Christ taught the apostles to administer it. Sometimes in the fields, we would get a hard rain, and the grain would get heavy. The grain would go down and would not stand until the reaper laid it down the same way. It was hard to harvest. It caused some of the kernels to get blown away with the chaff because it couldn't be beaten out of the straw properly. I loved harvest time. Dad let me run the machine, but he kept a close eye on me from a distance. It was important that the settings on the combine and machinery were set right. We wouldn't want good kernels to be blown away like chaff. We wouldn't want chaff to go into the bin with the good kernels.

5/22/13

As I walked the track today, I was pondering a truth and making some connections from my childhood days on the farm that really stayed with me. As a boy, I really wanted to be able to do all the things that men do on the farm. Dad let me do a lot of things in the field that were beyond my years, and I know that in order for him to do that he had to settle for less than the best. One thing he never let me do was plant corn. One thing farmers wanted with corn planting was straight rows, and the most important row was the first path through the field, because all the other paths through the field would work off the first path. If you got a hitch in the row on the first pass, every row would have a hitch in it after that. I sat on the fender as Dad planted, and he said, "Son, I'll show you how to make a straight row." He said, "You need to pick out something on the horizon that is way on the far side of the field and drive straight toward it. Never take your eyes off it. You can't look back, because if you do the steering wheel will turn and you'll have a crooked row." I watched him do it many times, but that is one job he never let me do.

I practiced his technique with other things. With a disk or a mower or with whatever I was doing, I would practice making straight rows, especially the first row. I would stand up on the tractor and focus on the landmark. If I needed to look back to check the implement I was pulling, I knew I had to stop the tractor. If I turned my head, my shoulder would turn, and there would be a crook in the line. It wasn't absolutely necessary to have everything be perfectly straight, it just gave me something to do while I was doing my work. Everything looked nicer with straight rows.

The reason I thought of this as I walked the track today is because I was thinking about living the Christian life in all circumstances and how I have learned to practice keeping my eye on the landmark all through life. One of my prayer partners picked up on this without me saying anything about it, but I am writing about it now. He said, "It seems to me you know how you should live, and you're trying to live it out that way". That is exactly right. I think I know how God wants me to respond to all this in my life, and I am trying my best to walk it out the way he wants me to.

5/25/13

Today, Elijah prayed to receive Christ. It was all God, and nothing of me; in fact, I tried to put him off. I have been trying to connect with him for some time, and it just wasn't working out. I began wondering if he was as interested as he said. As I finished my walk on the track, there he was. He said, "Let's sit in the shade and talk. It's a hot day here."

We sat down, and the first question he asked was, "How is it that you and your wife have been married for fifty-two years?" I said, "Well, we are both Christians. We realize our lives are not about us, and they belong to the Lord." He said, "Is your wife a Christian?" I said, "Yes." He said, "Would you have married her if she wasn't?" I said, "No, I don't think I would. God doesn't want his children to become equally yoked with unbelievers and that means we need to be in equal agreements, not only in marriage but in business as well." He had more questions. I said, "Let me get my Bible. Otherwise I'm just giving you my opinion about things. I want you to get it from God himself." As I left he called me back, and he said, "Bob, do you think I could ever be a good Christian brother?"

I got my Bible, and we met in the courtyard. I wanted him to read it, but he said he didn't have his glasses. I asked Elijah where he thought Jesus came from. Elijah didn't know, but he broke the silence. He said "Can we pray?" I said, "Yes, what do you want to pray for? Do you want to become a follower of Jesus?" He said, "I do." I said a short prayer, and he prayed a salvation prayer repeating after me. He was sincere, and he was prepared by God before I came. He was like a really red tomato just ready to fall off the vine. The Lord had so completely done the work.

It was a thrilling day for me. It's been two months since I have been able to introduce someone to the Lord, and the Lord knew I needed that too. I am always amazed that there are people all over that God is speaking to. We are probably walking by them every day and not noticing, because we are too busy or too preoccupied.

5/27/13

A friend sent me the book *Authentic Christianity* by Ray Stedman some time ago. I'm reading it for the second time, and parts of it for the third time. His book is about the signs of life of new Christians and then goes into three possible choices Christians can make as they become older in the faith. He says, "Inevitably, sooner or later, the old natural life begins to reassert itself. The glow begins to fade from Christian worship, and Bible reading becomes less and less rewarding."[6]

According to Stedman, first, the young Christian may continue his decline to the point of dropping out of all Christian relationships, neglecting the Bible, abandoning prayer, losing interest in spiritual things, and falling back into the previous life style. Second, the young Christian may become aware of his cold and rebellious heart, become frightened by the thought of regressing to what he was before, and repentantly cast himself upon God's mercy, renewing his trust in God's promises. Third, and the most likely possibility, is that the new Christian may discover what millions of others before him have learned: it is possible to avoid the pain and humiliation of these cycles of repentance and renewal by maintaining an outward facade of spiritual commitment, moral impeccability, and orthodox behavior. One can simply maintain an outward reputation for spiritual maturity that is satisfying to the ego, even thought he is inwardly haunted by the fact that his "Christianity" is a hollow shell. Such an outwardly Christian lifestyle is so prevalent today that a new Christian can hardly be blamed for adopting it and regarding it as normal. He drifts into it with only an occasional twinge of doubt or a rare, faint pang of conscience.

38

6/5/13

I do believe that prayer moves the hands of God, and he moves the hands of man. Yesterday, I was reading in my room when the social worker came into my room and said we needed to meet. He told me that the BOP in Washington signed off on the papers on May 20, which was almost two weeks ago. One would think that in twenty days it should be ready to come back from the judge; if so, the social worker will tell me I must be out of here within forty-eight hours. The judge needs to set up the court order, and, of course, the IRS will be there and can protest. More than likely, this should go through.

6/6/13

I am saddened today because of all the guys around me—you could call them friends—who are drug dealers, bank robbers, armed robbers, and many different things. It just hit me that as I ask them about their time so many have been down for fifteen to thirty years already and still have eight or nine to go. They are people just like me. You can't pick them out. I know they need prison, but it just seems like the sentences are so very long. I'm not criticizing the system at this moment; I am just sad for so much wasted life, lost life, lost relationships, and the lack of hope for a future if they ever get out. A number of them have life sentences. They are just like the man next door to you. I wonder if there isn't some way people could be taught, on first offenses, about what will happen to them if they continue; perhaps they could be given a shorter sentence as a trial run. Some are considered career criminals because they have offended three times. That's mandatory, and I can see that as right. I don't know, it's just my heart going out to these guys.

This morning I received the news we are looking for. My release has been approved, and tomorrow I will be on my way home. Isn't that amazing? Thursday morning I was sitting in my chemo chair with the needles in my arm but no medicine going through because the pharmacy hadn't' mixed my bags yet. Three nurses came to me seeming pretty happy and said, "Mr. Goris, we have good news for you. Your release has been approved. Do you want to continue with this treatment, or do you want to quit?" I said, "I want to continue, but I want to get it done and get out of here." They assured me the bags would be there shortly.

Two hours later, I was still waiting. Another nurse came along, and I said, "When will I be released?" She said, "I don't know, but it needs to be tomorrow because we aren't allowed to keep you over the weekend." I said, "Unhook me. I want to call my wife." She said, "Oh, I'm sure your wife would rather you have this treatment."

Two-and-a-half hours later, I was finally finished with my treatment. I went back to my floor and asked the head nurse when my release would be. She called R & D. They said the earliest would be 8:30. I figured that could be any time before noon, but I was going to be ready. I wanted to talk to Jan because she had met Tom who had just flown in to visit me. I wanted to stop her because she was staying in Charlotte two-and-a-half hours away, and I wanted to tell her to pack her stuff for going home. We were told that Jan would be the first to know of my release so when I called her I said, "Well what do you think of the news?" She said, "What news?" I said, "I'm getting released." She couldn't believe it was real. I told her to turn around and go back to Charlotte and pack up all her things to go home. She did and then came for the afternoon visit with Tom.

That afternoon they told me to pack up my stuff because I would be leaving Friday. I told them to put me down for 8:30 a.m. I spent the rest of the night and early Friday morning getting rid of my stuff. I handed most everything out because what we consider junk here is pretty valuable there. I tried to take care of my friends.

I am ecstatic that the time has finally come. It's still quite unbelievable to me and will be until I'm in the car heading for home. Jan will pick me up at 8:30, and we will drive through the weekend. It will be quite an experience.

I also have feelings of strange sadness. Different here in Butner than Duluth. There are so many guys with such long sentences, and it's painful for me to think of the waste of human life. I wish there were better answers and alternatives to corrections.

I also have feelings of great gratitude for what God has done and what he has let me see and experience: the relationship with prayer partners and for all relationships that I have had for years that I am sure are now much deeper. I'm sure there will be a lot of contemplating on the way home and in the days to come.

From Jan

After two-and-a-half months, as I was driving to Butner for my week-end visit, my cell phone rang. It was to be Bob's last call from prison. I heard him say, "I'm being released tomorrow at 8:30 a.m. Go back to Charlotte and pack your bags; were going home!" Words cannot describe the joy in hearing the news. I turned around, headed back to Charlotte, packed my belongings, and said good-bye to the sweet family that took me in.

6/7/13

I got up early and took my clothes and bedding to the laundry and was supposed to get a receipt for it. There was nobody there; I threw the stuff in a big hamper they had and an inmate said, "I'll sign that for you; they never look at it anyway." I found a cart and went to my room and loaded my bags of books and other property on the cart. I went to the waiting area on our floor by the elevator and waited for my name to be called. I know how they are on remembering to call, meaning that 8:30 could be any time between 8:30 and noon. Sometimes, they lock down the elevators, and you can miss appointments. At 8:30 a.m., for some reason, the gate to the elevator opened. Nobody was around so I just pushed my cart through. The elevator was there, and the door opened. I went to the first floor where R & D was, but I still hadn't been called.

The big steel door to the hallway to R & D is always locked, and a guard needs to open it. An inmate was coming through from the other side and said, "You want to go here?" I said, "Yes," and I shot through the door. My next big fear was showing up without being called. In Duluth that would have been a fatal mistake. This was all very dramatic for me. I was down on the first floor without being called. I could get a shot for this. It was starting to feel more like a prison break than a release. As I got to the door an inmate was just coming out and said, "Here, you can go in here." I said, "I don't know if I can." I saw a guard in there and said, "Can I come in?" He said, "What do you want?" I said, "I'm supposed to leave at 8:30, and my wife is waiting for me." He said, "Well nobody is out there, and nobody called." I said, "You'd better check." Jan and Tom were waiting for me. The guards gave me a speedy check out and didn't even look in my boxes; they just wanted me out of their hair. In fifteen minutes, I was outside with Jan and Tom. We got outside the visitor center where the shrubbery was manicured and looks so great. I said, "Wow, I didn't know

I was living in paradise." We laughed about how it all went. It was almost like a jail break. Nobody called me, and nobody told me to go. If I hadn't taken the matter into my own hands, I probably wouldn't have gotten out of there until noon. It seemed to be all legal—at least nobody shot at us as we left.

It was so great to be free. After breakfast we parted ways with Tom. He took the renal car back to the airport and flew home. Jan and I had the next three days, which we had looked forward to so much, and it was wonderful. We stopped for gas, and I got out of the car and felt like I should wait for a guard to walk ahead of me. I went into the gas station with five dollars cash in my pocket and bought a newspaper. That was so great.

The drive through the Blue Ridge Mountains was so nice. The country was so beautiful, the trees were greener, the cars were newer, and it just seemed that everybody has such a good life and affluence.

We planned to travel short days but drove until midnight the first two nights because we stopped so much and wanted to get to Amy in Kansas City and see them. In Kansas City, Amy had a bunch of friends who are prayer partners over to celebrate with food and prayer. Matt's family, who live only about twenty minutes from Amy, came too. They met some of the prayer partners. It was a great time.

Sunday night we got into Minneapolis late so we stayed with Tom and Jill at their new place in Bloomington. We slept in Lydia's bedroom. Monday morning, bright and early, we were at the probation office to meet the PO. He's a nice man. I only have to send in an e-mail report once a month, but I am under supervised release for three years. I'm not supposed to leave the state for the first two months. I told him my life expectancy, and I said I feel strong right now and would like to visit my grandchildren in Dallas and in Kansas City while I still have strength. He said he could ask the judge but usually that is not done in the first two months. I said I'd rather he not ask the judge, because I just don't want my name coming up in front of her more than necessary.

Later, as we were driving home, the phone rang. It was the PO. He said he had called the judge and she said she would give permission due to the circumstances.

It's hard to take it all in. We went to a picnic in the park with Lisa's church. Experiencing the worship was just overwhelming to me. I couldn't sing, although I wanted to very much. Then the expressions of joy and love to me from the people really did me in. I was very emotional. I thought, "I hope I can get used to this."

Sunday, we went to our home church in Willmar. For three years I was wondering how that would be. There was hesitancy on my part, but I thought I needed to break the ice. The experience was so wonderful. So much love, grace, and acceptance; it was just overwhelming, but it was so good. I'm so glad we went. We stayed with my sister Marcy. It was good to be with her. Our extended family has grown so much closer through all of this.

This coming weekend my grandson, Levi, is having his graduation party here, and there will be many prayer partners from Lisa's church as well as extended family in attendance. We are also planning to have a thanksgiving celebration at the Willmar Evangelical Free Church on June 27. We are going to honor God for his faithfulness, forgiveness, grace, and mercy. I pray that it will be a time of encouragement for others who are going through hard times. Our family will lead some worship, I'll do some speaking, and we will pray. All the good that has come from this is from God's hand, and he blesses us even when we are unworthy. It's all about God and his goodness.

At the same time, everything is hard to do now that I am home. I have to get a new phone service and figure out what to do for a computer. We are so thankful for the nice apartment we have here with Lisa and Craig. It's a real garden apartment. Right out our door is a beautiful garden that Jan keeps herself very busy in. We have grandchildren stopping in and running through. It's really great. It's so nice to have the little ones around.

I am feeling strong although the emotions that are tied to my experiences of the grace of God at every turn are almost more than I can contain. Things like praying with family, singing, or looking at photo albums are very emotional for me. Meeting people who have prayed so much for me just brings me such overwhelming emotions of thanksgiving, and it is hard to adjust. I have much strength, but I know my strength dissipates quite quickly with activity. My voice is starting to come back and is getting stronger. I feel like somebody stole my clock, and I don't know what time it is with my life. While I am praying and hoping for, and expecting, many more days of life and useful service, there is something I just want to get done. I want to get all our prayer partners together to praise and thank the Lord, not only for what he has done for me but also for what he has demonstrated of himself. I look forward to a time to really cement in what we have learned about God, his character, and his mighty deeds. When I went to prison, I asked God to go before me, and he did. I asked him to be there with me, and he was. I asked him to be on the other side of it, and now he is. I am so thankful and have so much joy that I can't even speak of it right now.

From Jan

I was at the prison at 8:15 a.m. Tom had flown in for the weekend to visit. I was so thankfrul he was there. After so many changes and disappointments in prison rules, I was not sure if Bob would really be released this quickly, with less than a day's notice. At 8:35, I heard Bob's voice at the guard's desk. "I'm being released," he told the guard. "Well, then go," the guard replied.

Tom ran and got my car, opened the trunk, and Bob wheeled his cart with all his belongings down the sidewalk. The box contained books, packs of letters, one change of clothes, a pair of boots, and the new Bible I sent him three years before. It didn't look so new anymore. It was well worn and underlined from beginning to end, including the hundreds of pages of commentary after Revelation, which he studied and used for teaching in Duluth. Some pages were stuck together from reading them under the big maple tree by the chapel in Duluth.

We were on our way to freedom. We stopped for breakfast at the first exit we saw. Bob was more than eager to down a good breakfast of bacon and eggs, grits, pancakes, and coffee. Tom and I grinned as we watched him pick up his spoon to spread butter and jelly on his toast. He had not had a butter knife in his hands for three years.

We had seventy-two hours to get back to Minnesota and report to the PO. We took our time and enjoyed the lush green country and the beauty of a state we had not traveled through before. We stopped at Billy Graham's retreat center in Asheville. We walked into the chapel and up the stairs of the prayer tower. It was a fitting place for us to begin our life together again in prayer; we thanked God for his goodness and mercy toward us and for keeping us through these years of being apart. We thanked him for sustaining us through this journey and prayed for guidance for the days ahead.

39

7/9/13

Day-by-day, the Lord lets me realize the longings of my heart. I longed to be able to ride home with Jan in the car. There were days in Butner that I was sure I would have to be flown home, but when the day came, we drove, and I drove a lot of the time. We had a wonderful time. I longed to be with my whole family again and sing and enjoy them in our home. That has happened, and I still long to spend more time with each one individually.

I longed for a time of celebration in Willmar, and the Lord gave me that. Friends in our home church in Willmar set it up. Many came to our night of celebration. My whole family was there, and we led worship. The time of worship was so good. I could tell everyone was enjoying it so much, praising the Lord for all he had done for us. It was like we had been through this experience together. My voice even came back that night, and I have had it ever since. I can't remember for sure, but I think I even prayed that night with the group that I could control my emotions. That was just answered prayer. It was so good to look into the audience and see everyone enjoying their worship so much. It was so powerful and energizing for me. I tried to write something to say that night. I had notes, but I was not comfortable with what I wrote. I prayed and had others praying for me. I didn't say anything I planned to say and don't know what I said, but Jan said she was comfortable with what I said so I trust it was okay.

I really wanted to travel along the north shore of Lake Superior with Amy's family, and we did that. I desired to take some of my grandchildren through *First Principles*, and we started that on that trip. The twelve and fourteen year olds really got it, and I was so thrilled with their response and their ability to understand it. We have set up more times now to continue with it. God has granted me that. I still desire to do more with some of the others and have initiated some conversation with that. I believe God is going to work that out. This is my greatest wish yet for my life.

Some have said they wished I had said more about my health condition in Willmar. Actually, I forget I have cancer at times and it almost seems unimportant to me. This week I visited the VA hospital and met with my oncologist. The oncologist just refused to give any hope. He said one of the medications I am taking in pill form costs about six thousand dollars a month, and he said he doubts it will extend my life even fourteen days. He said, with the other meds I am taking, he would give me maybe six months. If he would add one more medication that he is thinking of adding, he would maybe give me eight months. I don't know when he is counting from, but I don't know that it makes any difference.

Then we met with another doctor about hospice for when that time comes. He said his area is broader than hospice. He was a Christian, a Mennonite, and that was nice. He was a very nice man, but they all work in the same time frame. It's hard to sit in front of a doctor and not believe what they are saying, yet I know that God is not concerned about statistics, and he is in control.

I think Jan and I were both moved (shaken?) by the experience with the doctors. We sat in the car afterwards eating a little lunch, and Jan asked me if I was afraid to die. I said I wasn't and then I cried more than usual. For the first time, I realized how strongly I desire to be with my family more and to teach some of the things I have learned and thought about through my life. I have found that some do want to hear, listen and learn, and I am so excited about doing that.

I know God knows the time..I think this must be the hardest part of the whole experience: I haven't really thought about the dying part all that much, maybe not enough. I do know that I have great peace with it but do not relate with any fear of it. This is not because of my goodness or my righteousness but only because I believe so strongly in Christ's righteousness. He has done everything for me so that my passing will not be death but a wonderful transformation. I am so blessed to still be alive. I thank God for every day of life he gives. I don't take any day for granted. I know many are praying for me, and I appreciate that so much. I have felt really well considering what is going on in my body. It's only been the last few days that I have felt more fatigue and some pain on my left side. I have taken a few pain pills again. With cancer, every time you feel a new pain or a recurring old pain, you wonder: is this cancer, or is this a result of the last test they did?

I have now been home for five weeks. The wonder of freedom still stays with me. Everything is like new. I don't think our car has left the garage without both of us in it more than twice. We do everything together. It has been very hard for me to think about leaving Jan. As we lie in bed together at night, I tell the Lord that I need grace that I just don't have yet. I don't want to leave my grandchildren. I have high hopes of being with them and teaching them. I am finding them so open to what I want to say to them.

It's Wednesday, and today is another day. It went much different than planned. We went to the VA early, expecting to get my first chemo treatment since I'm home. I had brought all my medical records in before so the doctor could study them. I did this twice. The first doctor just looked through them and gave them back.

On my second trip, I took the files along, just in case, and, sure enough, the oncologist needed them and wanted them scanned into the computer. The office person took them, said she scanned them, but evidently didn't and then gave them back. So when we got to the doctor, he didn't have my records of treatment, and I couldn't do the treatment. We did look at the new images they got last Friday and received very good news. The scan showed no cancer in the liver. I definitely had cancer in the liver before because when they opened me up they did a biopsy of the liver and the pancreas. Today, there is no cancer in my liver. The tumor on the pancreas is about one inch in size.

The doctor in Butner said the tumor was the size of an egg; it has gotten smaller. The doctor refuses to be encouraged, but we are. There may be no medical reason for this happening, but we believe God is at work. In addition to the chemo, he is using all the nourishment I am getting from all the things Jan is feeding me. We just are thanking God, and I really believe if I were still in Butner, I would not be alive anymore. The early release is another real answer to prayer. God is really showing us grace and mercy. I should have belief in all the future grace I will ever need, but I still find myself wanting.

Maybe that means my time has not yet come. There is so much more I want to do. I know God can do it without me, but maybe he is going to allow me to see it. As profoundly good as God has been, why should I ever doubt his goodness and his grace? I know that when the time comes he will give me grace to leave.

7/24/13

Yesterday was treatment day at the VA. It was a good day. The doctor finally read the medical reports I brought with me from Butner and compared the scans they did there in March with the scans they did here last week. The

Butner scans showed cancer in the liver, cancer in the liner of the intestines that hold them together, and a tumor in the pancreas. They were all confirmed by biopsies.

The new scan showed no cancer in the liver and no cancer in the liner of the intestines. The tumor in the pancreas has shrunk by 50 percent. He had to show a little optimism over this, but he still speaks in terms of the end being six to eight months from the day treatment started. His science only allows him to place me in the law of large numbers, and when I said the evidence shows we are making more progress and shows more progress than science says I should be having, he would only say that I am in the top of the class. By his expression, he gave credit to prayer only in the sense that it improves our attitude and attitude is important. As far as nutrition goes, he gives no credit for that. He said the medication I was getting in Butner was unconventional because I was getting three medications. He is sure the VA will not pay for the three, and he plans to drop that one. He has me on only one of the three now and is consulting with other oncologists about what the second one should be. I guess we need to go with their recommendation because I will have no say on that.

I do not have a problem with them calling the shots on the medication because I believe the greater reason for the improvement is the prayers of the saints and the nutrition and being home with my family. I eat almost no sugar, coffee, or tea. Yet in the waiting room for oncology, the table is filled with free coffee, cookies, and candy bars—they tell us it's all ours and that we can eat it all for free. It really is a different outlook.

7/27/13

As I get older, I appreciate the discipline my earthly father gave me. I didn't like discipline at the time, but now I value it more than ever before. Last night I was at a wedding and sat with an old friend who grew up in a Christian culture, but not American culture. They had their three small children with them, and it was a privilege to see children so well disciplined and so sweet and full of joy. We often think of discipline as a negative thing, but I believe that we should see it as one of the greater, enduring blessings of life.

I miss the discipline. Sometimes, now that I am out, I wonder if I am disciplined or being disciplined enough. I miss the accountability I had to others whom I felt the Lord had placed under my care and keeping. Today, I can go to pretty much any church I want. I can "enjoy" a service, but, otherwise, it doesn't seem to make much difference if I am there or not. I ask myself how long this should continue and if I am contributing to God's kingdom. Discipline is a good thing. It demonstrates we are worth another's time and energy. It shows us to whom we belong. It makes us confront, confess, and repent of our sins. It humbles us, and it brings us to our knees to weep over our sin. It also draws us closer to the embracing arms of our Lord and Savior. Discipline is a blessing.

Those without discipline are orphans. Parents who are not disciplining their children are emotionally and spiritually abusing them and are setting them on a path of self destruction. If we are not receiving the discipline of God, it shows that we are not his children and that he is not our father: "For the Lord disciplines the ones he loves and chastises every son whom he receives . . . for what son is there whom his father does not discipline . . . then you are illegitimate children and not sons" (Hebrews 12:6-8). The Lord disciplines those he loves—those he adores and has adopted into his family. Discipline is one of the surest signs of adoption; it demonstrates that we belong to God and are loved by God in a special saving way.

As we talked in Duluth together, Matt always said he never wanted to be the "people gatherer." He didn't like the one-on-one. He liked to teach but wouldn't be the guy bringing the people to class. I felt this was a dilemma and was concerned about how he could function this way. God has taken care of that. Matt wrote me recently, "I just find myself talking to people. Guys I've known for some time sit down by me and just ask me how I can be so interested in the Bible." He says he knows that he will never be able to just sit in his office, being a back room guy (as he explained himself before). He can't wait to be on the street, in a coffee shop ministry or somewhere he can be talking to people. This is the way the Lord disciplines and changes us from our old ways of thinking.

Rob wrote, "But Bob, I still stumble. I feel as though I stumble a lot. I feel like my faith is tested every hour of every day. Maybe that's normal but I don't like it. It saddens my heart to see how some other Christians behave. I used to think I could go to the chapel on Sunday service and count about sixty Christians there. But to be honest, a very small handful of them are. I can't understand why anybody would only want to be half-Christian and not commit themselves more. I feel like, for me, I need to do all I can for Jesus. The grace that he has poured upon my family has been so overwhelming that I can cry when I think of it all. I worry that I can't please him enough for all that he is doing for me. I have seen the Lord answer my prayers for me and for you. So why do I still worry? I still feel so inadequate. I feel I just can't do enough for Christ. Working with Matt has been great! He goes through things with me like you did . . ."

I replied to Rob, "Rob, that is the most beautiful thing about Christ. We cannot repay him; we cannot do enough. It would be an insult to him to think that we thought we could actually repay him for as great a work as he has done. All we can do is receive what he gives us and say, 'Thank you.'"

What we can and are to do is to magnify him. We are to keep him up close where he looks large to us, and when we talk about him, we don't talk about him in a small, unimportant way. There is a special place God has created in our hearts and lives where Jesus belongs. We tend to want to fill that place with other things. The best thing we can do to show our appreciation for Jesus is to not fill that place with other things. That means we shouldn't make "much" of other things. We are to make "much" of Jesus; we are to love what he loves and diminish (don't spend time with) the things he doesn't care about. That is how we show our gratitude to him for what he has done. That is all, but that requires our life. That means not living our life thinking about ourselves and what makes us happy. It means thinking about Jesus and what makes him happy.

It is a discipline to think this way. It's a new discipline, and a new way of thinking. It does not come naturally, and that is why it is a discipline. We must let the Holy Spirit discipline us. We must ask him to discipline us and to change our hearts away from the old things we liked to think about, worry about, and make much of. He must give us a new heart and new love for all that he loves and holds as important. This is discipline. We must learn to love it. We won't love it at first. We would rather just not go to church when we don't feel like it or not read the Bible when we don't feel like it. After we do this for a while, we will find that we do like it. We love what he loves, and we are bothered by what bothers him. Ask him to do it because only he can.

First stop, to change into civilian clothes, June 7, 2013

Summer 2013, visiting parks around Minneapolis

Thankful for a beautiful place to live with our daughter, Lisa, and her family in Elk River

With many of the grand children soon after Bob returned home

Children Lora, Lisa, Amy and Tom

"and he saw his son and his son's son, four generations—"
Tom, Grant, Grayson, and Bob, May 2014

40

I am a happy man. Jan and I thank the Lord for the life, health, and strength that he gives us. We thank him for each day not knowing how many we have left. I must admit that I wonder at times how this will end. We do know that for everyone, life must end at some time; still, we ask for a miracle, and at the same time we feel that every day we are seeing a miracle. Last Febuary, I was told I had two to four months to live. Soon, I will be on my fourteenth month. I know, at times, my story can sound like a sad story. To me it is not sad. I always wanted to minister. I had a hard time getting an audience in the church, and God gave me an audience in prison. He showed me the results of his work as his Spirit worked right before my eyes.

Nehemiah said, "Go and enjoy choice food and sweet drinks, and send some to those who have nothing prepared. This day is holy to our Lord. Do not grieve, for the joy of the Lord is your strength" (Nehemiah 8:10). I believe I was with those "who had nothing prepared."

Most of my life I felt very adequate in my ability to provide for myself and my family because the Lord blessed me. It was easy to credit myself with the good life the Lord had given us. When he allowed it all to slip away from us, we learned more deeply. We experienced Psalm 28:7, "The Lord is my strength and my shield; my heart trusts in him, and he helps me. My heart leaps for joy, and with my song I praise him (NIV)."

As we transferred what we made much of (the security we had built) to making much of the security that the Lord is, we experienced Habakkuk 3:18, "Yet I will rejoice in the LORD, I will be joyful in God my Savior (NIV)."

Now, with the cancer, I am experiencing each individual day as a gift: we truly say, "Though you have not seen him, you love him; and even though you do not see him now, you believe in him and are filled with inexpressible and glorious joy (1 Peter 1:8, NIV)."

I still ask the Lord every day to let me be used by him, to show me where he is working, and to let me join in and be a part of his big, eternal plan. As my strength grows weak, this happens in smaller and smaller circles.

As I think through my life, I am so thankful for a wife who loves the

Scriptures as much as I do. She loves memorizing verse even more than I do, and I owe my memorization of Bible verses to her. She really led me in that. The first passage we memorized in this last seven years came from my long nights with struggling how to pray. One night, in the middle of the night when I was frustrated with the "sameness" of all my prayers, I came upon Psalm 51. I shared it with Jan in the morning, and we both memorized it. We still say it together as we walk or drive along. Then we learned Psalm 16, and there were many more. We will continue to recite them as we face this next, and possibly the last, phase of our life together.

God is truly good. I hope this book will be an encouragement to many who face challenging situations in life. I hope it is a testimony to the fact that God is not limited by circumstances. Our hope in Christ is rock solid. He will give us all we need. He wants us to be satisfied in him. I must admit that, throughout life and without realizing it, I was finding many other things to satisfy me, and I really saw this more clearly as they were taken away. Today, I can truly say that God satisfies my soul. I am truly satisfied. I am a happy man.

About twenty years ago, while I was in a seminar, we were asked what would be the three most important things you would like to do the day before you die. I wrote down: walk a mile, read a chapter in a book, and have a meaningful conversation. I can still do all three. At the same time, I still have confidence that if the Lord takes away any or all of those three, he will keep me here as long as he has a purpose for me, and that is the most important thing—God's purpose.

41

On October 1, 2014, at 2:00 a.m. God's purpose for Bob's life was complete. I (Jan) was tapped on the shoulder by his sweet Cambodian nurse, Sarah. "He's gone," she whispered. For the past few weeks one of the family members slept in Bob's room each night. We knew his last breath on earth and the first breath in heaven was very near.

Prior to being admitted to the VA Hospital, hospice nurses had been coming to our home in Elk River for three weeks. Bob used every opportunity to talk about the Lord, the blessings in his life, and the peace and joy he was experiencing.

As the pain became more and more intense, the medication dosage increased. He kept a notepad in his pocket to record every hour, on the hour, handful of medication he would attempt to swallow. It became clearly evident his pain would need to be controlled with intravenous pain medications. Therefore, he was admitted to the VA hospital. He was also scheduled to undergo a procedure to reduce the pain. During the procedure a needle was inserted into the nerves around the pancreas and alcohol was injected into the nerves to destroy them, thus diminishing the pain. Shortly following the procedure Bob started experiencing a great deal of pain again, so it was obvious the pain was stemming from another source.

Following is an update of Bob's status that was sent to our prayer partners, family and friends on September 13, 2014:

This email is from Jill (Bob's daughter in law). I would like to update you concerning the procedure he had completed on Friday. We had great hopes it would relieve the intense abdominal pain Dad has been experiencing over the last several days which would also potentially reduce the oral pain medication. The procedure itself went well, but the outcome has been disappointing in terms of pain relief. Dad has continued to need intravenous medications with no decrease in the amount necessary for optimal pain control.

Even though he is in pain, he continues to be very pleasant and kind to everyone. He enjoys conversation and sharing his thoughts with all of us. Yesterday prior to going into the procedure, he shared it was impressed on his heart during the night that he needed to focus on "the prize." It is a gift that required a sacrifice and has been prepared and is waiting for us, and we need to look forward to it. There are many distractions that can keep us occupied and divert our focus, but we need to remember, amidst the busyness of life our eternal prize is waiting for us.

It is uncertain the number of days, hours, or minutes we will continue to have to enjoy him on this earth, but the time we have is priceless and precious.

Thank you for your continued prayers and thoughts. We are humbled by your interest and love for our family and feel the Lord's grace covering us, sustaining us, and encouraging us.

I had taken along four changes of clothing hoping he would be released back home and taking less pain medication, but the four-day stay was not to become a reality. As the pain became more intense, the intravenous medication had to be constantly increased and monitored.

Two of the three most important things Bob wanted to do the day before he died were now no longer possible, but meaningful conversation was still feasible and attainable.

The final weeks of Bob's life were spent with purpose and intent. Bob shared the Gospel and Christ's love to other patients, doctors and nurses. He spent time with each of the children and grandchildren sharing thoughts, aspirations, encouragement, and answering any question they had about life or death. There were no words left unsaid, no stones left unturned. The time was beautiful, innocent, precious, impactful, impressionable and memorable.

There were exceptional times of singing and praying. The music not only blessed us, but it also blessed the other hospice patients and nurses caring for us. We were also able to partake in communion with most of the family present. It was a special time of celebrating the ultimate gift of eternity for those who believe in the shed blood of Christ for the sins of the world.

As I realized the four-day stay was drifting into more and more days, I drove home to Elk River to regroup and make plans to stay with Bob for the rest of the days he had left to live. As his pain increased, my thoughts and prayers were focused toward his earthly release. Bob had been preparing me as best he could with final plans, my future, and things I would need to take care of following his death. For example, in the car manual, he carefully wrote the instructions with regard to where and when to get the wheels balanced and tires rotated. He was very meticulous about taking good care of what we had and what we owned. In life, and now in his last days, he was always concerned about my life, my future, and my wellbeing. He was a loving, devoted husband, and he modeled it well.

The care we received at the VA Hospital was wonderful! Each nurse and each doctor devoted his/her time, expertise, gentle spirit and tender care. The availability of the Fisher House was a blessing to our family. It is a home designed to accommodate the needs of veteran families who have loved ones receiving care at the VA Hospital. It was a place to share meals, rest and interact with families with similar experiences.

Being at the Fisher House brought back so many memories of sharing stories, meals, and rooms with women in Duluth when Bob was in prison. Women and children often stayed at the Agape House, a home provided for inmates' families when they came to visit. There are many similarities: brokenness, heartache, separation, pain, and loneliness. However, there is a marked difference: being a veteran is honorable; being an inmate is not. I was repeatedly reminded that regardless where we are in life, whatever the situation, we can make a difference. Bob's motto, adopted from John Piper, "Don't waste your life" was lived out in prison and during his months of enduring cancer.

As his concluding days drew near, the final most important thing Bob wanted to do the day before he died was no longer possible. He was no longer able to converse with us, as his body became increasingly weak yielding to the pain medication. His only means of communicating was to lift an eyebrow or blink an eyelid.

Many times we would gather around his bed waiting and watching for a slight response similar to watching a newborn baby. Entering and exiting this world are awe-inspiring events and have many similarities.

I read to him, sang to him, shared verses with him and just held his hand. I thanked the Lord for his life, his influence in my life, our family, our friends, the men in prison, the young men he mentioned throughout his career and countless others. I thanked the Lord for the extended months we had together. Time to walk, time to talk, time to recite Psalms, time to read, time to reflect on our lives, and time to spend with family. Even in those final days and then hours, sweetness prevailed.

This past summer we read the book, *We Shall See God*, a Charles Spurgeon classic devotional on heaven written and amplified by Randy Alcorn. It was wonderful material that brought much excitement, as we read and discussed what eternity would be like for those who believe in Christ their Savior.

Following is the last letter that Bob had intended to send to his prayer partners, family, and friends, and was sent out September 27, 2014:

This is Jill Goris (Bob's daughter in law) sending an update concerning Bob's status. Each family member spent time with him and has experienced "sweet moments" through his words of encouragement and testimony. Bob has stated he is waiting to go home with the Lord, and his work is done on earth. He is ready to go. He is not afraid. He has said his good-byes. It is time. So we are waiting with him and helping him to finish the race. He will have to cross the finish line without us, but we are by his side and encouraging him with singing, prayers, and just "being."

Dad wrote a final letter and thought he might add to the content, but he was never able to complete it. I am sending the portion of the letter he wrote knowing this will be his final words he has for each of you. You have all been an incredible tower of strength and source of encouragement for this servant of the Lord. You have prayed for him, prayed with him, prayed for fellow prisoners, wept with him, sacrificed for him, loved him, loved us, and we will be forever grateful for your abundant blessings and perseverance. We will never be the same having experienced this act of kindness and brotherly love. We will be in contact with you concerning the details of celebrating his heavenly homecoming. Bob wrote:

I believe this is the time to think about one of my last letters to you. The doctors were greatly disappointed the procedure was unsuccessful and probably more disappointed than me. I was not as optimistic as they were, because I was not sure the pain was coming from the pancreas. I have had a lot of time to think about pain while being in pain, and I believe I can see the Lord's blessing even in the midst of pain. The main reason I am writing this is I want you to know that pain also comes from God, and He uses it for our good.

In my pain, I saw our family pull together in a far greater way than

I ever thought I would experience. It caused me to evaluate the Lord's goodness in pain. One night when the pain was intense, I was wondering how can there be good in this? The Lord reminded me that we would not be having the great times together if it were not for the pain. He also spoke to my heart and impressed on me that my mind has been fixed on taking care of ending the things on this earth, and that has been keeping me from thinking about the things of heaven. So much time and energy is invested in things that don't matter.

Jan and I just finished reading Randy Alcorn's book on heaven. I remember a couple days ago we read about what we will be doing in heaven. I realized I would have to change a lot, and it scared me for a moment. Then I concluded, our Lord and Savior has already done all the preparing. He finished it all on the cross! When I leave this earth everything is done for me! All is prepared! That's what Jesus has been doing for me. Of course I knew all of this before, but the seriousness and the significance of it were clearer to me that night than ever before. I believe it has changed me a lot. I need to focus on heaven and let the Lord take care of all the rest...

While Bob was wasting away, I pondered the purpose of his body lying motionless, just breathing with no ability to communicate. It later became evident, and I believe it was for my sake; it was so I could release him more and more in those final days and final hours. The moment I was informed he had died, I was grateful his suffering was over, and he was praising the Lord he longed to see face to face.

Bob had written his obituary months before he died. He stated the reason for his death was: Died of a happy heart. He truly was a happy and fulfilled man when he left this earth. He was completely expended, as he finished the race.

Bob was a planner. He loved planning trips and events. When he was in Duluth, he asked Amy if she would mail him a road atlas. Seemed like a strange request as he was going—no where! When he was released from prison and we were driving home, he had the atlas in his hand. I said, "We have a GPS, so we won't need that."

"Well," he said laughing, "this is marked with all the places we are going to travel to." Almost every state had yellow markings indicating highways we had once traveled, airports we had once landed, or campgrounds he still hoped to take the grandchildren to. I was later informed that an atlas is a treasure to an inmate in prison. Men can still dream, plan, and try to imagine life outside the prison.

Bob not only wrote his own obituary, but he also spent time planning his own funeral. Many people do not want to plan their own funeral or even talk about it, but he had some definite ideas about what he thought should be done and said. He believed it should be a celebration! After all, heaven is a promotion! He wanted it to be a time of singing and praising the Lord with the content of the message focusing on the sovereignty of God and His goodness. I can honestly say the day was a celebration, and it included all that Bob had desired and requested. The sixteen grandchildren formed a choir and sang about God's faithfulness, and I was reminded of the night before Bob was sentenced to prison. That night we all sang around the piano, because singing hymns and worship songs with the family was a highlight for Bob.

After weeks in the county jail, prior to being transferred to Duluth Federal Prison, I asked Bob how he endured those trying weeks and his response was, "Singing with the family the night before I left sustained me. The songs continued to bless my soul."

I wondered how that could be. Now, weeks later after Bob's celebration service, the music of that day, the choir of our grandchildren, and our adult children leading in worship, I too can say, "The words and music have carried me through, and it has sustained me!"

I directed a children's choir for many years and remember telling the young singers they were each the most beautiful instrument the Lord had created. Their voices could be used for the praise and glory of God far better than any man-made instrument.

Many mornings I wake up with a song echoing through my mind, perhaps one verse of an old hymn, a new worship song or a tune from my childhood. I know the recollections are a gift from God, and I am a grateful recipient.

We will miss Bob dearly! We will miss his humor, his laughter, his teaching, his encouragement, his singing, his grilling, his planning, his dreaming with us, and so much more. He was a passionate man whose greatest joy was sharing Christ. The more he shared, the more passionate he became.

Now, we must all depart from where we have been and move forward. We will cherish and uphold the memories, the legacy, and the heritage left behind. We beseech the Lord to fill the vacant place in our home and in our hearts with His amazing grace.

"But whatever you do, find the God-centered, Christ exalting, Bible saturated passion of your life, and find your way to say it, live for it, and die for it. And you will make a difference that lasts. You will not waste your life." —John Piper

Reflections from Our Children

Tom

While writing this excerpt, 2 Timothy 3:16–17 is on my mind. It causes me to reflect on the impact my dad had on my life.

I learned a lot from my dad and rather than writing another book, I'm going to focus on a few pearls he taught me.

Work Ethic ~ Dad was not afraid of work or to work. Dad's workweeks were very demanding, so he was fully engaged in business, day and night, the duration of the week. However, we spent Saturdays outside mowing lawn (too much lawn), working with the horses, cutting the hay, and cleaning the barn and grove. On Sunday, we rested. Another important pearl.

Dad convinced me to start selling merchandise at a young age. In seventh grade, the first air pot coffee pots were marketed, and I bought 30 of them and sold them in a short period of time. By eighth grade, he introduced me to a family friend, Curt Miller, who took me under his wing and taught me to paint houses and barns. By my sophomore year, dad loaned me money to launch my own painting business. I was beginning to perceive and learn the benefits of work. Obviously, the concept of providing for myself was important, but it was also a vehicle, which allowed me to be engaged and involved with people.

Connecting with People ~ Another significant pearl and skill I witnessed in my dad was extraordinary people skills. I believe that was his greatest strength. In order to have outstanding people skills you need to have an intense interest in people. He loved, trusted, worked with and spent time with people from all walks of life. Perhaps a quality trait he acquired and cultivated from observing his father and something I desire to aspire to do as well. Dad referred to this type of investment as a "people collector" or "people connector."

Dad loved to help people see life differently, work differently, think differently and live differently. Approximately twenty-five years ago, Dad went to India for the first time. He asked God to help him love the people of India, as he did not feel he had the capacity to do so. Dad was very open with what he was processing, saw his lack of ability, asked God to change him, and then acted on his change by committing financially and emotionally to the people of India. God was faithful in answering his honest, candid prayer.

Lifelong Learning ~ Dad was a student. Interestingly, he did not do well in school, but he was a very wise man, and he never stopped learning. My dad always loved technology and technological advances. He had one of the first bag cell phones and many updates thereafter. He desired to stay current with computers, iPads, and gadgets, not just to have the latest style, but also to further communicate and educate himself and to identify and keep in touch with others.

My dad had many collections of books, tapes and CDs ranging from Zig Ziglar, Jim Rohn, Charles Spurgeon, R.C. Sproul, John Piper, many others but most importantly, the Bible. This learning developed and shaped his core values, his thoughts, and his life course that he fluidly extended to others through his family, ministry, work, friendships and relationships. He believed Scripture was not just something to be learned but to be lived out.

Dad always had an interest in business and ministry and were the topics he usually focused on and discussed when we spent time together. He desired to know the current details and specifics of my business interests, work projects, and pursuits, and it grew to a new dimension when he was in prison. Even in the hospital, dad wanted to hear the latest updates of my life. Dad's lifelong interest in me continues to be an inspiration.

Loving Mom ~ the most important earthly pearl. Dad's love for mom became more focused and strengthened over the past ten years. He made more time for her and concentrated his energy toward their marriage with more intentionality. Dad's appreciation grew for her during his years in Duluth. He loved mom's inner beauty and spoke very highly of her often. This has caused me to re-evaluate my own relationship with my spouse.

Dad taught me the goal of Scripture is not only to be learned, but it is also primarily to be lived. I watched my dad finish strong. The joy of the Lord was his strength. He made an eternal difference and left a legacy for us to follow. He will always be my hero.

Lisa

My strongest memory of Dad in my childhood was our dinner time. One of the principles Dad truly lived by was when you work, work hard; when you play, play hard. This was obvious during our evening meal gathering. Every night we had the table set by 5:50 p.m. At 5:59 p.m. Dad would walk in the door, and we would RUN to the table. He would sit down and begin with prayer at 6:00 p.m. As we ate, we talked about our day and occasionally, our conversation would end with Dad telling a joke which never seemed to end. He would laugh so hard, then cry through choppy sentences, and finally, the punch line would surface. Dinner would conclude with family devotions, and I don't ever remember Dad skipping this important time. Even if he had a 7:00 p.m. meeting, he would read while we ate squeezing everything in efficiently, so he could be back on the road in perfect time. If he was able to stay home for the evening, we had great conversations about the Scripture, and we all loved it.

Many times he asked me to play the piano while he worked or read. He loved it when any of us played our instruments, but he especially seemed to love piano. Sometimes, he would come and sit on the bench and say, "Play something I can sing." We would both sing, and it was really sweet!

I loved the "work hard; relax hard" idea, but the "play hard" often seemed a little over the top for me. He would spend so much time preparing for the activities such as harnessing the horses or waxing the skis, that we felt obligated to do this activity for eight hours to make it worthwhile.

I really enjoyed the buggy rides on summer days and stopping for picnics at noon. But, being afraid of animals and my dislike for sub-zero weather precluded me from enjoying many of these outings. Nonetheless, we all did it. Every time. Nothing got in the way of our having a "good time." We always sang in our coming and going, so that made the "fun" more enjoyable.

In Dad's last weeks in the hospital, he loved company and conversation. He even continued to teach us what he was learning in the hospital bed. He grew stronger in his intent to do this as he grew older, and decided he would "sing until there was no more song in him."

As each grandchild visited and his own children sat by his bed, he would teach and share about God's glory. He wanted to prepare and be ready to be in God's presence. So as we visited, he was careful to control conversations and not be distracted by trivial things. After a long day of conversations, I asked him if he wanted to watch a little news. He said that he was trying hard to break ties with this world to be ready for eternity, and watching television would not help him do this. So we sat in silence. He prayed. He meditated.

Dad always pushed himself to do what was necessary. He ate with no appetite, swallowed pills knowing they would make him sick, went for walks, and participated in family times when it would have been much more comfortable to stay on the couch. In the final days of taking food, it became clear that he could no longer keep it down. In such a sweet, child-like way he asked, "Do you suppose its ok if I don't eat anymore?" He knew this was a deciding moment toward the end.

God's Word became his very bread and water. In the last days while he was quite sedated I read Psalm 103 to him. I didn't know if he was aware of anything at all. I only knew that occasionally he would signal that he was awake with a raised eyebrow or some vocal sound. After reading verse 5, "He satisfies your desires with good things that your youth is renewed like the eagles", he groaned. And again after verse 14, "For He knows our frame and remembers that we are dust."

His response let me know that he was being sustained by God's words. Some of his last words spoken, as he was becoming increasingly difficult to understand were in response to the question, "Are you doing ok, Dad? Are you happy?" He slowly but strongly said, "Oh, yes."

The long good-bye at the hospital was a gift from God. As each one said their final words, Dad gave a blessing, "The Lord bless you and keep you; and make His face to shine upon you, and be gracious to you; the Lord lift up His countenance upon you and give you peace" (Numbers 6:24–26).

May God keep us faithful, as He kept Dad faithful until the end.

Amy

It was really a joy and privilege to be his daughter and to be raised in our family. He was one of my closest friends in life, and I loved him very much. He was pretty specific about not focusing on himself when he was gone, but he wanted us to glorify the Lord and fix our thoughts on Him. But there is one other person that played such an important role in his journey that I want to honor, and that's my mom.

The night before he passed away I was talking to her on the phone and she said, "You know, it was such a privilege to be married to him." She said, "We were team mates, and we were partners." And those of you who knew them, that's exactly how it was. You really didn't see one without the other, and Dad certainly would not have been who he was without Mom. They worked hard, but they also played hard. They were both passionate about life and our family.

I remember as a child, dinner was always served at 6:00 p.m. Mom was a wonderful homemaker, and food was really important to us! She always made home such a special place, and when Dad walked in the door, it was family time.

They had a lot in common, but they also balanced each other in ways they were different. Mom would say Dad was her spiritual leader and mentor. In the last years and months, they spent a lot of time in the Word together. They memorized many passages together, and when Dad was in Duluth they would say those passages together over the phone. Sometimes, they would recite it together while she was visiting him.

In the last weeks of Dad's life, when Dad was barely speaking, she was quoting Psalm 51. She would say a line, she would wait, and Dad would say the last word. She would say another verse and wait…and he would finish it. She did a whole chapter like that. They were so in the Word together, and I know it was the Word of God that pulled them through these last years.

Dad took really good care of Mom her whole life. He loved her so much! But, she also took really good care of him. Throughout his time in Duluth, Mom visited him faithfully, almost every weekend and through all kinds of weather. She embraced circumstances that were not natural for her. She also decided it was a time to find God's purpose in that season and was very steadfast in her support of Dad.

When Dad was diagnosed with cancer, she again took up the fight. She even moved to Butner, North Carolina, to be close to him while he was in the cancer center for prisoners. After his release, they returned home to Minnesota. She drove him to countless appointments at the Veteran's Hospital in Minneapolis. She did everything she could to support him in his fight against cancer. (I'm sure he drank more green smoothies than he would care to tell you about.) If there was something she could do, she did it! She took her role as "helper and completer" very seriously, and she did everything, and more, to enrich his life in all circumstances.

It was beautiful to witness their marriage. The love that they had for each other was normal to me. As a child growing up, I thought that was how every marriage was, but the older I got I realized that it was unusual and quite a remarkable marvel. It was a deep love, a deep commitment and a deep faithfulness to each other, to the Lord, and to our family. One evening during his final days in the hospital, we were gathered around his bed. Dad said to Mom, "And we are still in love."

"Yes," she replied, "we still are." She loved and served him faithfully until the end.

So, I honor you, Mom, and I love you. We are so proud of you for how you have walked this journey. You are a beautiful example of a godly wife and mother. The Bible says, "A wife of noble character, who can find?" He did find you. And you found him. And it was a good match.

He was an amazing dad and a wonderful grandfather to my children. I am eternally grateful for his impact on my life and my children's lives. His investment was deep. His commitment to us was unwavering. His love for us was steady in every season of our lives. I have so many happy memories and so many blessings and truths, which I've learned from him. I will miss him greatly, and I already do. I look forward to the day when I will see him again and together live in the eternal presence of God!

Lora

Being the daughter of Bob and Jan Goris is a gift of grace from God in my life. Psalm 100:5 states, "For the Lord is good; His steadfast love endures forever, and His faithfulness to all generations." By God's grace, I have been the recipient of observing God's faithfulness from one generation to another through the lives of Grandpa and Grandma Goris and Mom and Dad. Surely, the Lord has been faithful.

God's faithfulness was displayed in conversations I had with Dad from an early age until our last goodbye. I recall, as a teenager, being in the hot tub with snow piled all around and discussing doctrine. Dad could articulate deep thoughts that captivated my attention and formed in me an appreciation for guarding doctrine. Doctrine mattered and affected my life in practical ways. Dad was never one for much small talk, but he was always up for a meaningful conversation about life or spiritual issues. If the conversation didn't have a specific purpose, it usually was fairly brief.

In formidable years, I wanted Dad's thoughts and input in my life. I recall calling home when I needed to speak to him about specific decisions or issues I was facing. Dad pointed me to God and God's purposes throughout my life.

I was blessed to spend six days at the hospital near the end of Dad's life and have sweet conversations. His last words to me were the blessing of the benediction, "May the Lord bless you and keep you. May the Lord make His face to shine upon you, and be gracious to you. May the Lord lift up His countenance upon you, and give you peace both now and forever."

The Lord has been faithful in allowing me to see Dad live obediently according to His words in James, "Count it all joy...when you meet trials of various kinds, for you know that the testing of your faith produces steadfastness...that you may be perfect and complete lacking in nothing." Dad was a man of strength in trials great and small. I never heard Dad complain about circumstances. I recall sitting around the dinner table (trying to engage him in small talk) asking him how his day was. "Good," was his standard reply. I remarked to him that he always gave me that answer, and I was trying to have some conversation with him! His reply was that every day and every kind of day was a good day.

In the last years, Dad's character, faith, and attitude were tested in the fire of an arrest, trial, a guilty verdict, and prison. Dad's attitude in trials was tested, and truly he came forth as gold. Dad was joyful, obedient, steadfast, and trusting. God's grace, kindness, and faithfulness were on display for many to see.

Some of the kids' highlights during prison visits were Dad's funny stories about life on the inside, stories of ministry and men, and their grandpa's delight over them. Prison was a joyful place to go and visit. One winter visit Chris, I, and Nana (Mom) took our five children skiing to a ski hill outside of Duluth. Dad expressed being so happy that day imagining the kids skiing; never expressing a bit of sadness. He wanted to hear every detail about it. "Count it all joy..."

God's faithfulness and grace were also evident as Dad ran hard after the Lord in his last years of life. He and Mom prayed every day for purpose. Near the end when his pain was out of control for several days and the hospital staff was a little baffled, I asked if he was discouraged. He smiled and said, "How could I be discouraged? God has been so good to me. The world thinks pain is such a bad thing. Pain isn't so bad. God has purpose for me even in pain."

Dad had such energy for life, for ministry, for people, for learning, for growing. During his last visits to Texas, he was so energized by reading the Bible with our children. He took them through Bible studies, and he and Mom gave our older children their first study Bibles. Dad wrote long notes to each child in the front cover. He was so happy to meet with our children, to meet with our friends, to meet with strangers...anyone he could talk to about the Lord, the Gospel, and God's purposes for life. Dad loved life and loved people. He was so energized by hearing people's stories and helping them see God's sovereign purposes for their lives.

Psalm 78:4 says, "We will not hide (things we have heard) from (our) children, but tell them to the coming generation the glorious deeds of the Lord, and His might, and the wonders that He has done." Surely, the Lord has been good. His grace, goodness, and glory have been on display. The Lord redeems and restores, give purpose and meaning, satisfies and fulfills our desires. God has been faithful and exceedingly kind to bless our family with Dad, with Papa. Someday soon we will be together again. It will be a great day!

Endnotes

1 Walid Shoebat, *God's War on Terror: Islam, Prophecy and the Bible* (Top Executive Media, 2010).

2 John Bunyan, *The Complete Works* (Philadelphia: Bradley & Co., 1871), 70.

3 John Eldredge, *The Sacred Romance: Drawing Closer to the Heart of God* (Nashville: Thomas Nelson, 1997).

4 Ibid.

5 Francis Schaeffer, *True Spirituality: How to Live for Jesus Moment by Moment* (Tyndale House Publishers, 1971, 2001), page xx in the Introduction.

6 Ray Stedman, from *Authentic Christianity,* "Ch. 1: The Great Imitation," found at http://www.raystedman.org/authentic-christianity/the-great-imitation.